# The Guide to Case Anaysis and Reporting

Fourth Edition

# AL EDGE, Ph. D

SYSTEM LOGISTICS, INC.
P.O. BOX 25776
HONOLULU, HAWAII 96825

# ACKNOWLEDGEMENTS

This book incorporates the contributions and experience of many people. First , I would like to thank Denis Coleman for his contribution to the original edition. Much of that original work is still present as we complete the fourth edition. Denis has moved on to a most successful career in computer software and we extend our thanks and best wishes. Next , I would like to thank my family for their support and assistance as editors, assistants, critics, and distributors. While space does not permit me to thank each of my colleagues at the College of Business, University of Hawaii for their assistance, a special note of appreciation is extended to Wolf Reitsperger, Jim Wills and Dave Bangert, for their advice; Naomi Wipf for secretarial support and to Ben Nagata for graphic assistance on the cover. Lastly, I would like to thank the following case authors for allowing me to reprint their work: Jeffrey Schuman (United Products), Michael and Robin Hergert (NEC Corporation), Rolf Hackmann (Crisis in Geneva), Ken Coelho and Donald Lecraw (Cambridge Products, Ltd.).

# THE GUIDE TO CASE ANALYSIS AND REPORTING

ISBN: 0-9602362

Fourth Edition, September 1991

# TABLE OF CONTENTS

## CHAPTER V.  HOW TO WRITE CASE REPORTS

## CHAPTER VI  HOW TO PRESENT CASE REPORTS

## SELECTED  CASES

## APPENDICES - RESOURCE MATERIAL FOR CASE ANALYSIS

# CHAPTER I    HOW STUDENTS CAN BENEFIT FROM THE CASE METHOD

## I.  HOW TO USE THIS BOOK

This book is a guide to the preparation, analysis, discussion, and reporting of cases.    It has advice for students that covers all case-related activities throughout the  semester.

Case analysis and reporting is more an art than a science;  there are no  "cookbook"  rules  that lead to brilliant analyses and presentations for each case.  This book  presents guidelines, checklists, and examples which describe the  "science"  aspect of  case analysis.  As students gain experience in case analysis,  they  will identify  further guidelines, checklist items,  and examples that lead them to more effective and efficient  analyses.  Also,  their instructors  will  contribute important material on case analysis.  Students should incorporate these additions into the book by notes  in the margins. Important passages should be underlined and clarified by written marginal comments.

This book attempts the difficult task of instructing the  student  in a  complex, creative process, called case analysis.  We  believe  this can  be  done  through  the use of checklists.  The  topics covered  by checklists in  this book are so broad that they require  chapters  or even  books  for a full treatment.  Nevertheless,  a  checklist  can  provide  worthwhile advice on the use of the topics by incorporating checklist  items  that  serve one of the  following functions.

* **The Outstanding "Do's"**:  Most tasks have elements that one strives to execute. For ex- ample,  during the in-class discussion, one  tries to word  contributions to be brief and to the point.  Concentrating attention  on  the "Do"  elements of a task  improves  its  overall exe- cution.

* **The Common Errors**:  In a similar fashion,  drawing attention to the common  errors made in a task improves the performance of anyone who makes that error.

* **Reminders about Theory**:  In applying an extensive theory to a problem  (e.g.,  industry analysis  to a case situation),  one must  be sure to relate all one's  knowledge to the prob- lem.   The systematic review afforded by the checklist ensures that no important  areas  of theory are inadvertently ignored.

## II.  WHAT IS A CASE?

A case  is a managerial situation of events and organizational circumstances  described in a factual manner.  It typically includes a chronology  of significant events in the organization's devel- opment;  summaries of important functional information (marketing,  financial, etc.),   opinions of management or employees,  and information about  the competitors and industry in general.

When students are assigned a case,  they do the following:

**Prior to class:**
   (1) Read the case.
   (2) Analyze the case situation and arrive at action recommendations for the characters in the case.
   (3) Reread and re-evaluate the analysis at a second sitting.
**During class:**
   (4) Participate in the in-class discussion of the case.
**After class:**
   (5) Write up brief notes on important ideas or events after the in-class discussion.

In addition, instructors usually assign written analyses of some cases during the semester. Some instructors also have selected students present the analysis of their cases orally to the class. This book is a guide for students to all the above activities.

## III. WHY CASES ARE USEFUL FOR STUDENTS

This section introduces specific action skills which students develop through the use of cases. Students can develop these action skills more rapidly and thoroughly by concentrating on them through all phases of studying cases. This section describes specific benefits that conscientious students gain from using cases. The goal of teaching with cases is to give the student the ability to act intelligently, rationally, and morally in business situations.

*"The great aim of education,"* said Herbert Spencer, *"is not knowledge, but action."*

The use of cases in education *(the case method)* is often contrasted with the use of lectures *(the lecture method)*. Cases impart action abilities to students by giving them practice in decision-making; lectures impart action abilities to students by giving them facts, principles, and theories which will guide them in decision-making situations. Both are used to the same end: to cause the student to act correctly in these situations. The nine action skills described in Checklist 1.1 give direction and motivation to students who are learning by the case method.

---

**CHECKLIST 1.1 ACTION SKILLS REINFORCED BY CASES**

**1. Think clearly in complex, ambiguous situations.** Many situations involve making a decision with information that is incomplete, conflicting, and ambiguous. Successful experiences with cases give students the practice and confidence necessary for clear, intensive thinking in ambiguous situations.

**2. Devise reasonable, consistent, creative action plans.** Most cases require the student to detail a course of future action. The student learns to devise and express plans that are:

   * **Realistic:** Do not assume ridiculous situations. Example: The firm will reduce production costs by making cuts in the wage rate.

   * **Consistent:** The parts of the plan must not contradict each other or rely on contradictory interpretations of evidence.

   * **Creative:** The plan transcends the immediate given information.

---

**3.** Apply qualitative and quantitative tools. In normal coursework, students learn the principles of these techniques and gain practice by small examples and problems. However, employment of these techniques in actual situations requires more knowledge than one typically gains by introductory theory and problems. Successful application requires ability to recognize circumstances where certain techniques are useful and to assess the accuracy of those techniques relative to impending decisions. Cases give the student practice in using these tools in realistic situations.

**4. Recognize the significance of information.** Theories and observations of modern management have shown that managers must sift through a mass of information, both formal reports and informal channels (the grapevine). The manager's task of defining problems and their solutions demands the ability to classify information.

**5. Determine vital missing information.** Successful decision-makers must know where, and when, to seek more information. Cases give the student practice in seeking information to solve problems.

**6. Communicate orally in groups.** Both the in-class discussions of cases and small group discussions preceding or during class are an integral part of learning by cases. The ability to listen carefully to others, to articulate one's views, and to rapidly incorporate the views of others into one's position are all important skills for managers.

**7. Write clear, forceful, convincing reports.** Managers and their staffs must express themselves in writing. The best way to improve your writing skills is to write; hence, the usefulness of the case report.

**8. Guide students' careers.** Many students are unaware of the day-to-day tasks and responsibilities of managers. The wide variety of actual situations described in cases gives students valuable knowledge about the functions of many job positions. Students can use these experiences to determine their own capabilities, limitations, and interests, and thereby make better career planning decisions.

**9. Apply personal values to organizational decisions.** Modern industrial society forces managers to make decisions which trade among business profits, government expenses, and the welfare of individuals and the public. This area of ethics and social responsibility is important and problematic in a professional education. The process of stating and defending positions in case discussions sharpens a student's awareness and maturity in the area of value and moral judgments.

*"The essential fact that makes the case system ... an educational method of the greatest power is that [it makes] the student ... an active rather than a passive participant."*
--Wallace B. Donham, Dean of the Harvard Business School, 1919-1942.

3

# IV. STUDENT RESPONSIBILITIES IN CASE DISCUSSION

A successful lecturer needs less effort and cooperation from students than does a successful case teacher. Although having students read material before lectures is useful, a good lecturer can deliver an interesting and informative lecture to an unprepared class. Although provocative questions by students during a lecture can add relevance and comprehensibility, an experienced lecturer can anticipate questions and include the material in the lecture. On the other hand, student preparation and participation is vital to successful teaching with cases. The in-class discussion degenerates when students are unprepared or unwilling participants. In this way, participation in case discussions is as important as participation in seminars. Thus, this subsection (Checklist 1.2) enumerates the expectations most instructors have of their students.

---

## CHECKLIST 1.2  STUDENT RESPONSIBILITIES IN CASE LEARNING

1. **Experience case situation.** Most cases describe situations of actual or disguised organizations. This gives students the opportunity to step vicariously into an organization's situation and feel the excitement, responsibilities, and tension of a real management situation.

2. **Enjoy yourself.** The case method places duties and pressures on students. Many shy away from the prospect of speaking before the class, and many dislike the routine of having to prepare before every case. However, every student is in the same situation and careful performance of the duties are vital to the earning experience. Studies are more pleasant for students who relax, enjoy the amusing parts of any predicament, and develop a class *esprit de corps.*

3. **Enter the case discussion.** Good students not only participate, but make contributions to the class discussions which often alert the instructor and fellow students to new steps for the analysis.

4. **Help manage the group discussion.** Students must consciously attempt to develop a lively, interesting discussion.

5. **Attend class regularly.** The case discussion is the centerpiece of case teaching; students who do not attend class gain little.

6. **Master the facts before every class.** Students may not have time to fully analyze each case before the class. However, some minimal preparation is necessary to follow the discussion and to make even superficial contributions. The lead-off question is impossible to answer if the facts have not been mastered.

7. **Analyze most cases before class.** Students should go beyond a mastery of the facts and analyze most cases during the semester (i.e., identify the issues and formulate logical, consistent action plans for the case's situation).

8. **Tolerate the instructor.** The task of the instructor is at least as difficult when using cases as when using lectures. The case facts, alternate analyses, and relevant industry data must all be thoroughly mastered.

---

# V. HOW TO CONTRIBUTE TO IN-CLASS DISCUSSIONS

The quality of the in-class discussion is an important determinant of the enjoyment and value that students derive from case teaching. Lively class discussions are entertaining and motivate future preparations. Significant discussions provide material for thought and valuable experiences for the participants. The "DO's" and "DO NOT'S" for case discussion are presented below.

---

**CHECKLIST 1.3  "DO'S" FOR CASE DISCUSSIONS**

1. Prepare before class
2. Push your ideas
3. Keep an open mind
4. Relate outside experience
5. Be provocative
6. Learn from other students
7. Recognize flow of discussion
8. Prepare a lead-off question
9. Be constructive

---

**CHECKLIST 1.4  "DO NOT'S"  FOR CASE DISCUSSION**

1. Do not make sudden topic changes
2. Do not repeat yourself
3. Do not repeat others
4. Do not use unfair hindsight
5. Do not be put off by bad experience
6. Do not overplay one theme

# CHAPTER II  HOW TO ANALYZE CASES

## I.  WHAT IS CASE ANALYSIS?

A case is a managerial situation of events and organizational circumstances described in a factual manner. A case puts you at the scene of the action and provides the relevant information for analysis. It may involve a whole industry, one organization, or some part of an organization. Case analysis gives you practice in bringing experience, theory, qualitative techniques, quantitative tools, and ingenuity to bear on the formulation of action plans in real (or realistic) situations. Although case teaching has many benefits, it best serves to give you practice in diagnosing an organization's situation and formulating action plans.

The activities in learning by the case method are so different from those in learning by the lecture method that it takes some time to adjust to the new demands. Traditional teaching requires you to learn theory and facts and to apply them to problems that are given. Cases can require that you determine the problem, select the appropriate tools, and formulate a plan of action, all in the absence of complete information. Further, there may be no one "correct" action plan. These complications, all typical of job experiences soon to confront you, embody the challenges and opportunities of case analysis.

As one case writer indicated:

*"The purpose of giving you a case assignment is not to cause you to run to the library to look up what the company actually did, rather, to enhance your skills in sizing up situations and developing your managerial judgment about what needs to be done and how to do it. The aim of case analysis is for you to bear the strains of thinking actively, of offering your analysis, of proposing action plans, and of explaining and defending your assessments".[1]*

## II. FRAMEWORK FOR CASE ANALYSIS

This chapter presents a 6-step framework for analysis of cases. The framework gives students a concrete method to organize their activities in case analyses. Figure 2.1 A FRAMEWORK FOR CASE ANALYSIS identifies the STEPS, TASKS, and METHODOLOGY appropriate for case analysis.

------------

[1]Thompson & Strickland, "Strategic Management", 5th Ed.,(BPI/Irwin, Homewood, IL) 1990, pg 287.

```
FIGURE 2.1   A   FRAMEWORK  FOR  CASE  ANALYSIS

      STEPS                     TASKS                   METHODOLOGY

  1.  Comprehend case       Speed  read case          Take notes
      situation             Read case carefully       Underline

  2.  Diagnosis of strategic   Categorize and         External analysis
      issues & key problem        analyze data            Industry analysis
                               Identify strategic  issues     Trend analysis
                                  & key problems           Decision tree anal.
                                                           Gap analysis
                                                           Portfolio analysis
                                                           Strategic  mapping
                                                        Internal analysis
                                                           SWOT analysis
                                                           Financial analysis
                                                           Breakeven analysis
                                                           Organizational analysis

  3.  Define strategic issues   Develop hypotheses     Brainstorming
      & key problems         Explicitly define  issues &
                                problems

  4.  Generate strategic     List strategic options   Experience
      alternatives                                    Decision models
                                                      Research
                                                      Creativity

  5.  Evaluate & select      Recommend preferred
      strategic alternative     alternative

  6.  Defend  implementation  List questions about
                                workability of solution
                              Develop a defense
```

## A.  Example Case

This  section contains the text of the case "Standard Oil  Company  of  Indiana".   The  case is used to illustrate the steps in  the  case analysis framework.   Later it will be used to illustrate a written case report  and  to  illustrate an  oral  case presentation.   We  have selected this case because it  is interesting,  brief,   and an excellent vehicle to demonstrate case analysis and reporting.

When  reading  the  case,   remember to become involved in the situation.    Pretend that you are to advise the management of  Standard Oil.    What would you recommend?

# STANDARD OIL COMPANY OF INDIANA

[paragraph 1] In July 1965, Indiana Standard had annual sales of over $2 billion and ranked ninth in the country in terms of invested capital. Indiana Standard was organized in 1889 by the Standard Oil Trust. The company has experienced a phenomenal growth because of its early establishment in the Midwest, where the greatest potential oil market in the world was located.

[paragraph 2] Standard's refinery was built in Whiting, Indiana, and is one of the largest in the country and also one of the first oil refineries in the West. The principal function of the company at this time was to supply kerosene, lubricants, greases, and other petroleum products to the various Standard marketing companies across the nation.

[paragraph 3] With the advent of the automobile, an increased demand for gasoline and motor oils was foreseen by Standard's executives. This foresight prompted the company to build and operate company-owned service stations. This pioneer development met the expansion of the automobile market and made gasoline and motor oil easily attainable for motorists.

[paragraph 4] In 1911 the Supreme Court divested the Standard Oil Company (New Jersey) from the Standard Oil Trust. This action resulted in the Trust being broken; the thirty-four companies owned by the holding company became free, independent, and separate. Indiana Standard was one of these thirty-four companies, and it came out of the dissolution owning three large refineries and the marketing organization for the Midwest; however, the company was left without any pipeline system to ship its crude oil to the refineries. This problem was not solved at first because the company remained a refining and marketing company. For some time, crude oil was obtained from the Prairie Oil & Gas Company and other small organizations. The Prairie Company continued to ship the crude oil to the refineries as it had done before.

[paragraph 5] The rapid expansion of the gasoline market led to the crude oil shortage in 1916. Again, the foresight of its executives enabled Indiana Standard to overcome this possible problem. In 1909 the officers realized the future demand for oil and told the company's chemists to come up with a method to extract more gasoline from crude oil. The process set up by Burton to achieve this end involved cracking crude oil through the use of high temperature and pressure.

[paragraph 6] The Burton invention allowed Indiana Standard to produce two barrels of gasoline for every one that was produced before from crude oil. The invention also opened the eyes of other chemists in the oil industry to the fact that chemical changes could be obtained in crude oil. This resulted in a new interest in research and many new products from crude oil.

[paragraph 7] The company owes most of its advances and market standing to the Burton process. The process left Indiana Standard with one of the industry's best research divisions, which it maintains to this day. This research has kept its products high in quality and has resulted in many new products for its customers.

[paragraph 8] The increasing demand for gasoline and other oil by-products made the company start buying pipelines in 1921. The company again realized the potential market openings and began to build its own pipelines in 1938. In 1939 its first fully-owned and built pipeline was opened, built from Sugar Creek to Council Bluffs. By the early 1950's, Indiana Standard owned a total of 16,128 miles of pipeline.

------------------

Adapted from: Zeigler, Raymond J., "Standard Oil Company (Indiana)," in Business Policy and Decision Making, Appleton-Century-Crofts Div. of Meredith Publishing Co., 1966.

[paragraph 9] The most important event in Indiana Standard's history was the acquisition of stock of American Oil Company. American became wholly-owned by Indiana Standard in 1954. This acquisition increased the number of states Indiana Standard marketed in from the original 15 to 48.

[paragraph 10] As stated, Indiana Standard has had a phenomenal growth since its start in 1889. Now, Indiana Standard is the dominant refiner and marketer of petroleum products in 15 midwestern states under the Standard brand name. The growth may have been phenomenal but the oil industry as a whole was increasing at a terrific rate.

[paragraph 11] A comparison of Standard of New Jersey and Indiana Standard brings to light many interesting points on Indiana Standard's standing in the oil industry in the U.S. The size and volume of New Jersey Standard's business places it far ahead of Indiana Standard. The Indiana company has total assets of over $3 billion, only about one fourth of New Jersey's

[paragraph 12] The sales volume of the two companies shows that Indiana is ranked nineteenth in the top 500 industrial firms in the U.S.; New Jersey has annual sales above $10 billion, while Indiana has annual sales of $2,147,761,000. Part of New Jersey's large size and sales volume may be attributed to the large amount of earnings every year. New Jersey makes seven times as much net income as Indiana every year. This also may be one reason for Indiana Standard's decline in market standing. Indiana and New Jersey are almost even in dividends paid per share each year; New Jersey has many more shares outstanding. This means that even though Standard of New Jersey pays slightly higher dividends, it is retaining more money.

[paragraph 13] Indiana Standard is ranked ninth in the country for the amount of invested capital. However, its rate of return is only 6.8%, 349th in this category.

[paragraph 14] Many of Indiana Standard's problems arise from the company's attempt to overcome this low rate of return. The company has a firm belief that increasing efficiency will enable it to increase its rate of return. One major step towards efficiency was the introduction of a project system in the research department. The project system was set up by an outside consultant named A. D. Little. The system consisted of a cut in the department budget of $1 million, a large manpower lay-off, and stringent bookkeeping.

[paragraph 15] The new system also resulted in the elimination of two levels of supervision between the bench chemists and the individual directors of each division. Because of this and the manpower lay-off, the system may or may not help increase the rate of return. The cut in levels of supervision will curtail the amount of communication within the divisions; this increases the span of control a supervisor has and means less time available for each employee. The lay-off may result in the employees feeling insecure in their jobs because of this decrease in communication; however, the company does not admit that this is one of its problems and there is no evidence that it is trying to overcome its lack of communication.

[paragraph 16] The cut in the budget of $1 million has reduced the amount of research the company can do. The company will need higher sales through new and better products, and research is the only means to this end. Nevertheless, the company feels that its cut is justified because of the use of newly acquired computers.

[paragraph 17] The computers determine each day's run at the Whiting refinery. The efficiency of the company has been increased by the project system and the use of computers, but the number of employees has been decreased dramatically. In the seven years between 1956-1963 the total employment of Standard decreased by 14,000 employees. The Whiting refinery itself had decreased the number of employees from 8200 to 2800. Better communication seems to be the only solution to the problem of insecurity created by this large lay-off.

[paragraph 18] Another problem that Indiana Standard now confronts is being faced by the entire oil industry. Crude oil is becoming scarce. One of Standard's mistakes was in exacerbating this problem by selling its overseas rights to Standard of New Jersey. Many wells are being discovered overseas by Indiana Standard, but the U.S. Government had set a limit on the amount of oil that could be imported. This quota was set right after Indiana's sale to New Jersey and was based on the number of oil wells owned by the company at that time.

[paragraph 19] Indiana Standard recognizes this problem and has taken great strides towards overcoming it. One step was the acquisition of the Indiana Oil Purchasing Company. This company has the job of purchasing crude oil for Standard from the wildcat drillers in the United States. Another step has been the increase in Standard's overseas operations. The operations have been extended by building new refineries overseas to handle the higher output of the oil wells so that the company can meet the expanding foreign market for oil and its by-products.

[paragraph 20] Price wars and intense competition are two road signs of the oil industry and are creating problems for many oil companies. Indiana Standard and many other oil companies make the biggest percentage of their profits from gasoline sales. A price war could have disastrous effect on their plans; however, there are two major ways to avoid these problems. The company could diversify its product lines to lessen the reliance on gasoline sales, or the company could expand its sales operations so that a price war in one area would not affect its entire operation. Standard has taken the second alternative and is using the subsidiary American brand name to market its products outside the fifteen Midwestern states. The only way Standard could meet the other alternative would be to increase research. New products could be developed from increased research in oil.

## B. Practice Exercise

Now that you have read the "The Standard Oil of Indiana" case, take a few moments and jot down what you think is the **Strategic Issue or Key Problem** in the Standard Oil Case. Do this before reading ahead. No one expects you to come up with a great answer (if there is such a thing) but it can be very insightful to look back at your answer after reviewing a more complete analysis.

The Key Problem is:

_____

_____

_____

_____

_____

_____

*"Practically no problem in life. . .ever presents itself as a case on which a decision can be taken. What appears at first sight to be elements of the problem rarely are the important or relevant things. They are at best symptoms . And often the most visible symptoms are the least revealing ones."*

-- Peter Drucker

## STEP 1:  COMPREHEND CASE SITUATION

Perhaps the most important step in case analysis is the identification of the most significant and most critical issues facing management.  An organization is so complex and dynamic that it is difficult to identify the underlying problems that deserve management attention.  However, problems must be correctly defined before they can be solved.  The first three steps of this framework involve the definition of problems.

Herbert Simon (among others) has identified the important first step in decision-making as "intelligence".  Here, the term "intelligence" refers to the "C.I.A." use of the term-gathering information about the internal and external environment.  A manager reads memos, reviews staff reports, scans computer reports, talks with customers, and meets with colleagues to gain knowledge about the internal and external environment of the organization.  All this information, both formal and informal, gives managers the awareness that leads to defining problems, which in turn leads to solving those problems.

Students simulate the awareness by reading the body and exhibits of a case, and any accompanying teaching notes.  The casewriter has done most of the legwork; the student begins by assimilating the results.

Cases are designed to teach the art of carefully searching the environment and weighing all information to come up with effective action plans. The actual reading of the case can be divided into two steps: (1) a speed reading of the case and, (2) a careful reading which includes underlining and marginal notes.

Many cases deliberately present extraneous details so students practice sifting through information to distinguish the relevant from the irrelevant. Extensive weeding out of irrelevant information is not done at this first reading of the case.  Information which at first sight appears irrelevant may well prove useful when the situation is fully understood. Thus, as one does this reading, the mind should freely accept any information in the case,  yet take special note of facts which may later prove significant.

### EXAMPLE OF "COMPREHEND CASE SITUATION"

In order to comprehend the Standard Oil case situation, the student first reads the case along the lines suggested above.  Next we recommended that the student underline what appears to be the most significant information in each paragraph (these might be classified as possible symptoms of a problem).   We provide in Table 1 the words we selected as possible significant information for the example case (Standard of Indiana).  This selection process is not all that scientific and can be the result of many factors such as experience or intuitive judgment. Information that may identify trends, strengths or weaknesses of the firm, and comparative data are often viewed as significant information.

## TABLE 1. UNDERLINED WORDS IN THE STANDARD OIL CASE

| PARAGRAPH | WORDS SELECTED AS MOST SIGNIFICANT INFORMATION |
|---|---|
| 1 | phenomenal growth. . .early establishment...greatest potential oil market |
| 3 | increased demand. . . company owned service stations |
| 4 | divested. . .remained a refining and marketing company |
| 5 | rapid expansion. . .crude oil shortage |
| 6 & 7 | Burton invention. . .best research division |
| 8 & 9 | increasing demand. . .acquisition. . .American Oil Co. |
| 10 | dominant refiner and marketer. . . industry increasing at a terrific rate |

| 11,12 & 13 | Comparative Data | Indiana | NJ |
|---|---|---|---|
| | Sales | $2.15 Bil. | $10 Billion |
| | Total Assets | 1/4th | $12 Billion |
| | Net Income | | 7 Times |
| | ROI | 6.8% | |

| | |
|---|---|
| 14 | problems arise from attempts to overcome low rate of return. . . cut in budget. . . manpower layoff |
| 16 & 17 | reduced research . . . problem of insecurity |
| 18 | another problem. . .crude oil becoming scarce. . . mistake selling overseas rights |
| 19 | acquisition of the Indiana Oil Purchasing Co. |
| 20 | price wars and intensive competition. . . profits from gasoline sales |

## STEP 2: DIAGNOSIS OF STRATEGIC ISSUES AND KEY PROBLEMS

The case analysis is leading toward a definition of strategic issues and key problems. The word "problem" includes not only its everyday meaning of a perplexing situation, but indicates both areas needing corrective action and areas of opportunities for new actions.

As John W. Gardner noted many years ago, *"We are all continually faced with a series of great opportunities, brilliantly disguised as unsolvable problems."*

The general acquaintanceship with the case situation was the first step in this process. This second step is to scrutinize the evidence to identify and investigate general areas where issues and problems may exist. There are a number of "Do's" and "Do Not's" in identifying the problems, which are summarized in Checklist 2.1.

The activities of the student in the diagnosis step begin with some categorizing of the data. This clumping of the data leads to identification of strategic issues and problem areas, i.e., situations exhibiting unusual behavior, conflicts, changes, stagnation, etc. The student must draw on experience, a thorough mastery of the case facts, and creativity to identify these areas. These problem areas may be redefined as the analysis proceeds. After the problem areas are defined, the student takes each problem area in turn and brings together all the facts to understand what is really happening in the case.

The way that one intellectually identifies problem areas is described by William Pounds:

*" The word problem is associated with the differences between some existing situation and some desired situation...the process of problem finding is the process of finding differences."*

## PROBLEM AREAS IN THE STANDARD OIL CASE

**PROBLEM AREA NO. 1**   Historical Precedence - Standard of Indiana began its operation as the marketing arm of Standard of NJ [paragraph 4].   Has this precedent been an influence on its strategic approach to doing business?   One might hypothesize that the marketing managers who were running the division before divestiture continued on as top management after divestiture. Couple this with its major expenditures, American Oil Co. [paragraph 9] and the Indiana Oil Purchasing Co. [paragraph 19] and the divestment of its drilling rights [paragraph 18]. Considering these facts, one could argue that Indiana's strategic emphasis is on marketing not so much because this is the most profitable segment of the industry but due to historical precedent.

**PROBLEM AREA NO. 2**   Performance - In the Standard Oil Case there is data available (paragraphs 11,12 & 13) which compares Indiana to the New Jersey company.   This data can be used to generate new information.

| Existing Data: | Indiana | New Jersey |
|---|---|---|
| Sales | $2.15 Billion | $10 Billion |
| Total Assets | $3   Billion | $12 Billion |
| Net Income | | 7 times |
| ROI | .068 | |

Using the DuPont formula   ROI = Turnover(TO) x Profit Margin(PM)

$$\text{where:} \quad TO = \frac{\text{Sales}}{\text{Total Assets}} \qquad PM = \frac{\text{Income}}{\text{Sales}}$$

We can calculate new information: turnover, profit margin, net income, and ROI for both companies.

| New Information: | Indiana | New Jersey | Difference NJ Over IND |
|---|---|---|---|
| Sales | $2.15 Billion | $10 Billion | 4.6 times |
| Total Assets | $3   Billion | $12 Billion | 4   times |
| Net Income | $ .2 Billion | $ 1.43 Bil. | 7   times |
| ROI | 6.8% | 11.6% | 42% |
| Asset Turnover | .717 | .833 | 13% |
| Profit Margin | 9.3% | 14.0% | 34% |

A review of these findings clearly shows New Jersey's superiority of performance. But more important, this new information, gained using the DuPont formula, provides understanding about New Jersey's higher performance (ROI 42% greater). The reason for the high ROI is due to higher turnover and higher profit margins but the real difference is in profit margins (34%). Therefore, one of the key questions is **why does New Jersey have such high profit margins when compared to Indiana?**

**PROBLEM AREA NO. 3** Source of Supply - Indiana Standard has de-emphasized the drilling and supplying of crude oil and has been content to buy from others. The purchase of American Oil Company represents a large investment in the retail end of the business, which in turn meant even greater demand by Indiana Standard for crude oil. It would appear that during periods of increasing demand for oil and intermittent scarcity of supply there would be increasing pressure on the cost of purchasing crude oil for firms that did not have control of their sources of supply.

**PROBLEM AREA NO. 4** Indiana Standard's Approach - The approach to overcoming a low ROI (a symptom not the problem) appears to be based on the assumption that the company is operating inefficiently (budget cut $1 million, layoffs, reducing levels of supervision). Although this may be true (turnover, a measure of efficiency, is low compared to New Jersey) it does not explain the major difference in profit margins (34% difference).

At this point we have identified four key differences between actual and desirable situations. We are now ready to move to the next step in which we will formulate the strategic issue.

---

**CHECKLIST 2.1 PROBLEM IDENTIFICATION ADVICE**

**1. Do not confuse symptoms with problems:** The term "symptom" has the same meaning in case analysis as it does in medicine. If a patient has a high temperature and a headache, the doctor knows something is wrong, but must search carefully to find the cause.

**2. Do not make premature evaluations:** There is a tendency to apply value judgments to situations before making a thorough investigation.

**3. Do not blindly apply stereotypes to new problems:** Although one's past experiences are powerful tools in case analysis, they must not stifle creativity.

**4. Do not accept information at face value:** Information in organizations must be scrutinized in the same way evidence is in a court of law.

**5. Consider multiple causality:** It is a natural and perhaps useful human tendency to seek simple solutions to problems. This often results in seeking a single cause for a problem.

---

## STEP 3: DEFINE STRATEGIC ISSUES AND KEY PROBLEMS

The first two steps in case analysis lead up to this third step, formation of a precise statement of the strategic issues and key problems to be solved. This statement should explain the basic disequilibrium that underlies the situation. The general findings identified in step 2 above should be explained by the problem statement. Also, the problem defined should be the one that is most significant to the health of the organization.

# EXAMPLE OF "DEFINE STRATEGIC ISSUES & KEY PROBLEM "

In order to identify and define the strategic issue for Indiana Standard we need to develop a hypothesis which supports the conditions identified in the four problem areas earlier.

**Indiana Standard's strategic emphasis has been directed toward marketing which is a segment of the oil industry that is highly competitive. It has failed to protect its source of supply in an industry with limited supply and increasing demand. This failure has put the company at the mercy of small suppliers and wildcatters in times of scarcity, resulting in low profit margins.**

The following checklist describes important factors in the key problem statement.

---

**CHECKLIST 2.2   KEY PROBLEM STATEMENT ADVICE**

**1. State problem explicitly:**  Although one may intuitively understand the nature of a problem, one can not necessarily communicate the problem to someone else.  Translating a problem statement from thoughts into explicit words can be difficult but is necessary.

**2. Aim at significance:**  The problem selected must be a situation where action will produce important gains (or arrest large impending losses) for the organization.

**3. Distinguish short-run and long-run aspects:**  Many organizations face problems which have both short- and long-term aspects.  There are major underlying problems which eventually lead to immediate crises.  For example, a company finds that it is hard-pressed to meet next month's financial obligations.  This crisis must be solved (i.e., secure cash for next month) and the causes of this crisis remedied.

---

## STEP 4:   GENERATE STRATEGIC ALTERNATIVES

Many people find difficulty in generating more than one or two alternative solutions to a problem.  However, with careful thought, students can devise a great many solutions to an organization's problem.  It is an excellent idea to initially generate as many alternatives as possible, even though some may be irrelevant. Further study and modifications may well transform one of the ordinary or impractical solutions into the one selected as best.  To generate useful alternatives, one must often reach into oneself to bring out ideas and create fresh solutions. The following checklist describes sources for conceptualizing alternatives.

---

**CHECKLIST 2.3   SOURCES OF ALTERNATIVES**

**1. Experience:** Here one recalls how others (or oneself) have solved similar problems. These ideas may have come from personal contacts, reading, course notes, movies, etc.

**2. Decision Models:** Frequently, one applies quantitative tools in the case analysis that precedes alternative generation - for example, break-even analysis, return on investment, or decision tree analysis (see Chapter IV).  Alternative solutions may follow directly from such analyses.

---

**3. Research:** One can undertake systematic study to find alternatives. One searches trade journals, finds leads to articles in the Business Periodicals Index or Funk and Scott's, or follows other standard procedures for locating information in the library (see Appendix C).

**4. Creativity:** It is not always possible or practical to use experience, models, or research to generate alternatives. Then one must create a fresh approach. Often this creative process is aided if one returns to the analysis at a later time, or perhaps bases a fresh solution on a solution generated by one of the above methods.

A key consideration that arises later in the evaluation of each alternative is its practicality. When implementation is an issue, the specification of the alternatives may have to include a plan for implementation.

## EXAMPLE OF "GENERATE ALTERNATIVES"

The analyst compiles as many ideas for alternative solutions as possible. Some of the alternative solutions in the example case are:

* Indiana Standard can integrate vertically by entering the production end of the business.

* Indiana Standard can undertake long term contracts with large oil producers.

* Indiana Standard can look for joint ventures or mergers with oil producing companies.

* Indiana Standard can diversify in order to reduce its reliance on oil.

* Indiana Standard can encourage research and development to pursue the conversion of coal and oil shale to gasoline, and the usage of solar energy.

## STEP 5: EVALUATE AND SELECT STRATEGIC ALTERNATIVE

The first step is to make a T-account for each alternative. In one column, the student places "advantages" and in the other, "disadvantages". The process of listing advantages and disadvantages of one alternative often suggests further consideration for other alternatives. The student may return several times to each alternative until nothing more can be added. Often one creates a new solution as all the pieces fall into place during this procedure.

When one has performed this exercise, then one must select the best alternative. This intuitive decision is one of the enigmas facing proponents of quantitative analysis. If one alternative is inferior to another in every merit category, then it can be eliminated from further consideration. However, each alternative usually has some advantages not possessed by other alternatives. This leads to difficulties in objectively comparing alternatives.

There are several issues that often arise in the evaluation of alternatives. These are described in the checklist below.

---

**CHECKLIST 2.4   ALTERNATIVE EVALUATION CONSIDERATIONS**

**1. Relationship to organization:** A good alternative solves the problem within the framework of an organization's objectives, policies and (usually) procedures. The student must recognize all the organization-specific criteria when scoring alternatives. The alternative that is best for one organization might well not be the best one for another.

**2. Probability of outcomes:** With careful reasoning, one can predict possible outcomes of given alternatives. For example, a managerial reorganization can lead to harmony, disharmony, or have no effect. It is much more difficult to assess the probabilities of these outcomes. Nevertheless, successful decision-making requires the ability to judge the likelihood of such outcomes.

**3. Timing:** There are two ways in which the time dimension can be critical to the success of alternatives. First, execution of the planned actions will take some length of time. The availability of resources, personnel, and the response of the economic and competitive environment may change in that time. In other words, the student should be sure not to plan today's solution for tomorrow's environment. Second, organizations tend to solve problems only after they have been in existence for some time. As a result, harmful attitudes and practices may have grown in the organization. In selecting the best alternative, it is important to distinguish between actions in the past that would have avoided the problem and actions today necessary to rectify the situation. In other words, do not apply yesterday's solution to today's problem.

**4. Differential advantage:** When an organization develops a new product, market, or service, it must consider the competition. This question of competition reduces to a question of differential advantage. What reason is there to believe the organization can do better than existing or prospective competitors? Are costs less? Does the organization have special expertise? Does it have a better distribution system? Is it better financed? If the organization cannot find some differential advantage, then perhaps the alternative should be redefined so some segment of the market is entered where the organization does have an advantage over competition.

**5. Strategy of acceptance:** Even after all outcomes of each alternative have been identified, the value of the outcomes assessed, and their probabilities of occurrence estimated, the task of selection is not complete. One must use a strategy (or criterion) of acceptance. Although the question of selecting the best alternatives (even from ones with well-defined outcomes) raises issues that are still unsolved, one can distinguish two strategies useful for case outcomes. First, one can take an expected value approach. Second, one can apply a "minimax" approach -minimize the maximum loss.

---

## EXAMPLE OF "EVALUATE AND SELECT STRATEGIC ALTERNATIVE"

In an organization the size of Indiana Standard, more than one solution can be pursued. Thus, the recommendation is to both:

* Integrate vertically by entering into oil drilling and supply operations.
* Direct special R & D efforts toward breakthroughs in increasing energy sources by conversion of coal or oil shale to gasoline and usage of solar energy.

The problem with these solutions relate to their feasibility. Indiana has the resources to undertake extensive efforts in each area, but should carefully pursue a consistent strategy and monitor progress. The advantages of vertical integration include:

1. The industrial process can be timed to take full advantage of the vertical integration. For example, refining can be designed to maximize the offering of one type of crude oil.
2. Organizational plans can be securely formulated without fear of interruption. For example, retail service stations can be assured of the supply of a uniform grade product.
3. The integrated supply system can optimize transportation and inventory investment.
4. Complete data from well-head to gas station is available for planning and decision-making.
5. The intra-firm transfers can be made more rapidly because of a reduced need for bargaining and contracting.

Although R & D is not likely to lead to advances as significant as the Burton process, breakthroughs may be possible in the areas of alternate energy sources and conversion of other fuels to motor oils. The Indiana laboratories are equipped to undertake research at low cost compared to the potential long-run advantages.

*"More important and more difficult is to make effective the course of action decided upon. . . Nothing is as useless as the right solution that is quietly sabotaged by the people who will have to make it effective."*

--Peter Drucker

## STEP 6: DEFEND IMPLEMENTATION

Treatment of the implementation phase of a decision is problematic in case analysis. Although the workability of alternatives was considered in the evaluation of alternatives, the task cannot have been exhausted at that point. There is an endless stream of details - cost calculations, time-phasings, resource allocations, personnel motivations - involved in the implementation.

In the case analysis framework here, the final step is to prepare to defend the recommendations. This is excellent preparation for the in-class discussion, because any action plan will be subjected to many questions about its workability.

The activity of the case analyst for this step is to list as many significant questions as possible that probe the workability of the action plan, then to think through a defense of the plan for each question. The following checklist identifies areas where many action plans can be attacked at the implementation phase.

## CHECKLIST 2.5 IMPLEMENTATION CONSIDERATIONS

**1. Limitations of Personnel:** Many action plans can be challenged on the grounds that they require skills and abilities beyond those possessed by the organization's personnel. An organization, for the most part, must live with the capabilities of its existing management, staff, and labor. The action plan may challenge individuals, but must not require individuals to accomplish tasks which they are incapable of performing.

**2. Control System:** The workability of an action plan is enhanced by specifying adequate controls. A control system is a set of procedures to ensure that the action plan is proceeding in the fashion envisioned. Thus the control system contains the original objectives, a sequence of activities necessary to achieve those objectives, and milestones to measure progress along the way.

**3. Motivate Behavior:** The action plan may require some individuals to significantly alter their attitudes or jobs. The action plan should indicate how this is to be accomplished.

**4. Contingency Plans:** One way to attack a plan is to question what will happen if some part of the plan does not turn out as intended. For example, if initial sales of a new product are low, does the action plan fail? Is there adequate financing? Is a new advertising approach possible? Can inventories be sold at cost to reduce further losses?

## EXAMPLE OF "DEFEND IMPLEMENTATION"

In this step, the analyst poses and answers questions about the workability of the recommendations. Since answering the questions is so open-ended, the example here contains only the questions. There are two parts to the action recommendations for this case, so there are two sets of questions.

The vertical integration recommendation can be questioned as follows:

* The case had ample evidence that management was more interested in the marketing end of the business. Does management have the interest and competence to execute this plan?

* The investments will take a long time to realize pay-off because of the time lag between exploratory drilling and oil recovery. Can Indiana Standard wait?

* Does the growing independence of foreign oil-producing countries make foreign investments in oil recovery too risky because of threats of nationalization?

* What effect will this decision have on morale in the Indiana Oil Purchasing Company?

The part of the solution where R & D is directed to pursue other energy sources can be questioned as follows:

* There is no known energy source cost-competitive with oil for providing automobile propulsion. Does the alternative have a reasonable prospect for success?

* Suppose a technique for converting coal to gasoline is perfected, can Indiana Standard generate funds for the huge facilities that would be necessary to perform the conversion on an industrial scale?

* Suppose Indiana Standard develops a coal conversion technique and invests in facilities. What happens if another company discovers a more efficient method of conversion?

**NOTES:**

**NOTES:**

22

# CHAPTER III  STRATEGIC CONCEPTS FOR CASE ANALYSIS

## I. INTRODUCTION TO STRATEGIC CONCEPTS FOR CASE ANALYSIS

In recent years definitive work primarily by Michael E. Porter[1] represents important new concepts in strategic thinking and is the major focus of this chapter.  Several frameworks to organize a student's thinking in strategic terms are presented.

Fundamentally,  strategy deals with the allocation of resources, it is essentially a commitment to undertake one set of actions rather than another.  Strategic thinking in case analysis requires three basic activities:

1. Understanding where the firm has been and why it has either succeeded or failed to achieve expected results.

2. Identifying future trends or events that can change these results  (either positively or negatively).

3. Evaluation of the current strategy and then deciding whether or not to change it,  and the degree and type of change necessary.

Developing  strategy  is an analysis-driven exercise, not  an activity  where  you  succeed by sheer effort and intuition.   Determining the best strategy ideally needs to be grounded in a probing assessment of a firm's external environment and  internal situation.

## II.  INDUSTRY ANALYSIS - The External Environment

The essence of formulating a competitive strategy is to relate a firm to its environment.  The environment  we focus on is the industry in which the firm competes.   Forces outside the industry are important  but  only in a relative sense; since  changes  outside  the industry typically affect all firms equally.

The intensity of competition in a given industry is not a  matter of  coincidence  but  rather is rooted in its underlying economic structure.   Competition in an industry depends on five competitive forces  shown in Figure 3.1.   These five forces are:  threat of  entry, intensity  of rivalry among firms, pressure from substitute  products, bargaining  power of buyers, and bargaining power of suppliers.   The collective  strength  of these forces determines the  ultimate  profit potential  in the industry.   The goal of industry analysis for a  firm is to find a position in the industry where it can best defend  itself against these competitive forces or where it can influence them in its favor.

------------

[1]See Michael E. Porter, "Competitive Strategy", ( Free Press,  Macmillan Publishers,Inc.,NY) 1980,  also "Competitive Advantage",  1985 and "The Competitive Advantage of Nations", 1990  by  the same publisher.

Knowing these underlying sources of competitive pressure helps to (a)highlight the critical strengths and weaknesses of the firm, (b) clarify the firms position in the industry, (c) identify the areas where strategic changes may yield the greatest payoff, and (d) points out the areas where industry trends hold promise as either opportunities or threats. Understanding these forces will also prove to be useful in considering areas for diversification.

Industry analysis is the fundamental building block for formulating a firm's competitive strategy. The following discussion and checklists will assist you in using the five forces to understand the structure of the industry and in identifying a firm's strategic position in that industry *(May the force be with you)*.

## FIGURE 3.1   FIVE FORCES DRIVING INDUSTRY COMPETITION

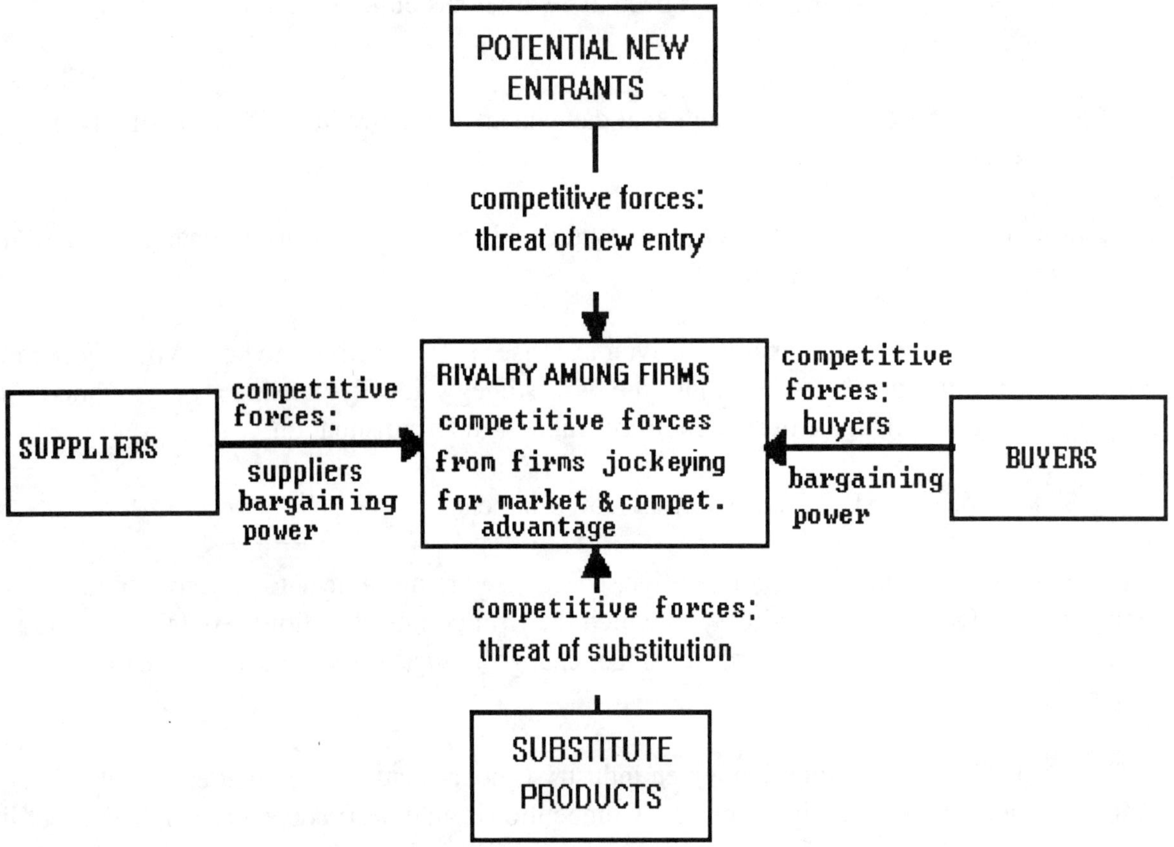

Adapted from:  Michael E. Porter,  Competitive Strategy,  (Free Press, Macmillan Publishers, Inc., N.Y.) 1980, pg 4.

## A.   THE  FIVE  FORCES

**1.   Threat of Entry** :   The threat of entry into an industry depends on the barriers to entry that are present, coupled with the reaction from existing firms that the newcomer can expect. The barriers to entry are presented in Checklist  3.1.

24

```
CHECKLIST 3.1   EVALUATING BARRIERS TO ENTRY

1. Economies of Scale - Does the product/service lend itself to economies of scale (decline
in unit cost as volume increases)?  Economies of scale deter entry by requiring entrants to come
in at large scale.

2. Product Differentiation - Is the product/service differentiated?  Differentiation creates a barrier
to entry by forcing entrants to spend heavily (advertising, promotion,etc.) to overcome existing
customer loyalty.

3. Switching Costs - Is the cost of switching from one supplier's products to another high (involves
such things as employee training, new ancillary equipment, etc.)?  If the costs are high the new en-
trant must offer a major improvement in cost or performance in order to get the buyer to switch.

4. Capital Requirements - Is there a requirement to invest large financial resources in order to
compete?  Large capital requirements create a barrier to entry.

5. Access to Distribution -  Does the product/service require extensive outlets for its distribution?
A barrier to entry can be created if the new entrant needs extensive outlets for the distribution of
its product/service.

6. Absolute Cost Advantages - Additional cost factors that can result in barriers to entry are:
        *  Proprietary product technology
        *  Access to raw materials
        *  Favorable location
        *  Proprietary learning curve
        *  Government subsidies

7. Government Policy - Governments can restrict or eliminate entry into a given industry.

8. Expected Retaliation  - If the firm enters is there likely to be retaliation by competitors?
```

**2. Intensity of Rivalry Among Firms**: Rivalry takes the form of jockeying for position--using tactics such as lowering price, additional advertising, new product introduction, and increased customer service. Intense rivalry occurs because a competitor either feels the pressure or sees an opportunity to improve position.

Some forms of competition, primarily price competition, are very volatile and can hurt the entire industry in terms of profits. Price cutting can be matched by the competition and once matched can lead to price wars. Price cutting has a direct impact on profit margins and is a tough form of rivalry. On the other hand, promotions such as advertising expenditures often increase demand or enhance product differentiation in the industry for the benefit of all firms. Rivalry can be "cutthroat" or it can be "polite or gentlemanly" depending on a number of interacting factors. Factors that determine the intensity of rivalry are presented in Checklist 3.2 Rivalry Determinants.

CHECKLIST 3.2    EVALUATING RIVALRY DETERMINANTS

**Rivalry can become intense (cutthroat) if:**

1. There is slow industry growth (It becomes a market share game).
2. There is intermittent overcapacity in the industry.
3. The products are perceived as commodities. Buyers base their decision on price and service only.
4. There are high fixed costs which create strong pressure to fill capacity. High storage costs have the same affect.
5. The firm size is balanced. If the industry is dominated by a few large firms, these leaders can impose disipline or play a coordinating role (price leader, etc.) thereby limiting price cutting, etc. For a measure of balance see Herfindahl Index.(chapter IV, pg. 57).
6. The competitors differ in structure and origin (such as foreign corporations), often have differing goals and strategies on how they compete. The industry may find it difficult to establish "the rules of the game".
7. A number of firms are committed to the product and have high stakes in gaining success.
8. There are high exit barriers which may keep firms competing even with low or negative returns. The major sources of exit barriers are:

   * Specialized Assets
   * Fixed Cost of Exit
   * Strategic Interrelationships
   * Emotional Barriers
   * Government and Social Restrictions

**3. Pressure from Substitute Products**: All firms compete with industries producing substitute products. Substitutes limit potential returns by putting a ceiling on prices the industry can profitably charge. Checklist 3.3 presents "The Determinants of Substitute Threat".

CHECKLIST 3.3    DETERMINANTS OF SUBSTITUTE THREAT

**Substitute products offer a threat when:**

1. The price-performance offered by the substitutes is attractive relative to the firm's product.
2. The switching costs are low. Buyers are more willing to accept substitute products.
3. There is a high propensity for buyers to substitute. In high profit industries, substitutes are more likely to come into play given they increase competition through price reduction or performance improvement.

**4. Bargaining Power of Buyers**:    Buyers bargain for lower prices, higher quality or more service and play competitors against each other -- all at the expense of the industries' profit potential. Checklist 3.4 Determinants of Buyer Power presents the factors that determine the impact of the buyer on the industry.

```
CHECKLIST 3.4 DETERMINANTS OF BUYER POWER

A buyer has bargaining power if:

1. The buyer purchases in large volume relative to seller's sales.
2. The buyer's switching costs are low.
3. The seller faces high switching costs.
4. The products are standard or undifferentiated (treated as a commodity).
5. There is a credible threat to backward integrate.
6. The product is unimportant to the quality of the buyer's products or service.
```

**5. Bargaining Power of Suppliers**: Like buyers, suppliers can exert bargaining power over the industry by raising prices, reducing quality, or services (or threatening to). Determinants of supplier power is presented in Checklist 3.5.

```
CHECKLIST 3.5  DETERMINANTS OF SUPPLIER POWER

A supplier group has bargaining power if:

1. It is dominated by a few firms and buyers are fragmented.
2. There is a lack of substitute products.
3. The buyers are not an important segment of the supplier's business.
4. The product is important to the success of the buyer.
5. The product supplied is differentiated.
6. There is a threat of forward integration by the supplier.
7. There are high switching costs.
```

## B. STRATEGIC GROUPS WITHIN INDUSTRIES

Up to this point we have focused our analysis on the industry as a whole and evaluating that industry using the five forces. However, in most industries there are wide differences among firms so that evaluation of the industry as a whole is not enough. Often the analysis can be more productive by evaluating strategic groups of firms within the industry. Groups of firms within an industry may vary on a number of strategic dimensions. Checklist 3.6 lists some of the more important dimensions.

```
CHECKLIST 3.6 STRATEGIC DIMENSIONS

1. Price - high price to low price
2. Quality - high quality to low quality
3. Size of the firm - large to small
4. Degree of Integration - forward to backward
5. Distribution Channel - company-owned to specialty outlets to broad line outlets.
6. Product line - broad to narrow
7. Technological Leadership - leader to follower
```

As Porter[1] notes strategic groups are present for a wide variety of reasons (different initial strengths and weaknesses, different times of entry, etc.) but once formed they tend to resemble each other in a number of ways. This characteristic permits use of the strategic map as an important analytical tool for displaying strategic groups. Figure 3.2 presents a typical Map of Strategic Groups.

**FIGURE 3.2   A MAP OF STRATEGIC GROUPS**

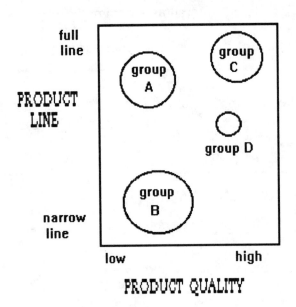

## C.   POSITIONING WITHIN INDUSTRIES

Every industry is unique and has its own characteristics. As a rule industries are relatively stable but can change over time as an industry evolves. Each industry (or segment of an industry) has different requirements for success. Competition in a fragmented industry often requires different resources and skills when compared to an industry controlled by a few giant corporations. In addition to industry analysis which provides a basis for responding to industry structure, firms must identify a position within the industry.

The key to effective positioning within an industry is competitive advantage. A firm will succeed relative to their competition, only if they develop some sustainable competitive advantage.

1. Competitive Advantage:   There are two basic forms of competitive advantage:   lower cost and differentiation.

   * Lower Cost -   is the ability to design, produce and market comparable product more efficiently than the competitor.
   * Differentiation -   is the ability to provide unique and value to a buyer in terms product quality, special features, or after-sale service.

Competitive advantage of either type, translates into higher productivity than that of competitors. The low-cost firm produces a product or service using fewer inputs than its competition. The differentiated firm gains higher revenues per unit than its competitors.

**2. Competitive Scope**: A final variable in the positioning equation is competitive scope, or the breadth of the firm's target within its industry. Scope is important because as a general rule industries are segmented. Typically industries have a range of product variety, many different distribution channels, and different types of customers. Competitive scope is generalized into two types - broad and narrow scope.

The type of advantage and the scope of advantage has been combined into the notion of generic strategies, or different approaches to superior performance in the industry. Each of these strategies, illustrated in Figure 3.3 represents a fundamentally different concept of how to compete.

### FIGURE 3.3   GENERIC STRATEGIES

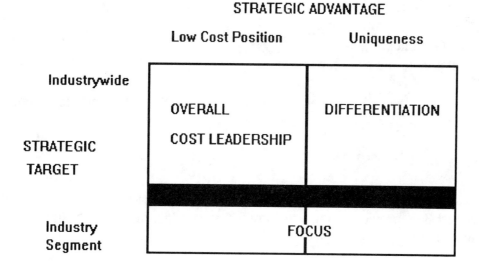

Source:  Michael E. Porter,"Competitive Strategy", (Free Press, Macmillan Publishers, Inc New York), 1980, p 39.

## D. GENERIC STRATEGIES

**1. Low Cost Leadership** - requires efficient-scale facilities, aggressive pursuit of cost reductions (from experience, tight cost and overhead control, avoiding marginal customers, etc.). A great deal of management attention to cost is required to achieve this strategy.

**2. Differentiation** - requires creating something that is perceived as unique in the industry. Approaches to this strategy can take many different forms (design or brand image, technology, customer service, etc.).

**3. Focus** - Like the differentiation strategy a focus strategy may take many different forms (aimed at a particular buyer's group, geographic market, or segment of a product line, etc.). The other two generic strategies are aimed at achieving their objectives industrywide, while the focus strategy is aimed at some particular target within an industry.

29

## III. SITUATION ANALYSIS - The Internal Environment

In the first half of this chapter we explained how to use industry analysis and strategic positioning to assess the relative attractiveness of the firm's external environment. This portion of the chapter is concerned with how to evaluate a particular firm's situation and how this might impact on their strategic positioning in their industry.

## A. STRATEGIC PERFORMANCE

The first step in this analysis is to determine the firms present competitive approach. Are they moving towards low cost leadership, trying to differentiate, focusing on a specific segment of the market or are they caught somewhere in the middle. The best evidence of how well the firm's strategic positioning is working is to look at their recent performance. Indicators of strategic performance[2] include:

1. The rise or fall of market share.
2. Increasing or decreasing profit margins.
3. Net profit and ROI trends.
4. Sales growth relative to the market as a whole.

The second step is to conduct a SWOT analysis ( a firm's strengths, weaknesses, opportunities and threats).

## B. SWOT ANALYSIS

This analysis involves evaluating a firm's internal strengths and weaknesses and its external opportunities and threats. Checklist 3.7 provides things to look for in conducting the analysis of strengths and weaknesses in a firm.

---

**CHECKLIST 3.7    INTERNAL STRENGTHS AND WEAKNESS**

Factors to consider in evaluating a firm's strengths and weaknesses include:

**1. Strategic Factors** - What is the firm's track record in implementing strategy?. See indicators of strategic performance above.

**2. Financial Factors** - Does the firm have adequate financial resources relative to the competition? Look at financial ratios, cash flow and return on investment (see Chapter IV Financial and Quantitative Tools for Case Analysis).

**3. Marketing Factors** - Does the firm have marketing capability? Look at product line, advertising and promotion, channels of distribution, etc.

---

[2] Thompson, A.& Strickland, A., "Strategic Management" , 5th Ed.,(BPI/Irwin, Homewood, IL) 1990, pg 90.

**4. Production Factors** - Where is the firm on the experience curve, do they have access to economies of scale, technology skills, manufacturing skills, proprietary technology? What is their position relative to R & D and product innovation?

**5. Management/Organization Factors** - Is management supportive? Do they possess the attributes that characterize successful firms? See "Attributes of Excellence"

Checklist 3.8 provides factors to look for in evaluating a firms opportunities and threats.

---

**CHECKLIST 3.8 EXTERNAL OPPORTUNITIES AND THREATS**

Some of the factors to consider in evaluating a firm's opportunities include:

1. Are there opportunities for market growth (i.e., new or shifting buyers needs) ?
2. Can we expand product line?
3. Should the firm diversify into related areas?
4. Is forward or backward integration a viable option?
5. Have trade barriers lowered in other markets?
6. Are there new industry trends to consider (i.e., emergence of an new industry segment, etc.)?

Some of the possible threats that a firm should consider include:

1. Increasing sales of substitute products.
2. Decreases in marketing trends (changes in custormer tastes,etc).
3. New entry of low-cost competitors.
4. Adverse changes in regulatory requirements.
5. Changes in trade policies and /or foreign exchange rates.
6. Customer or supplier integration.

---

## C. COMPETITIVE ANALYSIS[3]

In recent years analysts have begun to evaluate a firm's ability to gain and maintain competitive advantage. In a volatile, intensely competitive world, success comes from the capacity of a firm to respond and act. The steps used to evaluate the firm in terms of sustaining competitive advantage are:

**1. Basic Competence.** Companies compete on the basis of distinctive skill. Successful companies remain focused on their basic strengths, build on them, and de-emphasize activities that do not add value.

---

[3] See Michael E. Porter, "Competitive Advantage", (Free Press, Macmillan Publishers, Inc., N. Y.) , 1985.

**2. Time Compression.** Companies are increasingly competing on time whether it be from being first through innovation or faster cycle times for product development to just-in-time inventory and speedy response to market trends.

**3. Continuous Improvement.** When we speak of "quality" we're talking of more than just the concept of zero defects, we're talking about a total quality movement which embraces the idea of continual upgrading. This involves step-by-step product and process improvement based on measures, feedback, and learning.

**4. Relationships.** A final source of competitive advantage is based on collaboration across companies, especially supplier-customer partnerships.

The authors of "In Search of Excellence"[4] identified eight recurring attributes of excellence among the companies they studied. These attributes, presented in checklist 3.9, can serve as a basis for evaluating the organizational climate (operating values and attitudes of management) of the firm.

---

**CHECKLIST 3.9 ATTRIBUTES OF EXCELLENCE[4]**

**1. Bias Toward Action** - The firms are action oriented; the approach is "do it, fix it, try it." They don't analyze a problem to death before acting. They make progress in small steps rather than through sweeping changes. They are flexible, incremental, and responsive.

**2. Simple Form and Lean Staff** - The structure of the organization is a means to an end, not the end in itself. The best is often the simplest. Many of these firms are divided into small, entrepreneurial units that get things done. Staff is kept as small as possible to avoid bureaucracies.

**3. Closeness to the Customer** - The firm is "customer driven" in that they view the customer as an integral part of their business, rather than as an outsider. Above all, they strive to design goods and services to meet the customer's needs.

**4. Productivity Improvements Through People** - Successful firms believe that productivity can be improved by motivating and stimulating employees. They do this by giving them autonomy, feedback and recognition. They use progress charts, pins, and slogans all of which may appear simplistic but do in fact work.

**5. Operational Autonomy** - Successful firms authorize their managers to act like entrepreneurs, giving them the authority to make a wide range of decisions on their own.

**6. Focus on a Key Business Value** - Strong firms focus on a strategic value that is important to their success, but simple enough to be understood and internalized by all employees.

**7. Doing What They Know Best** - The successful firms know their strengths and build on them. They resist the temptation to move into other areas that require skills they do not have.

**8. Simultaneous Loose/Tight Control** - Strong companies control a few critical variables tightly, but allow flexibility and leeway in others.

---

[4]Peters, T., & Waterman B., "In Search of Excellence", (Harper & Row, New York), 1982.

In today's world, rivals compete on a truly global basis, gaining competitive advantages from an entire network of worldwide activities. They gain advantage by using the most productive mix of these from multinational sources.

---

**CHECKLIST 3.10    FACTORS TO LOOK FOR IN GAINING AND SUSTAINING COMPETITIVE ADVANTAGE[3]**

**1.   Does the firm see triggers of opportunity early  and  move aggressively to gain competitive advantage?** Such factors as reducing costs through economies of scale, cumulative learning, established channels  of distribution and brand name, are  competitive  advantages gained by early movers.

**2.   Does the firm gain information/insight that  is not sought or available to the competition?** Are they investing in R & D, looking in the right places, not worrying about conventional wisdom, and actively looking for new ways to compete.

**3.   Does the firm operate on the basis of lower order advantages  or higher order advantages?** Low cost labor, cheap raw materials,  which are relatively easy to imitate and therefore short lived. Or do they have higher order advantages (proprietary technology, brand image, high switching costs, etc.) which are difficult to match and therefore more sustainable.

**4.   Does the firm have  many competitive advantages  throughout the operation ?** Having many competitive advantages makes it much more difficult for competitors to overcome  (the more the better).

**5.   Does the firm sustain advantage by continued expansion and upgrading (moving  up the hierachy)?**

---

## IV.   TOOLS FOR EVALUATING STRATEGIC ALTERNATIVES

Having  completed  the external environmental  and  internal situational analysis the next step is to consider whether  the firm should continue  its present strategy ( with  some  fine tuning) or whether the firm needs to look at a competely different generic strategy.  Some of the analytical tools which can aid  you  in determining  the appropriateness of a particular alternative include:  performance  gap  analysis,   the growth/share matrix,   the GE business screen and,  the industry evolution matrix.

## A.   PERFORMANCE  GAP  ANALYSIS [5]

A performance gap represents the difference between  the projected future performance of the firm compared to desired performance.  Figure 3.5  offers one approach to strategic alternatives for closing  performance gaps  using breakeven analysis as  a  basis  of  evaluation.

-------------------

[5] Rue,L. & Holland P., Strategic Management: Concepts and Experiences, (McGraw Hill Inc.,New York),  1989, pg 148-152.

## FIGURE 3.5 STRATEGIC ALTERNATIVES FOR CLOSING PERFORMANCE GAPS

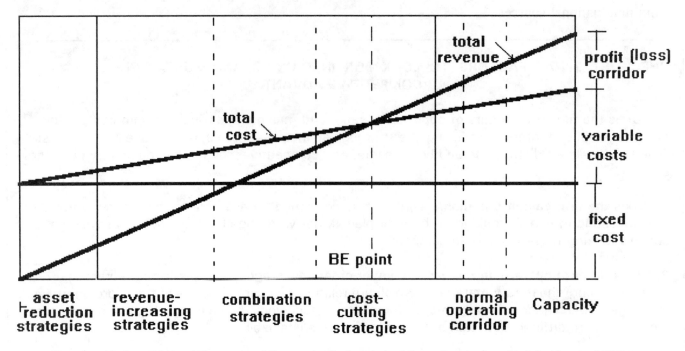

Source: Hofer, C.W., "Turnaround Strategies", Journal of Bus. Strategies, Vol.1, No. 1, 1980

## B. THE GROWTH SHARE MATRIX

A popular methodology developed by the Boston Consulting Group (BCG) was designed to assist in strategic evaluation and selection process. BCG describes the four quadrants of this matrix as cash cows, dogs, question marks, and stars. Figure 3.6 presents this matrix and recommed strategies for firms in a specific quadrant.

### FIGURE 3.6 THE GROWTH/SHARE MATRIX

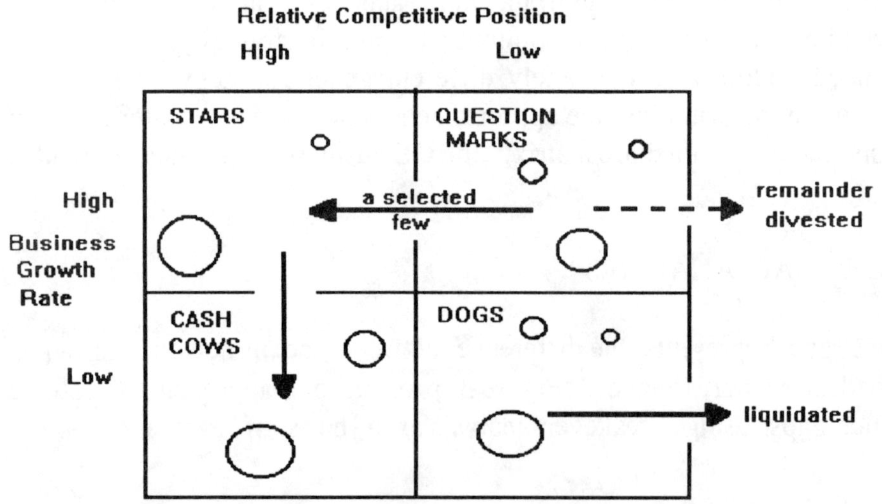

source: Adapted from B. Hedley,"Strategy & the Business Portfolio," Long Range Planning,Feb.1977,p.10.

## C.  THE  GE BUSINESS SCREEN

This matrix,  presented in Figure 3.7,  is similar to the Growth/Share matrix but provides a more definitive measure on both axes.  Both industry attractiveness and  business strength are rated as either high, medium, or low.

### FIGURE 3.7   THE  GE  BUSINESS  SCREEN
### BUSINESS STRENGTH/COMPETITIVE POSITION

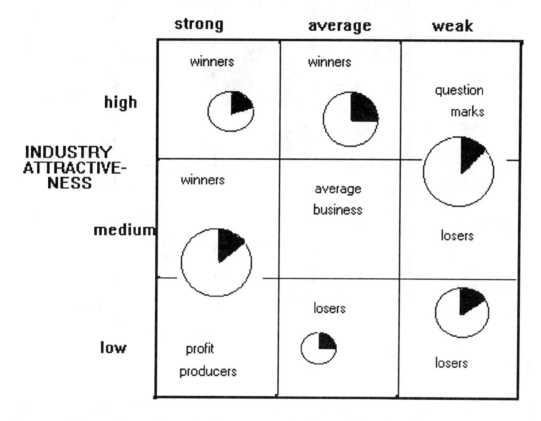

Source:  Adapted from Strategic Management in General Electric,  Corp. Planning  & Dev., General Electric Corporation.

## D.  THE  INDUSTRY EVOLUTION MATRIX

This matrix plots the firm's competitive position against the life-cycle stage of the product, market  and industry.  In figure 3.8,  the matrix shows  various enterprises of the firm as  pie slices (market share) of the  total industry (circles). Circle size represents the relative size of the industry.[6] The assumption in this analysis is that conglomerate organizations  should have businesses in all  stages of  their industry/product life cycles.

------------
[6]Charles W. Hofer, "Conceptual Constructs for Formulating Corp. and Business  Strategies,"  No. 9-378-754 Intercollegiate  Case  Clearing House, 1977.

35

# FIGURE 3.8 INDUSTRY EVOLUTION MATRIX

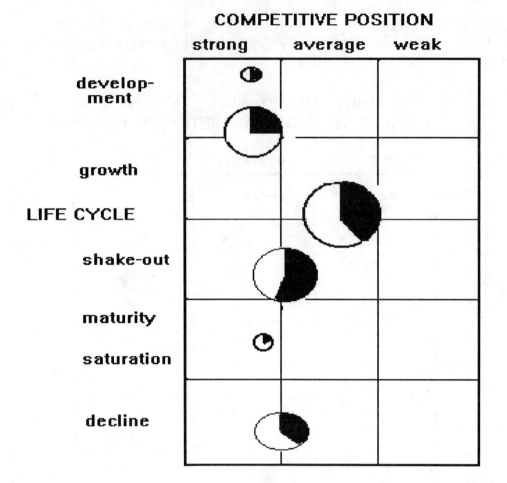

## V. GLOBAL ANALYSIS

The world has become a single marketplace. A firm that ignores this fact may find itself in jeopardy (about 80% of all U.S. products face foreign competition). Firms should go international if there are profitable functions (offensive or defensive) that can be performed abroad. According to Vernon and Wells[7] some of the reasons for going international are:

(1.) Become a financial intermediary.
(2.) Take advantage of technological lead.
(3.) Become geographically diversified.
(4.) Create a market aboard.

Checklist 3.11 identifies some of the advantages gained by going international.

--------------------------------

[7]Vernon R. & Wells, L., Managers in an International Economy, (Englewood Cliffs: Prentice Hall), 1981.

36

```
CHECKLIST 3.11   ADVANTAGES OF GOING INTERNATIONAL [7]

1. Gaining access to foreign capital markets.

2. Reduce problems dealing with exchange rate, devaluation and
   exports.

3. Increased sales potential.

4. Overcome trade barriers and political considerations.

5. Reduce transportation, labor and materials costs.

6. Make foreign investments that are under the firm's control.
```

The next step for the firm is to consider which products and services to take international. Rutenberg[8] developed a checklist to aid a firm in these considerations. His approach is based on three major considerations: (a) the capability of the firm, (b) the nature of the market and (c) costs and benefits of expansion.

```
CHECKLIST 3.12 CONSIDERATIONS FOR MARKETING ABOARD[8]

1) What are the present capabilities of the firm?
       a)  Would it dilute management attention?
       b)  Are products nontransferable?
       c)  Are technology or marketing skills unique?

2) What are worldwide markets like?
       a)  Do standards differ?
       b)  Are most markets dominated by others?
       c)  Is there growth and potential?

3) Can the firm undertake expansion aboard?
       a)  Is the firm already profitable?
       b)  Is technology unique?
       c)  Does the firm have good domestic marketing skills?

4) Can the firm work with or through a foreign national?
       a)  Employing local agents (independent agents).
       b)  Employing local representatives.
       c)  Entering into licensing agreements.
       d)  Forming a joint venture.
       e)  Acquiring local companies.
       f)  Forming a foreign subsidiary.
```

[8] D.P.Rutenberg,  Multinational Management, (Little Brown & Co., Boston) 1982.

**NOTES:**

# CHAPTER IV   FINANCIAL AND QUANTITATIVE TOOLS FOR CASE ANALYSIS

This section gives the student a compact review and reference to commonly used quantitative techniques. This is for students who are already familiar with the techniques, but who wish a convenient summary of the important practical aspects of the most utilized techniques.

## I.   ANALYSIS OF INCOME STATEMENTS AND BALANCE SHEETS

The two basic financial statements which measure an organization's financial situation are the balance sheet and income statement. Even though recent financial analysis has placed more emphasis on funds and cash flow statements, the balance sheet and income statement are essential for understanding the financial position and prospects of an organization. The financial statements given in this section are used to illustrate the calculation of ratios, the derivation of funds and cash flow statements, and return on investment.

## A.   THE BALANCE SHEET

The purpose of the balance sheet is to show a company's financial position at a given time, normally at the end of the accounting period. It provides a picture of the company's position in the same way a camera takes a photograph. The balance sheet is a listing of the resources of an organization together with the equities (i.e., the interests of creditors and owners) in those resources. Thus, a balance sheet reflects the results of all the financial transactions of the company. The balance sheet in Figure 4.1 portrays the financial condition of the Macro Corporation as of July 31, 1991 and July 31, 1992.

The assets are listed on the balance sheet until they are either wholly depreciated or transferred out of the organization. The equities of the creditors and owners are continually changing as a result of various transactions. Hence, the level of these equities and the assets at a given point in time are shown on the balance sheet. Even though the balance sheet reports the assets and equities, it does not identify either the causes or timing of changes in them. However, careful examination of a series of balance sheets reveals changes in the asset and equity structure. In this manner, relationships between items may be determined and trends discovered. The last part of this subsection considers such analyses of the balance sheets.

# FIGURE 4.1 THE BALANCE SHEET

MACRO CORPORATION
Balance Sheet
July 31, 1991 and July 31, 1992
(All Figures times $1000)

| ASSETS | JULY 31 1992 | JULY 31 1991 |
|---|---|---|
| Cash | $ 180 | $ 205 |
| Accounts Receivable | 590 | 490 |
| Allowance For Bad Debt | (13) | (10) |
| Inventories | 645 | 590 |
| Prepaid Insurance | 18 | 16 |
| TOTAL CURRENT ASSETS | $1420 | $1291 |
| Machinery & Equipment | $ 450 | $ 480 |
| Depreciation Allowance - Machinery & Equipment | (290) | (252) |
| Building | 400 | 400 |
| Depreciation Allowance - Building | (185) | (173) |
| Land | 24 | 11 |
| TOTAL FIXED ASSETS | $ 399 | $ 466 |
| Goodwill | 10 | 10 |
| TOTAL ASSETS | $1829 | $1767 |
|  | ==== | ==== |

| LIABILITIES AND EQUITY | | |
|---|---|---|
| Accounts Payable | $ 153 | $ 110 |
| Notes Payable | 90 | 79 |
| Accrued Taxes | 127 | 138 |
| TOTAL CURRENT LIABILITIES | $ 370 | $ 327 |
| Bonds Payable | 19 | 25 |
| TOTAL LONG-TERM LIABILITIES | $ 19 | $ 25 |
| TOTAL LIABILITIES | $ 389 | $ 352 |
| Common Stock | 500 | 490 |
| Retained Earnings July 31 | 940 | 925 |
| TOTAL STOCKHOLDERS EQUITY | $1440 | $1415 |
| TOTAL LIABILITIES AND EQUITY | $1829 | $1767 |
|  | ==== | ==== |

## B.   THE INCOME STATEMENT

The income statement reports the results ofa company's operation over a specific period of time. It identifies the inflow of assets (revenue), the outflow of assets (expenses), and the net increase or decrease resulting from the organization's activities. The income statement tells by the "revenue and expense" category the events of the accounting period. It answers such questions as: Is the organization moving forward (profits) or backwards (losses)? How fast ? What revenues and expenses are the key to the organization's performance? Figure 4.2 shows the income statement of the Macro Corporation.

**FIGURE 4.2    THE  INCOME  STATEMENT**

MACRO CORPORATION
Statement of Income and Retained Earnings
For the Year Ended July 31, 1992
(All figures times $1000)

| | | |
|---|---|---|
| Net Sales | | $ 3500 |
| Cost of Goods Sold | | 2040 |
| | | $ 1460 |
| Gross Profit | | |
| Less: Operating Expenses | | |
| Selling | $500 | |
| Administrative | 800 | 1300 |
| Gross Operating Profit | | $ 160 |
| Depreciation | | 60 |
| Net Profit from Operations | | 100 |
| Add: Other Income | | |
| Patent License | | 34 |
| Gross Income | | 134 |
| Less: Other Expense: | | |
| Interest on Notes | $ 12 | |
| Interest on Bonds | 2 | 14 |
| Net Income Before Tax | | $ 120 |
| Tax | | 50 |
| Net Income After Tax | | $ 70 |
| Less: Dividends | | 55 |
| Additions to Retained Earnings | | $ 15 |
| Retained Earnings July 31, 1991 | | 925 |
| Retained Earnings July 31, 1992 | | $ 940 |
| | | = = = = |

## C.   HOW TO COMPARE FINANCIAL STATEMENTS

Although  balance  sheets and income  statements for one accounting period are revealing, they do not by themselves portray the financial future of the organization.  One needs to compare a series of statements from one accounting period to the next to identify trends.  Such comparisons are facilitated by the conversion of dollar figures to percentages (i.e., by dividing each dollar figure by a key total amount). In horizontal analysis, one compares a financial component in an organization's statement with the same item in another statement at a different point in time.    Figure 4.3  shows the horizontal analysis of the balance sheet  for the Macro Corporation.   Here,  the two years are listed in adjacent  columns with  the current  figure  listed first.   The net dollar change column  is followed by a percentage change column.

41

# FIGURE 4.3  HORIZONTAL ANALYSIS

MACRO CORPORATION
Horizontal Balance Sheet Analysis
July 31, 1991 to July 31, 1992
(All figures times $1000)

| ASSETS | JULY 31 1992 | JULY 31 1991 | CHANGE ($) | CHANGE (%) |
|---|---|---|---|---|
| Cash | $ 180 | $ 205 | $ -25 | -13.9 |
| Accounts Receivable | 590 | 490 | +100 | +16.9 |
| Allowance for Bad Debts | (13) | (10) | -3 | +23.0 |
| Inventories | 645 | 590 | +55 | +8.5 |
| Prepaid Insurance | 18 | 16 | +2 | +11.1 |
| TOTAL CURRENT ASSETS | $1420 | $1291 | $+129 | +9.0 |
| Machinery & Equipment | $ 450 | $ 480 | -30 | -6.6 |
| Depr. Allowance - M&E | (290) | (252) | -38 | -13.1 |
| Building | 400 | 400 | 0 | 0 |
| Depr. Allowance - Bldg. | (185) | (173) | -12 | +6.4 |
| Land | 24 | 11 | +13 | +54.1 |
| TOTAL FIXED ASSETS | $ 399 | $ 466 | $ -67 | -14.3 |
| Goodwill | 10 | 10 | 0 | 0 |
| TOTAL ASSETS | $1829 | $1767 | $ 62 | 3.5 |
| LIABILITIES AND EQUITY | | | | |
| Accounts Payable | $ 153 | $ 110 | +43 | +28.1 |
| Notes Payable | 90 | 79 | +11 | +12.1 |
| Accrued Taxes | 127 | 138 | -11 | -8.7 |
| TOTAL CURRENT LIABILITIES | $ 370 | $ 327 | $ 43 | 11.6 |
| Bonds Payable | 19 | 25 | -6 | -31.5 |
| TOTAL LONG-TERM LIABILITIES | $ 19 | $ 25 | $ -6 | -31.5 |
| TOTAL LIABILITIES | $ 389 | $ 352 | $ 37 | 9.5 |
| Common Stock | 500 | 490 | +10 | +2.0 |
| Retained Earnings July 31 | 940 | 925 | +15 | +1.6 |
| TOTAL STOCKHOLDERS EQUITY | 1440 | 1415 | +25 | 1.70 |
| TOTAL LIABILITIES & EQUITY | $1829 | $1767 | $ 62 | 3.4 |
| | ==== | ==== | ==== | ==== |

Important factors are also highlighted by vertical analysis of financial statements. Accountants often refer to this type of statement as a "common-size" statement, since each item is expressed as a percentage of a common base. For the balance sheet, each component is usually expressed as a percentage of total assets. For the income statement, each component is usually expressed as a percentage of net sales. This form of analysis can be used to compare several companies in the same industry, or different divisions of the same company. The common size income statement for Macro Corporation is shown in Figure 4.4.

## FIGURE 4.4 VERTICAL ANALYSIS OF INCOME STATEMENT

MACRO CORPORATION
Vertical Analysis of Income Statement
For the Year Ended July 31, 1992
(All figures times $1000)
(All percentages are of net sales)

|  |  |  | Percent of Net Sales | Industry Average |
|---|---|---|---|---|
| Net Sales |  | $ 3500 | 100.0 | 100.0 |
| Cost of Goods Sold |  | 2040 | 58.3 | 49.5 |
|  |  | $ 1460 | 41.7 | 51.5 |
| Gross Profit |  |  |  |  |
| Less: Operating Expenses |  |  |  |  |
| Selling | $ 500 |  |  |  |
| Administrative | 800 | 1300 | 37.1 | 42.0 |
| Goss Operating Profit |  | $ 160 | 4.5 | 6.5 |
| Depreciation |  | 60 | 1.7 | 2.0 |
| Net Profit from Operations |  | 100 | 2.8 | 4.5 |
| Add: Other Income |  |  |  |  |
| Patent License |  | 34 | 1.0 | 0 |
|  |  | 134 | 3.8 | 4.5 |
| Gross Income |  |  |  |  |
| Less: Other Expense |  |  |  |  |
| Interest on Notes | $ 12 |  |  |  |
| Interest on Bonds | 2 | 14 | .4 | .4 |
| Net Income Before Tax |  | $ 120 | 3.4 | 4.1 |
| Tax |  | 50 | 1.4 | 1.7 |
| Net Income After Tax |  | $ 70 | 2.0 | 2.4 |
| Less: Dividends |  | 55 |  |  |
| Add to Retained Earnings |  | $ 15 |  |  |
| Retained Earnings July 31, 1991 |  | 925 |  |  |
| Retained Earnings July 31, 1992 |  | $ 940 |  |  |
|  |  | ==== |  |  |

## II. FINANCIAL RATIO ANALYSIS

Ratio analysis is a procedure to rapidly evaluate an organization's financial data to: (1) evaluate its current situation and (2) predict its financial future. The ratios are obtained by dividing one financial figure (e.g., current assets) by another (e.g., current liabilities) to give a decimal fraction (e.g., current ratio). The ratios are useful because they highlight relationships in the financial data that are often not apparent from a visual inspection of the individual items. Additionally, the comparison of ratios in one organization with those of similar organizations helps identify both problems and opportunities.

## A. STANDARDS

There are three types of standards against which an organization's ratios are compared:

**1. Past Performance Standard:** The past performance of the organization can be used as a standard to evaluate the present or predict the future. Trends in the ratios over time can be identified.

**2. Budgeted Standard:** Another standard commonly used by the analyst is the budget standard. The budget is a statement of what the company intends to do during a stated period of time. Ratios developed from actual performance can be compared to planned ratios in the budget to determine if objectives have been accomplished.

**3. Industry Average:** Many trade associations collect financial data from their members to prepare average ratios for the industry (see Key Business Ratios, Appendix B.).

## B. CLASSIFICATION

A five-category classification of ratios is useful for case analysis and reporting. These categories are:

**1. Liquidity Ratios** - These ratios measure the ability of a firm to meet its maturing debt obligations.

**2. Leverage Ratios** - These ratios compare the financing of an organization by debt to its financing by its owners, an important factor in determining the borrowing capacity of organization.

**3. Activity Ratios** - These ratios measure how efficiently a firm is using its resources.

**4. Profitability Ratios** - These ratios measure the financial returns that an organization earns per unit of its resources.

**5. Growth Ratios** - These ratios look at annual growth rates.

These ratios are often relevant to, and sometimes the key to, the analysis of the case. During the reading of the narrative in a case, one should look for symptoms of problems in an organization's liquidity, debt structure, resource usage, and profitability. Problems can be investigated by computing the ratios and comparing them against industry norms or the past performance of the organization (see Key Business Ratios, Appendix B.).

The remainder of this section describes in checklist format the most used ratios, and identifies their significance.

# CHECKLIST 4.1  LIQUIDITY RATIOS

An organization must be able to meet its maturing debt obligations.  Although a complete liquidity analysis requires a detailed cash flow forecast, the liquidity ratio can often identify anomalous conditions.  The example values are taken from the balance sheet of the Macro Corporation (Figure 4.1).

## 1.  Current Ratio

ratio = current assets/current liabilities

3.8 = 1420/370

This ratio measures the ability to meet short-term debt.  If it is small (less than 1.5), the organization may have trouble meeting maturing debts. If it is large (above 4), the organization may not be making best use of its short-term assets.

## 2.  Inventory to Working Capital

ratio = inventory/(current assets - current liabilities)

.61 = 645/(1420 - 370]

This ratio measures the fraction of working capital (current assets minus current liabilities) tied up in inventory. Low ratios (less than .75) are considered best for liquidity.  Inventories can spoil or lose value, so firms with a low ratio face less risk of losing liquidity.

## 3.  Current Debt to Inventory

ratio = current debt/inventory

.57 = 370/645

This ratio indicates the reliance of the organization on meeting its debts by funds generated from unsold inventory, the least liquid of the current assets.  If business turns bad, inventories will build and the organization will have difficulty paying suppliers.

## 4.  Quick Ratio

ratio = (current assets - inventory)/current liabilities

2.1 = (1420 - 645)/370

This measures the ability of an organization to immediately pay its short-term obligations. Since the inventory is typically the least liquid of the current assets,  this ratio is a more accurate measure than the current ratio of the firm's ability to quickly meet its short-term financial needs.

# CHECKLIST 4.2  LEVERAGE RATIOS

Leverage ratios compare the funds raised by debt with those provided by the owners. By using their own funds, owners maintain control but face increased personal investment. Use of debt gives the owners the opportunity to use someone else's money to make money. However, the company assumes the additional risk of having to meet fixed payments to creditors. Therefore, the use of debt (leverage) in the firm's capital structure is appropriate and desirable, but only up to certain limits.

In most case analyses, when leverage is an issue, a much more in-depth study is in order than a ratio analysis. However, a cursory leverage ratio analysis can often identify problems and opportunities for organizations. The numerical examples are taken from the Macro Corporation's balance sheet in Figure 4.1 and also the income statement in Figure 4.2.

**1.  Total Debt to Tangible Net Worth**

ratio = (current + long-term debts)/tangible net worth

.27 = (370 + 19)/(1829 - 389)

This ratio directly compares the equity of the owners with the funds provided by the creditors. The tangible net worth is the owner's equity (assets minus liabilities) less intangible assets. If this ratio is large, creditors will be cautious.

**2.  Current Debt to Tangible Net Worth**

ratio = current debt/tangible net worth

.26 = 370/1440

This ratio compares the short-term debt with the funds provided by the owners. If the ratio is large (greater than .75), then the creditors are cautious unless the organization has a strong innovative potential.

**3.  Fixed Assets to Tangible Net Worth**

ratio = fixed assets/tangible net worth

.28 = 399/1440

This ratio compares the owner's equity with assets that have a low turnover. If this ratio is low, further assets may have to be financed by a stock issue.

**4.  Times Interest Earned**

ratio = (profit before tax + interest)/interest

9.6 = (120 + 14)/14

This ratio measures the risk that a firm might not be able to meet its interest payments without unusual (and often embarrassing) maneuvers.

# CHECKLIST 4.3 ACTIVITY RATIOS

These ratios measure the efficiency of the operation of an organization. They are based on comparing revenue and expense categories over a given time period with the resources used to generate them. The numerical examples are taken from Figures 4.1 and 4.2.

## 1. Inventory Turnover

ratio = net sales for year/inventory

5.4 = 3500/645

This ratio approximates the number of times inventory is turned over in a given year. Although a high ratio is good (ratios vary greatly by industry), organizations with high ratios have to be careful of stockouts and delays in delivery for large orders. Its reciprocal multiplied by 365 gives the average number of days a product stays in inventory. There are difficulties associated with consistently costing inventory and sales to compute this index and problems in measuring the average inventory.

## 2. Collection Period

ratio = (receivables) (365)/net sales

62 = 590 x 365/3500

This ratio measures the average collection period for accounts receivable (i.e., the average number of days' sales that are due on credit). A ratio atypical of similar organizations is symptomatic of unusual management practices - some good, most bad.

## 3. Fixed Asset Turnover

ratio = net sales/fixed assets

8.8 = 3500/399

This ratio measures the efficiency of an organization's assets in generating sales. High values indicate productive (but not necessarily profitable) investments.

## 4. Working Capital Turnover

ratio = net sales/(current assets - current liabilities)

3.3 = 3500/(1420 - 370)

This ratio measures the efficiency of the use of working capital. A high value indicates efficient usage; however, if the value is too high, there may be insufficient working capital. Such situations can be diagnosed further by liquidity ratios.

# CHECKLIST 4.4 PROFITABLITY RATIOS

The end result of an organization's management, operation, sales, and marketing is the profitability. So many factors influence profitability that it is difficult to determine the cause of profits and losses; however, study of profitability ratios gives valuable clues to the causes of an organization's success or failure. These ratios differ considerably more from year to year than do the liquidity, leverage, or turnover ratios. The numerical examples here are taken from Figures 4.1 and 4.2.

## 1. Return On Net Worth

ratio = net profit after tax/tangible net worth
.05 = 70/(1819 - 389)

This ratio measures the earnings on the owne'r equity. (Tangible net worth is assets minus liabilities minus intangible assets.) This is a key figure in judging the success of management.

## 2. Sales Margin

ratio = net profit after taxes/net sales
.02 = 70/3500

This ratio measures the return on sales. It is useful in diagnosing the causes of an organization's success. For example, an organization may have a favorable overall profitability, generated from a low sales margin and high volume.

## 3. Productivity of Assets

ratio = (gross income - taxes)/total assets
.02 = (134 - 50)/3500

This ratio measures the productivity of the total resources committed to the organization. Comparison of this figure with past history and other organizations is useful in predicting an organization's future prospects.

## 4. Gross And Operating Margins

ratio = gross margin/sales
.42 = 1460/3500
ratio = operating margin/sales
.05 = 160/3500

These ratios begin to analyze details of operations. In case analysis, the issue raised typically requires more detail than is afforded by one set of ratios; however, comparison of these ratios over time can identify important trends.

```
┌─────────────────────────────────────────────────────────────────────────┐
│ CHECKLIST 4.5   GROWTH  RATIOS                                           │
│                                                                          │
│ 1.   Sales - Annual percentage growth in total sales.                   │
│                                                                          │
│ 2.   Income - Annual percentage growth in profits.                      │
│                                                                          │
│ 3.   Earnings per Share  -  Annual percentage growth in EPS.            │
│                                                                          │
│ 4.   Dividends per Share -  Annual percentage growth in dividends per   │
│                             share.                                       │
│                                                                          │
│ 5.   Price-Earning Ratio  -        Market price per share               │
│                                    Earnings per Share                    │
│                                                                          │
└─────────────────────────────────────────────────────────────────────────┘
```

## III.    FUNDS  AND  CASH  FLOW  STATEMENTS

The purpose of the funds and cash flow statements is to understand how the firm is using its financial resources. The income statement measures the profitability of the organization over a given period of time and the balance sheet measures the status of the organization at a given point in time. The flow statements provide more detail than the income statement or the balance sheet about why the organization has achieved its performance and the direction of its financial condition.

The three statements involved in analyzing flows of funds (i.e., working capital) are: (1) the schedule of changes in working capital, (2) the sources and applications of funds (often called the funds flow statement), and (3) the cash flow statement. Cases often contain several year end balance sheets from which the schedule of changes in working capital can be directly prepared. This statement shows the net changes in the accounts that constitute working capital (i.e., current assets minus current liabilities). The funds flow statement is more difficult to prepare and often requires more information than is given in cases.

Figure 4.5 contains the cash flow forecast for the Macro Corporation. Such a statement requires assumptions about sales, payment of debts and receivables, dividends, capital equipment purchases, etc. Intelligent financial planning of an organization requires the construction of a cash flow forecast. In case analysis, whenever liquidity ratios of an organization are low, a "quick and dirty" cash flow prediction is almost always mandatory.

## IV.    RETURN ON INVESTMENT[1]

Case analysts often face the task of evaluating and comparing the performances of companies, managements, and investment projects. A common method of evaluating performance is to compare the resources used with the profits earned. This form of measurement is called **return on investment**.

---

[1] Note: In computing "Return on Investment", one must be careful to note how Investment is being defined. Investment can be defined as Capital, Total Assets or Equity. The standard accounting definition states that ROI is computed by comparing net profit with capital. The important point here is that your terms be consistent when using these measures for comparison.

## FIGURE 4.5 CASH FLOW FORECAST

**MACRO CORPORATION**
Cash Flow Forecast
Aug. - Oct. 1992
(All Figures times $1000)

|  | Aug. | Sept. | Oct. |
|---|---|---|---|
| 1. SOURCES OF CASH (TOTAL) | 284 | 544 | 304 |
| a) Sales[1] | 280 | 290 | 300 |
| b) Patent Royalties | 4 | 4 | 4 |
| c) Sale of Equipment | - | 50 | - |
| d) Bond Issue | - | 200 | - |
| 2. USES OF CASH (TOTAL) | 289 | 304 | 414 |
| a) Raw Material [2] | 100 | 105 | 110 |
| b) Rent | 5 | 5 | 5 |
| c) Payroll | 60 | 70 | 75 |
| d) Selling and Administrative Expenses | 120 | 120 | 120 |
| e) Dividends | - | - | 100 |
| f) Interest Payments | 4 | 4 | 4 |
| 3. CASH AT START OF MONTH | 180 | 175 | 415 |
| 4. CASH AT END OF MONTH | 175 | 415 | 305 |

----------
[1] Assumes 10% of sales are for cash, 50% pay within 30 days, 90% within 60 days, 98% within 90 days, 2% uncollectable.

[2] Assumes 50% paid in 20 days, 100% in 45 days.

The simplest analysis is to compute the ratio of annual profit divided by assets. This is a useful measure of a single year's performance; however, it has two deficiencies. First, the single measure does not identify how the organization has achieved its profits. Second, the time value of money must be considered for multi-year investments. This subsection first considers a more complete analysis of an organization's profitability than the ratio of income to assets. It then reviews the present value technique of measuring the time value of money for investments. A useful measure of an organization's efficiency is the rate of return on assets, defined as:

NET INCOME/TOTAL ASSETS = NET INCOME/SALES X SALES/TOTAL ASSETS

This rate of return is often computed using the product of the two indices on the right side of the equation (where the "sales" terms cancel). The two indices on the right side of the above equation are interesting quantities in themselves:

RETURN ON SALES = NET INCOME/SALES
ASSET TURNOVER RATE = SALES/TOTAL ASSETS

The "asset turnover rate" measures the number of times that the assets produce their own worth in sales during the accounting period.

The DuPont Corporation has taken the above analysis one step further to evaluate its own performance. The "DuPont Formula" has been well received by many organizations. It combines the activity ratio and profit margin on sales to show how these ratios interact to determine return on total assets. The formula, modified somewhat, is set forth in Figure 4.6.

FIGURE 4.6  RETURN ON INVESTMENT CHART

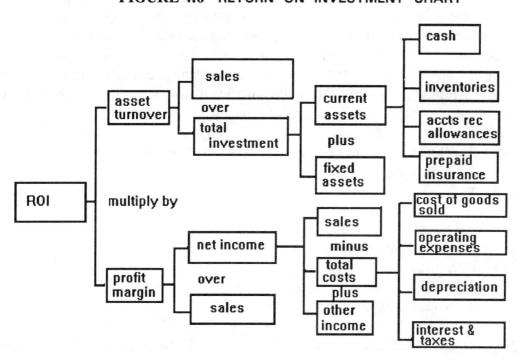

The upper section of the chart develops the turnover ratio. It shows how current assets added to fixed assets gives total assets. Total investment divided by sales gives asset turnover. The bottom section of the chart develops the profit margin (or return) on sales. The individual expense items, income taxes, and sales are combined to give net profits after taxes. Sales divided by net profits gives the profit margin on sales. The asset turnover multiplied by profit margin on sales gives the return on total investments, as the preceding formula showed.

51

The strength of this analysis is to emphasize both the end result, return on total investment, and the factors that produced it. Comparative analysis of the factors over a period of time aids in identifying key structural changes and in tracing back through the system to determine their origin. The particular selection of categories depends on the organization. For example, some organizations use separate categories for assets, which other organizations would group together under "miscellaneous assets". The art of applying this analysis is to select categories that best display significant factors in the organization's performance.

In evaluating investment projects extending several years, one must include the time value of money. The concept of time value of money is important, because money received now is of greater value than money received in the future. For example, if one were to receive two separate payments for a dollar, one today and one a year from today, the $1.00 received today is worth more because it could be put into a savings account to draw interest and be worth, say, $1.09 a year from now. Therefore, the time value computation weighs payments or receipts in the future less heavily that those which occur in the present. The process of moving money to be received in the future to a reference of an equivalent amount of money in the present is called determining the "present value" of money.

When one chooses investment projects, one tends to prefer projects with a greater present value. However, there are other complicating factors, for example, the risk of large losses, the amount of resource commitment, and the dependence of present value on the discount (i.e., interest) rate used. One often encounters very successful organizations who use only primitive methods (e.g., payback) in evaluating investment projects. The success of these organizations stems from their ability to devise good investment projects, not from their ability to scientifically select the best project. They would still benefit from correct financial comparisons of projects.

The formula for calculating the present value of a single payment in the future is:

**PV = F/(1+i)\*n**

Where:  PV = present value of a single payment
          F = future payment in year n
          i = interest rate
          n = years hence
          * = exponentiation symbol (e.g., 3*2=9)

The formula for calculating the Present Value of an Annuity (uniform payments over a number of years) is:

**PVA = F[(1+i)\*n-1]/[i(1+i)\*n]**

Where:  PVA = present value of an annuity
           n = number of years uniform payment to be made

The present value for a single future payment and the present value for an annuity for various years and interest rates are available in standard present value tables or can be calculated on inexpensive electronic hand calculators.

## V.  BREAK-EVEN  ANALYSIS

Break-even analysis is a useful analytic technique for case analysis.  Basically, this form of analysis is used to study the relationship between fixed costs (FC), variable costs (VC), and revenue (R).  It is a simple method for analyzing the interaction of cost and revenues at various potential levels of operation.      The typical presentation of break-even analysis is through the use of a break-even chart, as illustrated in Figure 4.7.  In addition to the cost-revenue relationship, the chart identifies the profit or loss path at various levels of output.

The break-even chart geographically presents the relationship between units produced and sold (volume) on the horizontal axis and the sales revenue and/or cost on the vertical axis.  The break-even point occurs when sales revenues (R) are exactly equal to the total cost (TC).  The fixed costs (FC) are items which do not change substantially as the volume of production changes.  As diagrammed in Figure 4.9, fixed cost items include such items as property tax, executive salaries, depreciation on plant and equipment and general office expense.  Variable Costs (VC) are those costs which vary directly with the change in production volume.  The chart identifies some of these costs as direct labor, direct material, other manufacturing costs, and selling and administrative costs.

### FIGURE 4.7  THE BREAK-EVEN CHART

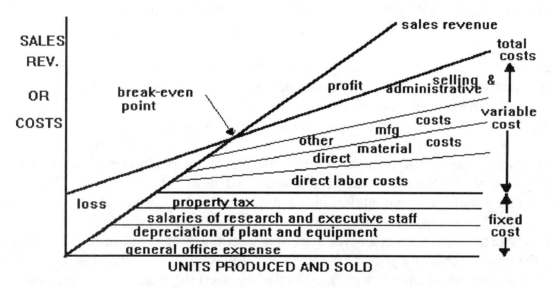

Break-even volume is defined as that volume of productive output at which sales revenue equals fixed cost plus variable cost.  It can be computed as follows:

1.  Let  R = revenue
        VC = variable cost
        FC  = fixed cost
        Z = profit

53

2) Then:    $R = FC + VC + Z$
    since   $Z = 0$ (at break-even)
            $R = FC + VC$ (at break-even)

3)  To solve for the break-even point in units:
            $P * U = FC + VC * U$, or $U = FC/(P-VC)$
        where: $P$ = price per unit
            $VC$ = variable cost per unit
            $U$ = number of units at break-even
            $*$ = multiplication sign

The primary advantage of using a break-even chart is that it reduces to a single diagram significant information regarding past, present, and future operations of a firm. The chart shows the impact of different levels of output upon profit at a given price, and answers such important questions as: If price is reduced, how much must the manufacturer increase output to maintain the present profit level? If price is increased, how much of a reduction in output can occur before profits are reduced? The break-even chart can also be used to analyze costs. By identifying the relative significance of each type of cost, it identifies the key areas for cost-reduction efforts.

## VI.  DECISION TREE ANALYSIS

A decision tree is a technique for graphically describing the alternatives in a decision problem. All possible courses of action for the decision are explicitly diagrammed, evaluated, and compared. It is an excellent technique to communicate complex situations to groups for both understanding and evaluation.

The decision tree is made up of decision points and chance events. A decision point is a series of alternatives or branches that are under the control of the decision-maker who may choose any of the branches to follow. A chance event is a series of outcomes or branches which occur with given probabilities. The exact profit or loss outcomes of each branch must be known.

As an example, consider the problem of a manufacturer facing production facility expansion. This decision hinges on market demand which, it is assumed, will do one of three things: rise, remain steady, or fall. If the manufacturer expands facilities and demand for the product rises, the company will enjoy the benefits of economies of scale and will realize a high profit. If demand declines, the manufacturer will have to spread fixed costs over fewer products and profits will suffer. The decision tree displaying the various decision points and chance events is illustrated in Figure 4.8. The diagram at node 1 (a node is a place where branches or "arcs" of the tree meet) shows that facility expansion will require an expenditure of $6 million. If the company expands and demand rises (there is a 60% probability that this will occur), the company can expect a yield of $1 million per year for 10 years.

# FIGURE 4.8    DECISION TREE

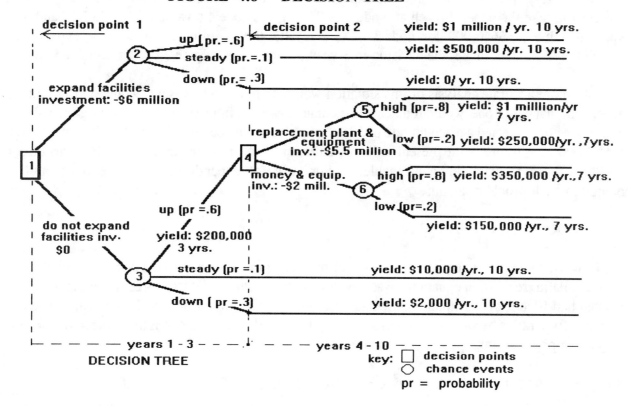

However, if demand remains steady (there is a 10% probability that this will occur) the yield drops to $500,000 per year for 10 years.  If demand falls (probability .3), then profit will be zero each year. There are similar chance events and decisions if management elects not to expand, as shown in Figure 4.8.

Decision tree models often use the concept of expected value to measure the relative value of the various alternatives. Expected value is the average payoff you could expect if you faced the same problem many times and selected the same alternative each time.  The expected value equation is:

Expected Value  =  sum of all outcome values times their probabilities.

The expected value to "expand facilities" (Node 1-2) is determined as follows:

| | | | |
|---|---|---|---|
| Expected Value (Node 2) = | 1,000,000 x 10 x .6 = | | 6,000,000 |
| = | 500,000 x 10 x .1 = | | 500,000 |
| | 0 x 10 x .3 = | | 0 |
| Expected Value of Operation | | | 6,500,000 |
| Less Investment | | | 6,000,000 |
| Expected Value of Decision to "Expand Facility" = | | | 500,000 |

Expected value calculations begin at the end of tree branches (the right side) and work back to the source node.

55

Similarly, one may calculate the expected value at node 5 ($450,000) and node 6 ($170,000), then elect to take the upper branch at node 4. This gives node 4 a value of $450,000, and thus an expected value of $646,000 for node 3. As a result, the major decision is not to expand facilities immediately, but to make the decision in 3 years. The expected value of this decision is $646,000.

A more accurate analysis of this situation would be to use the present value concept introduced earlier. In that case, one would replace the income streams in future years by their present values. For example, if one selected a discount rate of 12%, one would replace the $10 million income stream with $5,650,000 (this figure is the present value of an annuity of $1 million per year for 10 years discounted at 12%, a figure available in annuity tables). Similarly, all expenditures and revenues should be discounted in such problems as this.

## VII. BANKRUPTCY FORMULA

Edward Altman[1] developed a formula for predicting the likelihood of a company going bankrupt. The formula (a regression equation) was developed from a study of thirty-three manufacturing companies that had filed for bankruptcies paired against thirty-three similar but profitable firms. The formula combines five ratios by weighting them according to a firm's financial strength. Using this formula an analyst can predict bankruptcy a year in advance in 75-80 percent of the cases.

The formula is: Bankruptcy Index $= 1.2A + 1.4B + 3.3C + 0.6D + 1.0E$

Where:    A = Working capital divided by total assets
          B = Retained earnings divided by total assets
          C = EBIT divided by total assets
          D = Market value of equity divided by book value of total debt
          E = Sales divided by total assets

An Index:
                above 3 = good
        between 1.8 and 3 = questionable
              below 1.8 = bankruptcy

If the firm being studied is below 1.8, using the above formula, there is a 75-80 percent chance that the firm will go bankrupt.

--------------

[1] Altman E., "Exploring the Road to Bankruptcy", Journal of Business Strategy, Fall, 1983.

# VIII. A MEASURE OF INDUSTRY BALANCE

An measure of industry balance that is used by government to help decide when mergers of industry participants should or should not be allowed is provided by the Herfindahl Index.

The Herfindahl Index (HI) runs from 0 (perfect competition) to 10000 (monopoly). The index is calculated as follows:

$$HI = 10,000 \sum_i S^2_i$$

For example given there are four firms in the industry with market shares as follows: .25, .25, .25, .25. The Herfindahl would equal (10,000)((.25) +(.25) +(.25) +(.25)) or 2500. In general, industries with a Herfindahl in excess of 1800 are thought to characterize industries with reduced rivalry[2]

**NOTES:**

---

[2] See Oster, S., Modern Competitive Analysis, Oxford Univ. Press, 1990.

# CHAPTER V   HOW TO WRITE CASE REPORTS

## I.  INTRODUCTION TO REPORTING CASES

Case reporting gives students valuable training in communicating and selling the results of their analyses of strategic issues and problems.  These abilities in formal written and oral communication are vital to successful business careers.

The effective preparation and presentation of written and oral reports have several similarities. Both presentations are designed to meet needs of the audience.  In preparing both presentations, one must resist the temptation to begin the report before the analysis is completed;  this leads to extra work, poor argument development,  and superficial analysis.  Once the analysis is complete,  then the student faces the task of communicating the main results of the analysis to the reader or listener.

This communication involves: (1) selecting material appropriate for the presentation; (2) organizing the material for presentation;  and (3) using the media (oral or written) to convey the message. Choices in the selection and organization of the material depend upon the setting of the presentation. Such factors as the objectives of the report, the time constraints, the familiarity of the audience with the subject, and the analytic background of the audience are important considerations in selecting and organizing material.

This chapter covers the following areas of written report preparation.

1.  The selection and structuring of material for a written case analysis.
2.  A method of supporting logical arguments with evidence.
3.  Tips on ways to efficiently and effectively prepare written drafts.
4.  The task of putting together a professional looking final document.
5.  An example of a write-up for the Standard Oil Company of Indiana case.

We have found that,  properly directed,  students can achieve large improvements in their grammar and writing style with little effort.  Thus,  we have included an appendix in this book, "Appendix A: Guide to Effective Business Writing".  This guide decribes what to do about commonly made errors in punctuation,  grammar,  and compositional style.  We strongly recommend this appendix to students beginning a written report.

## II. ORGANIZATION OF WRITTEN CASE REPORTS

This section describes a general structure for a written report of a complex case where both the problem and its solution are to be defined by the case analyst.

The case report consists of three main parts:  the preliminary material,  the body of the report, and the appendices.   Each one of these items is a division of the three-point checklist,  "Organization of Written Case Report",  which is described in this section.  The remainder of this subsection discusses the points under each of these three divisions of the report.

## A. PRELIMINARY MATERIAL IN THE WRITTEN CASE REPORT

Report writers can become so involved with the content of the writing that they forget to make the document convenient for the reader. The preliminary material makes it convenient for the reader to access the material in the report - the more accessible the material, the more likely the report is to carry its message.

The first item in the written report is the preliminary material. Its individual items follow.

1. **Title Page**: Instructors may accidentally mix reports from various class sections, or leave reports in a colleague's office. The following information should appear on a report title page: (1) case title, (2) student's name, (3) date, (4) course and section, (5) class meeting time, and (6) instructor's name.

2. **Letter of Transmittal**: Some instructors ask students to include a cover letter for the reports. In these situations, the students pretend they are called in to make recommendations to a particular manager or management team in the case situation. The letter should contain: (1) name and address of writer, (2) date, (3) name of individual(s) for whom the report is prepared, (4) report subject, and (5) reason for the report. It should be no more than 250 words.

3. **Table of Contents**: All pages are numbered and the table of contents gives the page numbers of sections and, for short reports, subsections also. Many readers scrutinize the table of contents carefully to preview a report before reading. The division of the report into sections and the titling of the sections is often designed to make a table of contents that is useful for this purpose.

4. **List of Exhibits:** This is a listing of each exhibit number, its caption, and its page number. Readers frequently want to refer back to exhibits and have considerable difficulty in locating them without this list.

5. **Summary of Recommendations:** This section (300 words or less) summarizes the analysis. It is designed to serve as a compact summary for the busy manager who does not have time to read the report, as a guide for the careful reader who wants to understand the overall direction of the report before plunging into the details, and as a convenient reference for individuals who will use the report. In a term paper, this is the function of an abstract. In a case report, a list of recommendations, sometimes supported by key results from the analysis, serves the function of an abstract.

## B. BODY OF THE WRITTEN REPORT

The most important principle in report writing is to design the report for its readers. An important task in tailoring a report for a user is the balancing of material between the report body and the appendices. In most instances, the body of the report is kept as brief as possible by placing detailed arguments and extensive evidence in the appendices.

Good report writers consciously design length and emphasis for each section of the body of the report to best serve the reader of the report. A number of attributes of the reader bear on this decision. The writer should consider such questions as the following.

* What is the familiarity of the reader with the problem?
* What expertise does the reader have in the area?
* What conclusions are of importance to the reader?
* What are the preconceived notions of the reader?
* Why was the report requested?
* What does the reader have to know?

Descriptions of the individual items in the report body follow.

## 1.   Background Material and Facts

This section has two functions: (1) to give readers essential background material they may lack; and  (2) to clarify the report writer's understanding of the situation.   Instructors differ on the amount  of material they wish included in this section.   Students who have done little analysis tend to pad reports by rehashing material given in the case. The best approach for students is to ask the instructor how much background to include.

## 2.   Analysis

The analysis is the heart of the report.   It contains the logical thought  processes  used to develop the solution;   it  is  designed  to convince the reader of the advantages of the solution and thoroughness of the writer's case analysis.

There are some important considerations for the analysis section:

* Include  analysis of the external (e.g., Industry Analysis) and the internal environment (e.g., SWOT  Analysis).
* Include an analysis which is not merely a restatement of the facts.
* Develop arguments by short paragraphs.  Remember to consider only one main argument or  idea  per  paragraph.   Page-long paragraphs intimidate some readers and are often difficult to follow.
* Many  small  ideas  can  be put  together  by  use  of  point  form ("bullets"),  just as this section is arranged.
* Read  "Compositional Principles for Effective Writing" in Appendix  A.
* Clearly state assumptions made and reference any sources used.

## 3.   Statement  of  the  Strategic  Issue  &  Key  Problem

This section explicitly defines any major issues or problems.  As noted  in  Chapter II,  there can be confusion  between  symptoms  and  problems.    The purpose of this part of the report is to resolve any ambiguities,  and defend the selection as the underlying issue or problem.

## 4.   Solution and Implementation

This final section details the solution to the key problem and the steps for its successful  implementation.   Even though  the arguments for the solution and its form have been clearly established, further details,  justification,  and implementation considerations are included here.

## C. APPENDICES FOR WRITTEN CASE REPORT

The main purpose of the appendices is to include evidence and arguments which could not be placed in the body of the report. Reasons for exclusion are:

* The need to keep the body of the report brief.
* The material is too technical for many intended readers.
* The material is of only peripheral relevance to the report, but must be included for completeness (e.g., calculations that support key results in the report body).

Any material in the appendices should be referenced in the text. In addition, the title of each appendix should be chosen to describe its contents. The titles allow a reader to glance at the table of contents to determine the relevancy of material in the appendices.

## III.  HOW TO DEVELOP WRITTEN ARGUMENTS [1]

In developing written arguments, there is a tendency either to introduce only conclusions or to state many disparate facts and suddenly introduce a conclusion without showing how it follows from the facts. David Robinson has developed an excellent example to illustrate how facts and interpretations are combined to form strong written analysis.

The written case report attempts to present an orderly and logical flow of information and an interpretation of that information. That is, the report breaks down the information and relates it to a problem and its solution. The logical-flow process is demonstrated in Figure 5.1. In explaining this example, Robinson states that:

> "...a writer's presentation of one fact (fact 1) gives rise to a statement of significance. This statement of significance gives rise to statements of three additional related facts (fact 2, fact 3, fact 4) which, in turn, are shown to be significant before the writer logically introduces (fact 5) to support three more significant statements that, again in turn, lead to a logical conclusion."

One of the problems associated with the presentation of written analysis is the difficulty of telling a coherent story. The key to this problem is the development of good transition. Generally, this is accomplished automatically as one fact and its interpretation tends to set up the next fact. This concept is demonstrated in Figure 5.1. At some point, the writer will finish the chain of thought and go on to a new point. The writer may then use a short summary statement of the preceding arguments which relate it to the next topic, or simply make a summary and begin the new topic with a new paragraph or section. The reader should not be left with any doubt about the transition.

Graphs and tables are important devices in presenting factual information in supporting arguments. The inclusion of figures in the narrative (e.g., sales went from 120 in January to 130 in February, before dropping to 90 in March...) is tedious and inefficient. There are three important principles of graph and table usage.

---

[1]Robinson, David M., *Writing Reports for Management Decisions*, Merrill, 1969, p. 202.

**FIGURE 5.1   DEVELOPMENT OF WRITTEN ARGUMENTS**

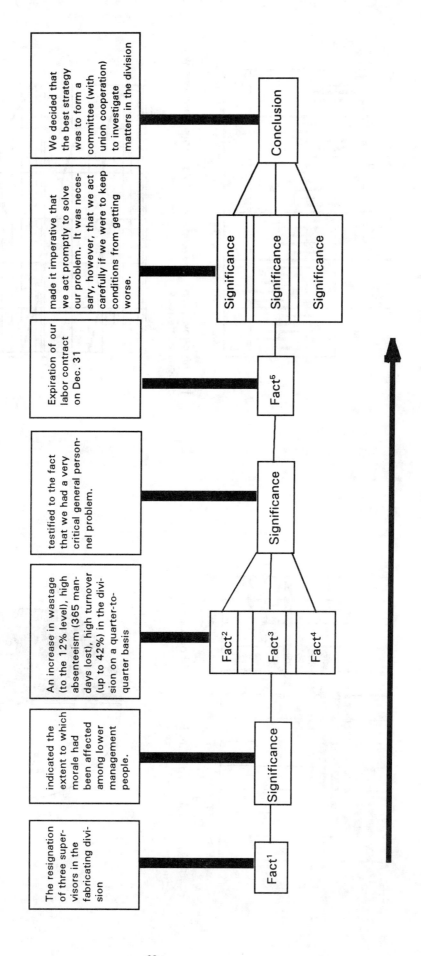

# FIGURE 5.2A EXAMPLE OF CHARTS AND GRAPHS

Source: Ewing, David W., Writing for Results, John Wiley & Sons, New York, 1974 (pp. 313 – 318).

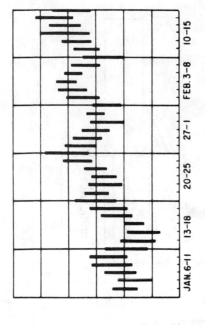

The *high-low graph* is a good way to portray variations within designated periods.

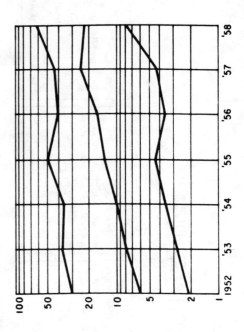

The *logarithmic graph* serves to show rates of change rather than amounts.

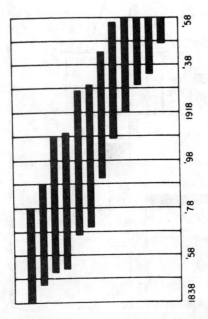

The *band* or *strata graph* can be used to show variations in time sequence.

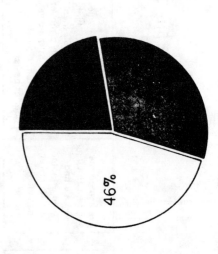

The *pie chart* is the most familiar form of area chart, another frequently used graphic form. The pie chart is used to represent component parts of a whole.

# FIGURE 5.2B EXAMPLE OF CHARTS AND GRAPHS

Source: Ewing, David W., Writing for Results,
John Wiley & Sons, New York, 1974 (pp. 313 – 318).

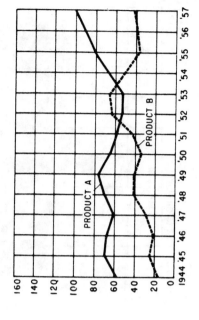

The *line graph* is probably the most frequently used of all visual reporting techniques. It is employed primarily to indicate a trend.

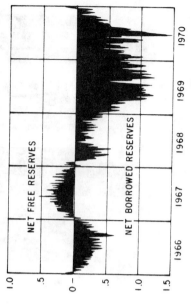

The *silhouette chart* is useful to accent plus or minus departures from a base, goal, or standard. In this illustration zero represents a state in which a banking system has neither free reserves nor borrowed reserves.

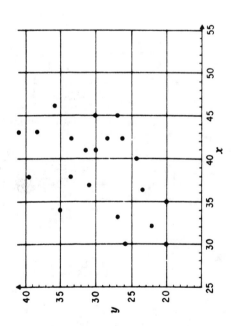

The *scatter diagram* is useful for showing the relationship (or lack of it) of two variables. This one shows a tendency for small and large values of x to be associated with small and large values of y.

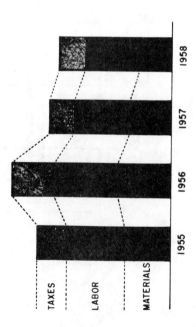

The *component* or *subdivided bar chart* provides the same information as a series of pie charts but in more manageable and compact form. The components of each bar can add up to 100% or to some absolute measure, such as sales volume, number of customers, material costs, and so on.

# FIGURE 5.2C EXAMPLE OF CHARTS AND GRAPHS

Source: Ewing, David W., Writing for Results,
John Wiley & Sons, New York, 1974 (pp. 313 - 318).

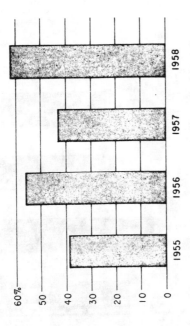

The *bar chart* runs a close second to the graph in popularity. This example is a simple bar chart. The bars can run vertically, as here, or horizontally, depending on the need.

The *grouped* or *compound bar chart* is useful for contrasting two or more variables over a period of time (as here) or in different localities, functions, organizations, and so on.

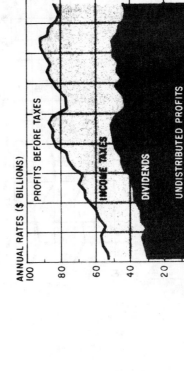

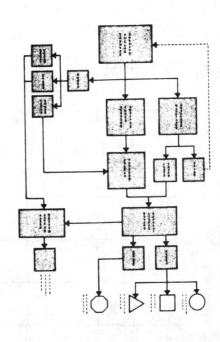

The *flow chart* is a favorite tool for portraying sequences in natural processes and organized operations, lines of command in organizations, time stages in development, and other subjects.

The *surface* or *stratum* chart shows trends in segments of a total amount. Note that the bottom layer is the only one that can be measured directly from the scale. Because an irregular layer gives the illusion others are moving up and down, too, it is a good idea to put the most irregular layers on top, if that can be done logically.

66

* All graphs and tables must be referenced in the text.
* Any graph or table should be clearly labelled so it can be understood without reference to the text.
* The purpose of a graph is to portray overall relationships, in contrast to a table which communicates specific numeric values. Thus, a graph typically has few grid lines and the axes are scaled to portray a visual feeling for the quantities involved.

Examples of graphs and tables are presented in figures 5.2A and 5.2B.

## IV. WRITING THE REPORT

There are a number of "Do's" and "Do Not's" in preparing a case report. These apply to the preparation of almost any written document. This section gives a number of tips and a few "Do Not's" which we have seen often in case reports. "Appendix A: Fundamentals of Effective Business Writing", is designed to accompany this secion. This appendix covers topics from common punctuation errors and weak sentence formation through correct paragraphing and forceful composition.

---

**CHECKLIST 5.1 HOW TO DRAFT REPORTS**

**1. Outline Before Drafting** - An outline of the contents of the write-up precedes writing the draft. It is both tempting and foolhardy to plunge into writing a draft before constructing a complete outline. Even with a good outline, enough redrafting will be necessary as new ideas occur during the writing. Considerable extra work and a less organized exposition is inevitable if a tight outline is not prepared before drafting begins.

**2. Draft Double-Spaced and in Pencil** - A draft should be easy to read and easy to change. Bad handwriting is made more legible by writing on every other line on one side of the page. The blank lines are convenient for corrections and additions. Nevertheless, students who can draft directly on a typewriter or a word processor should do so. Many students will spend thousands of hours over their careers preparing written documents; the case report is a good time to practice efficient habits.

**3. Cut and Tape Draft** - Most writers prefer to write first drafts quickly, even though the drafts that result contain many weaknesses - some sections or paragraphs are loose, ideas must be inserted, etc. When insertions or deletions do not fit on the draft, cutting and taping (or pasting or stapling) redrafted sections is the quickest way to incorporate the changes.

**4. Use Descriptive Section Headings** - The section and subsection headings serve as road maps for the reader. The table of contents should serve the reader as an outline of the report; many readers begin a report by scrutinizing the table of contents. The title of each section should decribe its contents; readers can more easily grasp sections when forewarned of their contents.

**5. Avoid Casual Errors** - Casual errors in punctuation, spelling and grammar can have a disastrous effect on the report's acceptance. The appearance of a quality report is destroyed by misspelled words and grammatical errors.

**6. Avoid Words that Prejudge** - A common weakness in case reports is the over-use of value-laden words that beg their own conclusions. The credibility of the writer is reduced by beginning reports with such phrases as "the high-handed action of the shop steward", or "the rip-off pricing of the product". The qualities ascribed to the steward and the product should be demonstrated in the report.

---

**7. Identify Sources** - Be sure to provide complete references to sources used to support arguments. If an expert is cited, give the person's name, position, and reasons why the person is an authority. If a study is cited, include details so the reader can judge the study's credibility - sample size, reputation of researchers, and techniques employed.

## V. PREPARATION OF FINAL DOCUMENT

In report writing, as in almost every facet of life, there is a confusion between content and cosmetics. The cosmetics refer to the exterior appearance of the report, while the content refers to the substance of the arguments and presentation in the report.

When instructors observe messy reports (dirty finger marks, typographical errors, no page numbers, etc.), they naturally expect to see sloppy content. Some students rebuff attempts by instructors to have them submit professional-looking reports by arguing that it is "hack work" to take care of these details. However, sloppy reports will create a strongly negative impression of the author and the failure to do the "hack work" can negate even the most professional content. In addition, the details of preparing a professional report require much more work than commonly supposed. The disciplines of rereading and correcting the draft, proofreading to find the typographical errors, knowing how to set margins, etc., require knowledge and concentration. These are necessary skills in business. Thus, we offer the following tips on preparation of the final document.

---

**CHECKLIST 5.2   ADVICE ON THE PREPARATION OF THE FINAL DOCUMENT**

1.   **Read Draft Aloud Before Typing**
2.   **Type on Good Paper**
3.   **Correct Typed Copy**
4.   **Type Double-Spaced**
5.   **Use Wide Margins**
6.   **Number All Pages**
7.   **Proofread for Typographical Errors**
8.   **Consider Using Word Processing**

---

### EXAMPLE OF A WRITTEN CASE REPORT

The case given in Chapter II, **Standard Oil of Indiana**, is written up in this section, The instructions to the student for this assignment are:

*"Write a 1500 word report to the management of Standard Oil Company of Indiana recommending future strategy to maintain sales and improve profitability. Include a cover letter introducing the report."*

# STANDARD OIL OF INDIANA

## CASE REPORT

Written by:  Chris R. Kilroy
July 1, 1992

Submitted to:  Dr. D. Coleman

For Course:  MGT 345, Section 3
(Tues. & Thurs., 10-11:30)

Example: Letter of Transmittal (in actual report, should stand on a page by itself.)

Chris R. Kilroy
2512 Kalakaua Ave.,
Honolulu, Hawaii 96825
July 1, 1991

Management Committee
Standard Oil Company of Indiana

Dear Sirs and Madams:

I have just completed the project to develop a long-term strategy for Indiana Standard. An exhaustive analysis of market conditions and study of Standard Oil of New Jersey has resulted in the formulation of two promising long-term strategies for Indiana Standard. The enclosed documents summarize the recommendations and describe the analysis which led to these recommendations.

Please do not hesitate to call if you have any questions about this material, or if I may be of further service.

Sincerely,

Chris R. Kilroy

Example: Table of Contents (In actual report, should stand on a page by itself.)

## TABLE OF CONTENTS

Example: List of Exhibits (May be on page with Table of Contents
otherwise on a page by itself)

NOTE:  All page numbers refer to example report.

Example: Summary of recommendations (In actual report, should stand on a page
by itself)

SUMMARY OF RECOMMENDATIONS

The oil industry faces a long-term supply scarcity, which makes the marketing end of the business hazardous and the production end potentially lucrative. Indiana Standard may increase its profitability from 6.8% return on investment toward Standard Oil of New Jersey's 11.6% by pursuing the following two strategies:

A. Integrate vertically by entering into oil drilling and supply operations.

B. Direct special R & D efforts toward breakthroughs in increasing energy sources and conversion of coal or oil shale to gasoline and usage of solar energy.

I. BACKGROUND INFORMATION

Standard Oil of Indiana was organized in 1889 as the marketing arm of the Standard Oil Trust. In 1911, the holding company was dissolved and Standard Oil of Indiana was spun-off as an independent company. The new company met the rapid expansion of the gasoline market and accompanying shortage of crude oil with the development of the Burton process, a method to extract twice as much gasoline from crude oil as was formerly possible. The company expanded its gasoline retailing operations with the purchase of The American Oil Company in 1954. Although Standard Oil of Indiana has achieved rapid growth, its financial performance is inferior to that of Standard Oil of New Jersey's.

Standard Oil of Indiana sold its overseas drilling rights to Standard of New Jersey, a risky venture in light of the scarcity of crude oil. Indiana's later response to this ill-advised sale was the acquisition of the Indiana Oil Purchasing Company. Thus, Indiana today finds itself in a competitive market, with difficulties in obtaining crude oil.

71

## A. INDUSTRY ANALYSIS

Two of the five forces (identified by Porter) that may be important in the analysis of Standard Oil of Indiana. These forces are 1) The Threat of Entry and 2) The Rivalry among firms.

1. The Threat of Entry - It would appear that the threat of entry into this industry is low due to the large capital investment , required distribution channels, etc. However, at the retail / wholesale level entry might represent a far greater threat. Small discount retail/wholesale gas stations may well represent an area of easy entry.

2. Rivalry Among Firms - As stated in the case there is a good deal of competition and price wars at the retail/wholesale level in this industry.

## B. SWOT ANALYSIS

1. Strengths
   Early entry
   Strong financial position
   Brand identifcation
   Strong distribution syster
   Experienced research and development

2. Weaknesses
   Lack of source of supply
   Low ROI

3. Opportunities
   Financially capable of differentiation

4. Threats
   Poor management performance may lead to take-over attempts Competition from discounters at the retail/whole sale.

## C. ANALYSIS OF THE STRATEGIC ISSUES

The analysis of the strategic issues is based on the following questions:

*   Standard of Indiana began its operations as the marketing arm of Standard of New Jersey. Has this historical precedence been an influence on its strategic approach to doing business?

*   Why is Standard of New Jersey's financial performance so superior to Standard of Indiana's?

*   Why did Indiana Standard sell its overseas drilling rights?

*   Are the budget cuts and layoffs in R & D going to solve the problem of low ROI?

72

## 1) FINANCIAL COMPARISON TO STANDARD OIL OF NEW JERSEY

Exhibit 1. compares the financial performance of Indiana Standard with that of Standard Oil of New Jersey. The calculations and derivations supporting this exhibit may be found in Appendix A.

One notes immediately that Standard Oil of New Jersey has a much higher ROI. This is achieved because they have a higher asset turnover rate (83% vs 72%) and a higher profit margin on sales (14% vs 9.3%). The high profit margin on sales is the main source of New Jersey's superior performance (plus 34%).

Exhibit 1 Financial Comparison to Standard Oil of N.J.

| ITEM | STANDARD OF INDIANA | STANDARD OF NEW JERSEY | DIFFERENCES N.J. OVER IND. |
|------|---------------------|------------------------|----------------------------|
| sales | $2.15 billion | $10 billion | 4.6 times |
| total assets | $3.0 billion | $12 billion | 4.0 times |
| net income | .202 billion | $ 1.43 billion | 7. times |
| ROI | 6.8% | 11.6% | plus 42% |
| asset turnover | .717 | .833 | plus 13% |
| profit margin on sales | 9.3% | 14.0% | plus 34% |

## 2) PRODUCTION OF OIL

Indiana Standard sold its overseas drilling rights in an industry with a long history of growing demand accompanied by a scarcity of crude oil. The stopgap measure of acquiring the Indiana Purchasing Company will not solve the long-term problems. In times of scarcity, Indiana Standard will once again be at the mercy of small suppliers and wildcatters.

A plausible explanation of this disinterest that Standard of Indiana has shown in the production end of the business is the marketing emphasis of the company, For example, the company was originally the marketing arm of The Standard Oil Trust. Also, in 1954, the company went further "retail" by purchasing the American Oil Company.

Unfortunately for Standard Oil of Indiana, the production end of the oil business appears to be more profitable than the marketing end.

Evidence to support this contention includes:

* The marketing end of the gasoline business is highly competitive, a condition which often leads to low profits.

* In times of scarcity, many buyers bid up the price of crude oil.

* There is no reason to believe the long history of scarcity of crude oil is ending. On the contrary, world supplies are fixed and demands of all countries are increasing rapidly with increased industrialization.

## 3. BUDGET CUTS IN R & D

The recent efficiency drive in the R & D division is not likely to solve long-term problems. The one million dollar budget cut only increases ROI from 6.80% to 6.83%. Also, R & D investment has long-term effects - for example, eliminating R & D entirely would probably result in large savings in the first year, but eventually lead to long-run starvation as competitors increased market share with unchallenged new products. R & D has been the key to much of Standard Oil of Indiana's previous success, for example, consider the Burton process.

Thus, the budget cuts and layoffs in R & D may be dangerous for long-run survival. It is wishful to think that a tighter control system, layoffs, and a one million dollar budget cut will lead independent-minded scientists to breakthrough discoveries.

## III STATEMENT OF THE STRATEGIC ISSUE

Indiana Standards strategic emphasis has been directed toward horizontal integration, a segment of the oil industry that is highly competitive. They have failed to integrate vertically to protect their source of supply in an industry with limited supply and increasing demand. As a result, the company is at the mercy of small suppliers and wildcatters in times of scarcity, resulting in low profit margins.

## IV SOLUTION CHOICE

### 1. Alternatives Considered

The key problem is to maintain a secure supply. This should lead to long-term security and improved profitability, perhaps even approaching the performance of Standard Oil of New Jersey. Possible methods to achieve this are:

* Indiana Standard can integrate vertically by entering the production end of the business.

* Indiana Standard can undertake long term contracts with large oil producers.

* Indiana Standard can look for joint ventures or mergers with oil producing companies.

* Indiana Standard can diversify in order to reduce its reliance on oil.

* Indiana Standard can encourage research and development to pursue alternate sources of energy.

2 Recommended Solution

In an organization the size of Indiana Standard, more than one solution can be pursued. Thus, the recommendation is:

a. Integrate vertically by entering into oil drilling and supply operations.

b. Direct special R & D efforts toward breakthroughs in increasing energy sources through conversion of coal or oil shale to gasoline and usage of solar energy.

The problems with these solutions relate to their feasibility. Indiana has the resources to undertake extensive efforts in each area, but should carefully pursue a consistent strategy and monitor progress.

The advantages of vertical integration include:

a. There is technical complentariness in oil processing. For example, refining can be designed to maximize efficiency for one type of crude oil.
b. Business plans can be securely formulated without fear of interruption. For example, retail service stations can be assured of the supply of a uniform grade product.
c. The integrated supply system can optimize transportation and inventory investment.
d. Complete data from well-head to gas station is available for planning and decision-making.
e. The intra-firm transfers can be made more rapidly because of reduced need for bargaining and contracting.

75

# APPENDIX A    FINANCIAL COMPARISON DERIVATIONS

The financial data can be analyzed as follows:

Data given in the case:

  Total Assets:  IND - $3 billion,  NJ - $12 billion

  Sales:          IND - $2.15 billion,  NJ -  $10 billion

  Net Income:    IND - ?,  NJ - 7 times IND

  ROI:            IND - 6.8%,  NJ - ?

We may use this data to compute some revealing financial ratios:

  Asset Turnover: IND - 2.15/3 = .707, NJ - 10/12 = .833
  (follows from: asset turnover = sales/assets )

  Net Income toSales: IND -.204/2.15 = 9.3%,
  NJ - 1.428/10 = 14%
  (follows from: net income to sales = net income/sales)

  Net Income:  IND - .204 billion,  NJ - (7) (.204) = 1.48 billion
  (follows from:  ROI - net income/total assets)

  ROI: IND - 6.8%,  NJ - 1.48/12 =  11.56%

The results of the above computations are the following
comparisons:

  Asset Turnover:  NJ's is 13.5% higher than IND's.

  ROI:  NJ's is 41.9% higher than IND's.

  Profit Margin (Net Income to Sales):  NJ's is 33.5% higher
  than IND's.

# CHAPTER VI    HOW TO PRESENT CASE REPORTS

## I.    INTRODUCTION TO ORAL PRESENTATIONS

One skill above all others rapidly earns a reputation for unusual competence.  It is the ability to stand on one's feet and deliver clear, forceful, interesting speeches.  Anyone who aspires to a management position will be frequently called upon to deliver extemporaneous and prepared remarks to audiences of all sizes.  The oral case report affords students an excellent opportunity to develop their abilities in public speaking.

The selection and organization of material for an oral case report is not the same as for a written case report.  The written report is a detailed, logical development of arguments.  The oral presentation must hold the interest and attention of the audience before anything is accomplished; thus, oral reports cannot use intricate arguments or examples with many details.  Audiences are easily bored by arguments and examples they can not follow.  The most important rule in preparing an oral presentation is:  include only material that is essential to the main argument and present it in a simple, straightforward fashion.  This means that some illustrations, clarifications, and content that would be included in a written report are left out of an oral presentation.  Both oral and written case reports are designed to make best use of their respective media.

The next section describes a general outline for a case presentation.  Although the outline itself is not literally applicable to every case, it illustrates the principles to be applied in any presentation.  The third section of this chapter is complementary to the outline.  It gives tips on successful speaking techniques that are useful in any public speaking situation.  Then the last section exemplifies a presentation of the case given in Chapter II, Standard Oil Company of Indiana.

## II.    ORGANIZATION OF PRESENTATION

This section describes a general structure for an oral case presentation.  It divides the speech into three parts: introduction, body, and conclusion.  Students need not follow this outline literally, but should combine ideas mentioned here, their instructor's suggestions, material from other sources, and their own ideas to adapt the structure to fit the particular situations of their presentations.

## A.  OUTLINE OF ORAL CASE PRESENTATION

### 1. Introduction for Oral Case Presentation

The purpose of the introduction is to interest the audience in the remainder of the talk.  When introductory material is vital for understanding of later arguments, it should be repeated later, as needed.  Audiences have short memories and may not listen carefully at the beginning.  In written reports, one can refer back to earlier sections.  In oral presentations, the early parts of the speech cannot be replayed by the audience.

The introduction may be divided into the following three segments.

1.1 **Get Attention of Audience:** The toughest moments in any presentation are the nervous last minutes preceding the start of the talk and the first few seconds of the presentation. One is tempted to lessen nervousness through reducing the uncertainty in the presentation by either reading or memorizing the speech. It is forbidden to read or memorize a case presentation. The lack of spontaneity will bore the audience. The audience came to hear a case presentation, not a reading of a case report. Nevertheless, the first sentence of the presentation can be memorized to ensure a smooth start.

1.2 **Outline Talk:** A speaker must briefly outline the organization of the presentation to the audience immediately after the start of the talk. Listening to a speech without an outline is like taking an auto trip without a roadmap. One is constantly lost, doesn't appreciate the scenery, and can't tell when the destination has been reached. The outline does not tell the entire story of the analysis, but includes a few intriguing details and presents a simplified description of the talk's organization. Sometimes the listeners' task is simplified when the main topics are listed on visual aids.

1.3 **Background and Facts:** This part of the speech presents only information that is both pertinent to the impending analysis and is interesting to the audience. The background material in a written case report often includes all necessary information. When a report is written, the reader can skim dull sections and refer back as required. In oral presentations, the audience has no such capability, so the background information is confined to a bare minimum. Audiences are easily bored with the presentation of details; they need constant theme development highlighted by interesting and amusing examples. Audiences may well forget facts presented here by the time they are needed in the later analysis.

## 2. Body of Oral Case Presentation

2.1 **Problem Statement:** After the introductory material, the problem is clearly stated so the audience knows the theme of the remainder of the talk. When chalkboard is available, it often proves useful to write a few words describing the problem. This statement should justify to the audience that this is indeed the central problem in the case, rather than just a symptom of the problem. One way to organize such an argument for oral presentation is to first consider the apparent problems that were rejected during the analysis. These are made more dramatic for presentation by arrangement in order of increasing plausibility.

2.2 **Alternatives and Analysis:** There are often many plausible solutions to the problem. Pertinent ones may be presented in an order that leads up to the alternative selected as the solution for the problem. The alternatives may be evaluated either as they are presented, or after all alternatives are presented and an evaluation scheme is developed. The overriding principle is to keep the talk interesting and understandable. This often means that important material reviewed during the analysis, which would be included in a written report, is left out of the oral presentation. The presentation of too much material more rapidly than an audience can understand is the most common weakness in case presentations. If the audience feels a promising avenue was not pursued, then the question period at the end of the speech provides adequate opportunity to demonstrate the thoroughness of the analysis.

2.3 **Implementation Plan:** The audience is interested in knowing how the problem solution will be implemented. There are often messy technical, financial, and personnel problems to be dealt with in the plan of action. Only major points are included in this part of the presentation. In order to make this story interesting and entertaining for the audience, the details can be filled in, as required, during the question period.

## 3. Conclusion of Oral Presentation

**3.1 Restatement of Problem and Solution:** Audiences may forget even major points unless they are repeated several times. In the beginning of the conclusion, the key points in the analysis may be repeated. The speaker is not to give a brief rehash of the talk (i.e., review only key highlights) and need not begin by saying "In conclusion." Some new material may be introduced for the purpose of maintaining audience interest. (It is usually inappropriate to introduce new material in the concluding section of a written report). One method of concluding in an interesting fashion is to summarize the key points in the presentation around one aspect of the case situation. For example, one could say, "Now, let's review the alternatives from the viewpoint of the vice president," or, "Let's consider the worst possible outcome and review each of the alternatives."

**3.2 Benefits and What Must Be Done:** After the brief review, a few comments that help sell the case solution are in order. The presenter should have demonstrated thoroughness and objectivity to this point in the presentation; now a few positive, yet subtly introduced, remarks on the benefits and future actions may sway the audience. A good talk has a strong ending. A few self-serving statements with emotional appeal praising the worth of the analysis and benefits of the action plan may be convincing and certainly will be provocative.

**3.3 Questions:** An advantage of an oral presentation is the opportunity for dialogue with the audience during and after the presentation. For most presentations, questions during the talk are for clarification only and not on matters of substance. It is senseless to continue a presentation if the audience is not able to follow because earlier material has not been understood. On the other hand, it is disruptive to the flow of the talk to answer detailed questions about justification and analyses during the presentation. Also, the remainder of the argument may depend on the point being discussed, so one embarrassing question can undermine audience confidence before the full scope of the analysis has been advanced. Thus, a presenter might indicate at the beginning of the presentation that questions of clarification are welcome during the talk, but that questions of substance should be reserved until the end. The presenter should be gentle but firm in handling questions and not waste time with insignificant questions that require detailed explanations. Audiences like strong speakers who make the best use of the group's time, even at the expense of some individual's curiosity.

It is useful to have some brief notes on additional material. The material can be included in the talk if the presentation moves more rapidly than anticipated, or can be discussed during the question period if there are too few questions.

## III. TIPS ON PUBLIC SPEAKING

There are many fine books on public speaking which explain principles and techniques of this important endeavor. However, the student who is faced with a case presentation has no time for a course in public speaking, so this section gives key tips on public speaking. Most of these tips come from our observations of common strengths and weaknesses in case presentations.

## A. ADVICE ON PUBLIC SPEAKING

### 1. Eliminate Nervousness During Speech

All inexperienced (and most experienced) speakers are nervous before speaking. Public speaking is perhaps a unique human activity in its property of stirring butterflies in the stomach of would-be participants. Even world-famous speakers have admitted to nervousness at early stages of their careers. Mark Twain (then Samuel Clemens) described the hours before his first public speech as pure terror. In *Roughing It*, he claims to have seriously contemplated feigned illness, flight, and even suicide rather than face his first audience. Almost all speakers find that once they begin a presentation, the nervousness passes. In fact, the nervousness is useful in stimulating concentration and "psyching-up" for the occasion. There are two ways to combat nervousness. First the student must act confidently; the confidence often follows.

William James, the famous American psychologist, has written:

> "Action seems to follow feeling, but really action and feeling go together; and by regulating action which is under the more direct control of the will, we can indirectly regulate feeling. Thus the sovereign voluntary path to cheerfulness ...to sit up cheerfully and to act and speak as if cheerfulness were already there. If such conduct does not make you cheerful, nothing else on that occasion can."

Second, the speaker should be thoroughly prepared. Thorough preparation builds the confidence that defeats nervousness. Many speakers fear that they will forget what to say and the talk will finish in 5 minutes rather than 30. In fact, these events almost never happen and thorough preparation further lessens this likelihood. If one fears finishing early, then one should prepare optional material which can be included if time allows. Otherwise, the speaker who fears an early finish may prepare too much material and risk being cut off in the middle of the exposition.

### 2. Speak from Brief Notes

There are two important "Do Not's" in public speaking. Do not memorize the speech and do not read the speech. Some speakers find it useful to write out the speech beforehand; however, do not make the mistake of bringing this copy to the podium. A written copy cannot be followed without reading.

Speech memorization falls into the same category as speech reading, except it takes much more work. Nevertheless, it is permissible to memorize the first line of a speech. Sometimes this helps conquer the initial nervousness because the speaker knows that the talk will start easily. However, further memorization is counter-productive; one memory lapse may destroy the entire presentation.

### 3. Rehearse

It is important to be prepared and confident in a speech, and to pace the timing correctly. One or two rehearsals are the best way to accomplish both these tasks. Many people find these rehearsals difficult, because it is disconcerting to present a speech to an empty room, a tape recorder, or a friend. During practice, the speaker may not be as "psyched-up" as during the presentation. Thus, if one can complete an acceptable rehearsal, one can look forward to a good presentation.

## 4. Pace and Gesticulate in Moderation

Nervousness can cause speakers to pace, gesticulate, and squirm so much that the audience is distracted. Polished speakers avoid any physical motion which distracts the audience. They do pace and gesticulate, on occasion, but with timing and technique which reinforces the presentation. Beginners must learn to control actions which distract the audience. If one must wrinkle fingers, one should do so behind one's back.

## 5. Speak to Entire Group

Experienced speakers maintain eye contact with the entire audience throughout the talk. They look at the center of the audience and occasionally glance to its left and right. This makes the audience feel involved in the presentation. Novice speakers often look only at their notes or gaze idly over the heads of the audience. A firm look at individuals in the audience is necessary. However, direct eye contact with individuals in the audience is not necessary - many speakers find that too distracting.

## 6. Observe Group for Feedback

Henry Ward Beecher was once asked by a minister how to keep a congregation awake during a sermon on a hot Sunday. Beecher responded that the usher should be equipped with a pointed stick, and whenever the congregation dozed, the usher was to use it on the preacher.

Speakers can look at the audience - are individuals attentive or fidgety, sitting straight with lively facial expressions or slouched with idle stares? The speaker is responsible for keeping the audience awake; no matter how poorly prepared the audience is or poorly ventilated the room, etc., the speaker is responsible for the audience.

When the audience's interest wanes, speakers can alter the rate, volume, and richness of their voices. They can move rapidly through material that is dull, in hopes that later material will prove more interesting. They can ask for questions. Good speakers read their audiences, dwell on interesting points, and stimulate interest whenever necessary.

## 7. Control Voice Rate and Quality

Speakers must enunciate with sufficient clarity and volume to be understood easily by all in the audience. By pretending to talk with one individual in the back of the audience, the speaker can judge the volume. Sometimes speakers are so rushed that they do not enunciate clearly. Speakers with this tendency need to slow down and speak carefully. Bringing the voice from deep within the chest often gives the sound a richer tone and more volume with less effort.

## 8. Use Microphone Correctly

A speaker using a microphone for the first time must be careful. The correct technique is to speak in a normal voice and maintain a constant distance (about 6 inches) between the mouth and the microphone.

9.    **Be Aware of Time Constraints**

Beginners often prepare more material than they can present in the available time. When this happens, most of the talk is filled with preliminary details, the analysis is rushed at the end, and there is no time for questions. One can combat this by preparing optional material, to be included only if time permits, and by correctly pacing the material during the presentation.

10.    **Keep Argument Simple**

The argument must be kept so simple that at least 80% of the audience can follow. If the audience cannot follow the gist of the speech, it will become alienated and bored. When speakers recognize that this has occurred (this happens to everyone at one time or another), they should invite questions or jump to a point where the audience can pick up the thread of thought.

11.    **Keep Visual Aids Simple**

Visual aids are useful adjuncts to an oral presentation. An overhead projection or slide should be very simple - a maximum of 45 words. The speaker can explain points which are highlighted or illustrated on the slide, but must not attempt to put the full explanation on the slide itself. The audience came to listen, not to read.

12.    **Use Chalkboard Intelligently**

Chalkboards are usually available in the rooms where case presentations are made. They may be used to emphasize key points and to preserve material that will be recalled later in the presentation. The white board is becoming popular for executive presentations. This is a board with a shiny white surface and one uses colored markers for writing. It provides better clarity than a blackboard.

13.    **Pretest Audio and Video Equipment**

Overhead projectors, slide projectors, tape recorders, and moving picture projectors should be tested before a presentation to guarantee they are in working order and that the volume, focus, and other adjustments are set correctly. If one uses audio tapes or motion pictures, one should be sure to identify where the tapes originated and their purpose in the presentation.

14.    **Consider Flip-charts**

Flip-charts or large cardboards are effective, but seldom used visual aids. They offer the same advantage of color as the white board and serve the same function as overheads without some of the disadvantages. Most overhead and slide projectors require that the lights be dimmed, which can make note-taking and staying awake difficult. As well, the cooling motors emit a soporific purr. The one danger in using flip-charts is that the writing will not be readable from the back of the room.

15.    **Consider Props**

On an a priori basis, the authors cannot justify the use of such props as a bottle of vodka for a case on distilleries, or a model train engine for a case involving railroads. Nevertheless, in thinking back to case presentations these authors have heard, the ones that have had clever props stand out.

16. **Be Committed to Your Talk**

If one acts confident, enthusiastic, and interested in a presentation, these infectious feelings are transmitted immediately to the audience. If a speaker acts disinterested in a topic, the audience will soon lose interest also. The audience deserves every opportunity to be educated, entertained, and even inspired by the speech.

IV.    EXAMPLE OF AN ORAL CASE PRESENTATION

This section describes an oral presentation for the case given in Chapter II, Standard Oil Company of Indiana. The section describes the content of a presentation which is organized by the topics suggested in III Tips on Public Speaking. This is followed by a mock-up of the notes that one would use as memory aids during the presentation.

A.    INTRODUCTION TO ORAL CASE PRESENTATION

1. **Example of "Get the Attention of Audience"**: One needs to begin the presentation with an "attention-getter." The comparison to Standard Oil of New Jersey (11.6% vs 6.8% return on investment) can be made dramatic by opening the talk with the following facts (easily derived from compound interest tables):

> *"Suppose you had two choices for investing $500 each year of your working career in a retirement fund. Let's assume you have two investment choices, the first earns the same rate of return on investment as Indiana Standard, and the second the same rate of return as Standard Oil of New Jersey. When you retire in 40 years, your annual retirement income would be $6,447 with Indiana-equivalent management, or $39,821 with New Jersey-equivalent management."*

This example is followed by a comment that there may be a long-term strategy which will allow Indiana to catch up with New Jersey.

2. **Example of "Outline of Presentation"**: As the outline of the talk is explained, one prints the following skeleton outline on the chalkboard:

(1)  PROBLEM

(2)  ALTERNATIVES

(3)  TWO ALTERNATIVES SELECTED

(4)  QUESTIONS

The following brief comments on each part of the presentation are made to interest the audience:

(1) Problem: The key to the analysis is correct definition of the "root" problem.

The problem to be outlined explains many of Indiana's weaknesses.

(2)   Alternatives: The vast resources available to Indiana Standard mean that solutions will have to be long-term and are important to the welfare of tens of thousands of employees.

(3)   Two Alternatives Selected: A fundamental change in business methods necessary to bring Indiana's profitability close to that of New Jersey. Long-term economic and technical forces must be predicted for Indiana to realize such large gains.

(4)   Questions: The speech will raise many interesting issues which may be explored during the question period. Questions during the presentation should only be for clarification of material presented.

3.  **Example of "Background and Facts":**   The presenter ties the following facts together into an interesting history of Indiana Standard:

*   Standard Oil Trust dissolved in 1911.
*   Indiana Standard in Midwest retail gasoline; orientation to marketing.
*   Burton Process in 1920's.
*   American Oil Company purchased in 1954.
*   Formation of Indiana Oil Purchasing Company.

B.   THE BODY OF PRESENTATION

1.  **Example of "Problem Statement":**   This presentation gets right to the point with a statement of the problem:

**"Standard Oil Company of Indiana has failed to protect its source of supply in an industry with increasing demand and limited supply. As a result, the company is at the mercy of small suppliers and wildcatters in times of scarcity, and its long-term profitability is in jeopardy."**

Second, evidence of the problem and apparent "self-destruct" activities of Indiana Standard are cited and explained:

*   Selling of overseas drilling rights to New Jersey.

*   Problems for Indiana Oil Purchasing Company still exist in time of scarcity, because of natural supply and demand behavior.

*   Purchasing the American Oil Company increased even further the supply requirements of Indiana Standard.

This part of the talk is closed with a comment about an ideal solution being one which finds a guaranteed supply and has an investment with an attractive rate of return.

2.  **Example of "Alternatives and Analysis":**   In a short presentation, one cannot go into the same detail as the case analysis given in Section 2.3.  Thus, this part of the presentation begins directly with the two recommended alternatives:

A. Integrate vertically - oil drilling.

B. R & D - Coal and oil shale conversion, solar energy.

The presenter writes the above skeleton on the chalkboard to be sure the audience remembers the alternatives.

3. **Example of "Plan Implementation":**

First, the presenter reviews the futility of the current R & D cuts - the million dollar savings only improves return on investment by 0.03%, and raises problems between creative scientists and a strict management. Second, the presenter discusses the supply problem in terms of Standard Oil of New Jersey's approach to investing in the supply end of the business, and Indiana's attempting to circumvent the problem by forming the Indiana Oil Purchasing Company. If the talk has progressed rapidly, or more time is available because a previous presentation finished early, then additional material is included here. The last two cue cards at the end of this section have additional material.

C. THE CONCLUSION OF ORAL PRESENTATION

1. **Example of "Restatement of Problem and Solution"**: The reiteration is introduced by saying, "Let's consider the long-term forces in the industry - What is world industrialization doing? What are the long-term sources of energy?" This leads into a brief review the problem and solution.

2. **Example of "Benefits and What Must be Done"**: One returns to an emotional level by briefly repeating the retirement example that began the talk. This motivates the statement that Indiana must look far into the future and make accurate predictions, must undertake significant changes in the ways they do business, and will need some "guts".

3. **Example of "Questions"**: The floor is now opened for questions. Sometimes, it takes a few seconds before the first question is asked, so the presenter should allow ample time.

The presentation above did not include alternatives that were rejected, nor did it detail the advantages of vertical integration. Thus, the presenter is armed with points in each of these areas, compiled on index cards, to be used should these areas be questioned. (See the last two cue cards at the end of this section.)

**Example of "Cue Card for Presentation"**

---

**CARD 1:** GET ATTENTION (2 MINUTES, CUMULATIVE TIME 2 MINUTES)

"SUPPOSE YOU HAD 2 CHOICES FOR INVESTING $500 EACH YEAR
OF YOUR WORKING CAREER IN A RETIREMENT FUND..."
* INDIANA  $6,447      (8.6%)
* NEW JERSEY  $39,821    (11.6%)

---

**CARD 2:** OUTLINE OF PRESENTATION (3 MINS., CUM. 5 MINS.)
   (Write boldface portions on board.)

(1)  PROBLEM - "ROOT" IS KEY
(2)  ALTERNATIVES - LONG-TERM, TENS OF THOUSANDS EFFECTED
(3)  TWO SELECTED - PREDICT LONG-TERM, PARITY WITH N.J.
(4)  QUESTIONS - CLARIFICATION DURING, SUBSTANCE AFTER

---

**CARD 3:** BACKGROUND (4 MINS., CUM. 9 MINS.)

*    TRUST DISSOLVED IN 1911
*    MIDWEST MARKET
*    BURTON PROCESS 20'S
*    AMERICAN OIL COMPANY (1954)
*    INDIANA OIL PURCHASING COMPANY

---

**CARD 4:** THE PROBLEM (6 MINS., CUM. 15 MINS.)

"FAILED TO PROTECT SUPPLY....MERCY OF WILDCATTERS IN
SCARCITY"
   SOME EVIDENCE:
*    OVERSEAS DRILLING SOLD
*    PROBLEMS FOR INDIANA OIL PURCHASING COMPANY
*    AMERICAN OIL PURCHASE - LARGE SUPPLY DEMANDS

---

CARD 5: THE SOLUTIONS   (5 MINS., CUM. 20 MINS.)
   (Write on board)

A.  INTEGRATE VERTICALLY - OIL DRILLING
B.  R & D - COAL AND OIL SHALE TO GASOLINE, SOLAR ENERGY

---

CARD 6:  IMPLEMENTATION   (4 MINS., CUM. 24 MINS.)

*  R & D CUT - 6.80% to 6.83% ROI ONLY
*  PROBLEMS WITH MANAGEMENT
*  NEW JERSEY`S CONTINUED SUPPLY ORIENTATION

---

CARD 7:  RESTATEMENT   (3 MINS., CUM. 27 MINS.)

*  LONG-TERM  -  POPULATION, INDUSTRIALIZATION
*  REITERATE  (POINTS ON CHALKBOARD)

---

CARD 8:  BENEFITS          (3 MINS., CUM. 30 MINS.)

*  RECONSIDER RETIREMENT CASE  ($6,447 AND $39,821)
*  MUST LOOK AHEAD AND USE "GUTS"

---

ALLOW 10 MINUTES FOR QUESTIONS

---

CARD 9:  ADDITIONAL MATERIAL - 1

ADVANTAGES OF VERTICAL INTEGRATION INCLUDE:

*  REFINERY DESIGNED FOR ONE TYPE OF OIL
*  UNIFORM GRADE OF PRODUCT CERTAIN
*  OPTIMIZE INTEGRATED INVENTORY AND SUPPLY SYSTEM
*  INTRA-FIRM TRANSFERS CHEAPER
*  COMPLETE WELL-HEAD TO GAS STATION DATA FOR
   DECISION-MAKING

**CARD 10**: ADDITIONAL MATERIAL - 2

ALTERNATIVE SOLUTIONS:

* LONG-TERM CONTRACTS WITH OIL PRODUCERS
* JOINT VENTURES WITH OIL PRODUCING COMPANIES
* DIVERSIFY TO REDUCE DEPENDENCE ON OIL

# SELECTED CASES

**NOTES:**

# CASE NO 1.    SYSTEM LOGISTICS INC.

The President of System Logistics Inc. is fond of saying that he runs the smallest publishing house in the world.  His assertion is based on the fact that System Logistics Inc., has, since its incorporation published just one book entitled " The Guide To Case Analysis and Reporting." The Guide, co-authored by Dr. Denis Coleman and Dr. Al Edge,  was first published in 1978 and is now going into its fourth edition.

## Background

The need for a guide to assist students in the preparation,  analysis,  discussion,  and reporting of business cases was perceived by the co-authors in 1977 and by 1978 they had incorporated, written the text, developed a brochure, and began publishing.  Shortly after publication began Denis Coleman left Hawaii to begin a very successful career in the microcomputer software industry in Menlo Park, California.

## Operations

System Logistics Inc. is a sub-chapter S corporation with Dr. Edge as president and his wife and two daughters serving as directors.  Originally,  the text was printed and distributed from Hawaii, but since the 3rd edition the printing and distribution are handled out of Denver, Colorado  by family members.  This change has proven to be most satisfactory since it lowers freight and printing costs. In the earlier editions the text and graphics were developed using a word processing program on an IBM PC computer.  Photo ready copy was developed using a  standard daisy-wheel printer. The photo ready copy was printed locally.   Depending on expected demand the company would print between 3000 and 5000 copies.  The printer would box and deliver the finished product to the point of distribution.

The 4th edition is being developed in a similar fashion, but this time with the use of an IBM PS-2 computer and a desk-top publishing program (Altus pagemaker).  In the earlier editions the Guide underwent only minor revision but this time more extensive changes are planned.   This is necessary because of relatively new developments in management theory, especially in the area of strategic decision-making and competitive analysis.  Much of the standard information such as quantitative analysis, how to present a case, how to write a case, the fundamentals of effective business writing, and how to use the library for research will remain with some up-dating.

## MARKETING

The marketing of the Guide is accomplished by direct mail.  With each edition, a brochure is developed,  and mailing labels are purchased from a mailing list service company.   The mailing list is selected from a catalog of college faculty lists. The list purchased for the first three editions focused on "Business Policy" and contains address labels for approximately 2,100 Business Policy Professors. In this situation, promotions are directed at the professors who teach case oriented courses. Although the ultimate consumer is the student, it is the professor who determines which books are required. Each brochure lists the benefits of the guide, a table of contents,  and provides a card  to be returned in order for the professor to receive a free examination copy. Typically, the effectivity of the brochures is about 20%, that is the company receives about 420 requests for examination copies from the 2100 brochures mailed.

Exhibit I provides sales figures of the "The Guide" for the last seven years.

---

## EXHIBIT I   TOTAL NUMBER OF BOOKS SOLD

| YEAR | NO. OF BOOKS SOLD |
|------|-------------------|
| 1984 | 2097 |
| 1985 | 2266 |
| 1986 | 2034 |
| 1987 | 1730 |
| 1988 | 1466 |
| 1989 | 1666 |
| 1990 | 1400 |

---

In discussing sales Dr. Edge noted that in recent years very little effort has been made to increase sales. "The Guide has been treated as a sideline business, closely related to teaching Strategic Management at the University of Hawaii." Recently, it was decided that the time is right for a major change and renewed effort. There is potentially a growing market for an alternative to the standard case book, since more and more professors are looking for greater versatility in their case courses. The Guide offers one such option where the professor uses it along with selected cases that he or she may have available or cases obtained by some other means such as "A Case Clearinghouse" or a zerox copy shop such as Ditto's.

About two years ago the company received a letter from The Case Clearinghouse of Great Britain and Ireland.[1] They noted that "The Guide To Case Analysis and Reporting" was one of the best book of its type in the field and offered to serve as European distributor. Since they are a non-profit organization, it is considered high praise indeed and now about one third of all sales go to that clearinghouse for distribution to their member schools.

Some problems for consideration are:

1. Low sales volume. The larger publishers send sales representatives to the schools to encourage the professors to adopt their books. System Logistics Inc., has no direct personal contact with the professors, but relies on brochures and free examination copies to sell the text. The lack of sales representatives isn't a big problem, since the sales representative can only bring the text to mind and encourage the professor to read it. The professor still has to read it and feel it will benefit the student and his teaching.

2. The high return rate. Up to this point the company has had too liberal a return policy for a paperback book. All undamaged books are accepted with a small handling charge. The return problem, which only exists in the U.S. sales, is due in a large part to professors who like the text but are not willing to make it "required", and list it as a "recommended text." Often they optimistically have their bookstore order a large number of books assuming that the students will buy the recommended text. Unfortunately, only a very small percentage of students purchase recommended texts, and as a result most of these books are returned.

---

[1] Recently the Case Clearing House of Great Britian and Ireland has changed its name to The European Case Clearing House.

3. Slow payment by bookstores. Many bookstores like to sell the text before making payment to the publisher. This involves as long as six months between their receipt of the books and payment. System Logistics Inc., has done little to encourage early payment and would like to speed up cash flow.

Recommendation

With these facts in mind, briefly recommend what strategy should be pursued as the company prepares for the next edition.

_____

_____

_____

_____

_____

_____

_____

_____

_____

_____

_____

_____

NOTES:

94

# CASE NO. 2    UNITED PRODUCTS, INC.

Having just returned from lunch, Mr. George Brown, president of United Products, Inc., was sitting in his office thinking about his upcoming winter vacation--in a few days he and his family would be leaving from Boston to spend three weeks skiing on Europe's finest slopes. His daydreaming was interrupted by a telephone call from Mr. Hank Stevens, UPI's general manager. Mr. Stevens wanted to know if their two o'clock meeting was still on. The meeting had been scheduled to review actions UPI could take in light of the company's sluggish sales and the currently depressed national economy. In addition, Brown and Stevens were to go over the financial results for the company's recently completed fiscal year--they had just been received from UPI's auditors. Although it had not been a bad year, results were not as good as expected, and this, in conjunction with the economic situation, had prompted Mr. Brown to reappraise the plans he had for the company during the upcoming year.

## COMPANY HISTORY

United Products, Inc., established in 1941, was engaged in the sales and service of basic supply items for shipping and receiving, production and packaging, research and development, and office and warehouse departments. Mr. Brown's father, the founder of the company, recognized the tax advantages in establishing separate businesses rather than trying to consolidate all of his operations in one large organization. Accordingly, over the years the elder Mr. Brown had created new companies and either closed down or sold off older companies as business conditions seemed to warrant. As of the mid-1960s, his holdings consisted of a chain of four related sales-distribution companies covering the geographic area from Chicago eastward.

In 1967, feeling it was time to step aside and turn over active control of the business to his sons, the elder Mr. Brown recapitalized and restructured his companies, merging some and disposing of others. When the restructuring process was completed, he had set up two major companies. United Products, Inc., was to be run by his youngest son, George Brown, with its headquarters in Massachusetts, while his other son, Richard Brown, was to operate United Products Southeast, Inc., headquartered in Florida.

Although the Brown brothers occasionally worked together and were on each other's board of directors, the two companies operated on their own. As Mr. George Brown explained, "Since we are brothers, we often get together and discuss business, but the two are separate companies and each files its own tax return."

During 1972, United Products moved into new facilities in Woburn, Massachusetts. From this location it was thought that the company would be able to serve its entire New England market area effectively, "Our abilities and our desires to expand and improve our overall operation will be enhanced in the new specially designed structure containing our offices, repair facilities, and warehouse," is how George Brown viewed the role of the new facilities. Concurrent with the move, the company segmented the more than 3,500 different items it carried into eight major product categories:

1. Stapling Machines.
2. Staples. All sizes and types.
3. Stenciling Equipment and Supplies.
4. Gummed Tape Machines.

5. Industrial Tapes.
6. Gluing Machines.
7. Work Gloves.
8. Marking and Labeling Equipment

---

* This case was prepared by Jeffrey Schuman, Framingham, Mass., published with permission.

In a flyer mailed to United Products' 6,000 accounts announcing the move to its new facilities, the company talked about its growth in this fashion:

> Here we grow again--thanks to you--our many long-time valued customers. . .
>
> Time and Circumstances have decreed another United Products transPLANT--this time, to an unpolluted garden-type industrial area, ideally located for an ever-increasing list of our customers.
>
> Now, in the new 28,000-sq. ft. plant with enlarged offices and warehouse, we at UNITED PRODUCTS reach the peak of efficiency in offering our customers the combined benefits of maximum inventories, accelerated deliveries, and better repair services.

By 1974, the company had grown to a point where sales were $3.5 million (double that of four years earlier) and 34 people were employed. Results for 1973 compared to 1972 showed a sales increase of 22 percent and a 40 percent gain in profits. Exhibit 1 contains selected financial figures for 1971, 1972, and 1973.

EXHIBIT 1  **Selected Financial Information, United Products, Inc.**

|  | Nov. 30, 1971 | Nov. 30, 1972 | Nov. 30 1973 |
|---|---|---|---|
| Current assets | $ 862,783 | $ 689,024 | $ 937,793 |
| Other assets | 204,566 | 774,571 | 750,646 |
| Current liabilities | 381,465 | 223,004 | 342,939 |
| Net worth | 685,884 | 750,446 | 873,954 |
| Sales | n.a. | n.a | 3,450,000. |

n.a. = not available

## COMPETITION

Mr. George Brown indicated that UPI does not have clearly defined rivals against whom it competes head-on with respect to all of its 3,500-plus items:

It is hard to get figures on competition since we compete with no one company directly. Different distributors carry lines which compete with various of our product lines, but there is no one company which competes against us across our full range of products.

On a regular basis, Mr. Brown receives Dun & Bradstreet's Business Information Reports on specific firms with which he competes. Mr. Brown feels that since the rival firms are, like his own firm, privately held, the financial figures reported are easily manipulated and, therefore, are not a sound basis on which to devise strategies and plans.

## MANAGEMENT PHILOSOPHY

When Mr. Brown took over UPI in 1967 at the age of 24, he set a personal goal of becoming financially secure and developing a highly profitable business. With the rapid growth of the company, he soon realized his goal of financial independence and in so doing began to lose interest in the company. "I became a rich person at age 28 and had few friends with equal wealth that were my age. The business no longer presented a challenge, and I was unhappy with the way things were going."

After taking a 10-month "mental vacation" from the business, George Brown felt he was ready to return to work. He had concluded that one way of proving himself to himself and satisfying his ego would be to make the company as profitable as possible. However, according to Mr. Brown, "The company can only grow at approximately 20 percent per year, since this is the amount of energy I am willing to commit to the business."

In 1974, at age 31, Mr. Brown described his philosophical outlook as " very conservative" and surmised that he ran UPI in much the same way as his 65-year-old father would. In describing his managerial philosophy and some of the operating policies he had established, he said:

I am very concered about making UPI a nice place to work. I have to enjoy what I'm doing and have fun at it at the same time. I cannot make any more money, since I'm putting away as much money as I can. The government won't allow me to make more money, since I already take the maximum amount.

I like to feel comfortable, and if we grew too quickly it could get out of hand. I realize the business doesn't grow to its potential but why should I put more into it. . . . The company could grow, but why grow? Why is progress good? You have to pay for everything in life and I'm not willing to work harder. . . .

Another thing. I am a scrupulously honest businessman and it is very hard to grow large if you're honest. There are many deals that I could get into that would make UPI a lot of money, but I'm too moral of a person to get involved. . . .

EXHIBIT 2   ORGANIZATION CHART--DECEMBER 1974

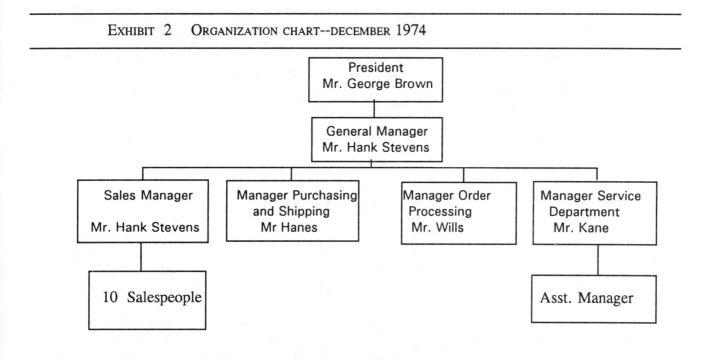

To me, happiness is being satisfied with what you have. I've got my wife, children and health; why risk these for something I don't need? I don't have the desire to make money because I didn't come from a poor family; I'm not hungry.

I have never liked the feeling of owing anything to anyone. If you can't afford to buy something, then don't. I don't like to borrow any money and I don't like the company to borrow any. All of our bills are paid within 15 days. I suppose I've constrained the business as a result of this feeling, but it's my business. The company can only afford to pay for a 20 percent growth rate so that's all we'll grow.

## ORGANIZATIONAL STRUCTURE

Upon returning to the company from his "mental vacation" in 1971 George Brown realigned UPI's organizational structure as shown in Exhibit 2 (the company does not have a formal organizational chart: this one is drawn from the case researcher's notes). With respect to the way his company was organized, George remarked:

> We have to have it on a functional basis now. We are also trying something new for us by moving to the general manager concept. In the past when I was away, there was no one with complete authority; now my general manager is in charge in my absence.

In discussing the new structuring of the organization, Mr. Brown was quick to point out that the company has not established formalized job descriptions. "Job descriptions are not worth anything. My people wear too many hats, and besides, we're too small to put it in writing." At present the company employs 34 people, including Mr. Brown.

Mr. Brown points out that he has never had a personnel problem. "All my people enjoy working here." He believes that "nobody should work for nothing" and has, therefore, established a personal goal of seeing to it that no one employed by UPI makes less than $10,000 per year. Mr. Brown commented on his attitude toward his employees as follows:

> The men might complain about the amount of responsibility placed on them, but I think it's good for them. It helps them develop to their potential. I'm a nice guy who is interested in all of my people. I feel a strong social obligation to my employees and have developed very close relationships with all of them. My door is always open to them no matter what the problem may be.

> I make it a policy never to yell at anyone in public; it's not good for morale. Maybe it's part of my conservative philosophy but I want everyone to call me Mr. Brown, not George. I think it's good for people to have a Mr. Brown. Although I want to run a nice friendly business. Employers and employees cannot mix socially; it just doesn't work out over the long run.

> This is not your normal business. I am very approachable; I don't demand much and I allow an easy open dialogue with my employees. Seldom do I take any punitive action. I'm just not a hard driving, tough guy . . . I'm an easy-going guy.

> It would take much of the enjoyment out of the business for me to come in here and run this place like a machine.[1]

> I find it hard to motivate the company's salesmen. Since we have so much trouble finding good capable men. I'm not likely to fire any that I have. This situation makes it hard for me to put pressure on them to produce.

> The bonus system, if you want to call it that, is I guess what you'd call very arbitrary. I have not set up specific sales quotas, or targeted goals for my inside people so, as a result, I base my bonus decisions on my assessment of how well I feel an employee performed during the past year.

> Recently, I've given some thought to selling the company. I could probably get around $3 to $4 million for it. If I did that, I'm not sure what I would do with my time. Besides my family and UPI there is not much that I am interested in. A couple of years ago when I took my extended vacation I got bored and couldn't wait to get back to the company

---

[1] When the case researcher arrived at the plant one afternoon, he observed Mr. Brown running around the office deeply involved in a water fight with one of his office girls. By the way, he lost.

## UPI'S PLANNING PROCESS

George Brown claims to be a firm believer in planning, "I find myself spending more and more time planning for the company. Currently, I'm averaging about 50 percent of my time and I see this increasing." As he described it, the planning process at United Products is really a very loose system:

We have no set way as to how we do the planning. Basically, the process is directed at ways of increasing the profitability of the company. I look at the salesmen's performance on a weekly and monthly basis and use this information in the development of the plans.

Since we have a very informal planning process, we only forecast out one year at most. The company's plans are reevaluated each month and, if necessary, new plans are set. Only on rare occasions have we ever planned beyond one year. However, I think the current economic and political situation may force us into developing plans that cover a two-year period.

I am familiar with commonly accepted theory about planning systems, but I do not feel it is necessary for UPI to institute, in a formal manner, any of those I've read about. We perform many of the activities advocated in the planning models, but we do them in a relaxed, casual fashion. For example, I am a member of many organizations connected with my business and receive industry newsletters on a regular basis. In addition, I receive input from friends and business addociates both inside and outside my line of business. Since we do not have a formal process, planning tends to be a continuous process at UPI.

Although goals are not formally developed and written down, Mr. Brown said he established targets for the company to achieve in the areas of sales, profits, and organizational climate:

1. Increase sales volume of business by 20 percent per year.
2. Increase gross profit margin 0.5 to 1 percent per year.
3. Make UPI a friendly place to work.

Mr. Brown feels that the company has been able to grow at about 20 percent a year in the past and should be able to realize that level in the future. In addition, he believes that sales growth is a necessary evil: "Those companies that don't grow are swallowed up by the competition, and besides, given the level of energy I'm willing to exert, I think 20 percent is a reasonable level of growth."

In the area of profits, the company actually sets no specific targeted figures other than simply an increase in the gross profit margin (as stated above). Mr. Brown observed:

We do not set a goal because we would not have a way of measuring it. I have no way of knowing how much money I am making until the end of the year, without considerable time and effort.

When asked about UPI's strengths and weaknesses, Mr. Brown indicated that the company had four areas of strength:

1. The number of different products carried.
2. The quality of its employees, particularly salesmen.
3. The absence of any debt.
4. Purchasing capabilities.

The major weakness he viewed as an inability to get and train new personnel--primarily in the area of sales.

## SALES FORCE

UPI's salesmen are not assigned a sales quota for the year but rather are evaluated based on Mr. Brown's assessment of the particular salesman's territory and initiative. He feels his salesmen make more than the salesmen of his competitors. Several of UPI's 10 salesmen have earned as much as $40,000 in a single year. All salesmen are compensated on a straight, sliding-scale commission basis calculated as follows:

8 percent for first $180,000 in sales.
7 percent for next $60,000.
6 percent for next $60,000.
5 percent for all sales over $300,000.

Mr. Brown is pleased with the sales success of his company and feels that United Products' greatest strength is its ability to "sell anything to anybody." Still, he perceives UPI's main problem as finding good salesmen. "There just aren't any good salesmen around, and this is a problem because salesmen are the lifeblood of our business."

## UPI'S MANAGEMENT TEAM

At the time of the company's reorganization, Mr. Hank Stevens was brought in as general manager and assistant to the president. Over the past several years, Mr. Stevens' areas of responsibility have grown to an extent where they now comprise approximately 80 percent of the activities that were formerly done by Mr. Brown. As a result of this, George Brown sometimes finds himself with little to do and often works only five hours per day. As he described it:

Hank's management discretionary power has increased steadily since he has been here--partly as a result of the extent of responsibility I've placed on him and partly due to his aggressiveness. As it now stands, he makes almost all of the daily operating decisions for the company, leaving me with only the top-management decisions. Let's be realistic, there just aren't that many top-management decisions that have to be made here in the course of a day. A lot of the time, I walk around the plant checking on what other people are doing and, I guess, acting as a morale booster.

When asked about the management capabilities of Hank Stevens, Mr. Brown responded by saying, "Hank probably feels that he is working as a very fast pace, but when you evaluate the effectiveness of his actions, he is actually moving forward at what I would consider to be a very slow pace. However, everything else considered, Hank is the best of what is around. I guess if I could find a really good sales manager, I would add him to the company and relieve Hank of that area of responsibility."

Mr. Hank Stevens

Mr. Hank Stevens, 32, joined UPI at the time of reorganization in 1970 after having graduated from a local university with a B.S. in economics. As general manager, Mr. Stevens' responsibilities included planning, purchasing, and sales management, as well as involvement in other decisions that affected UPI's policies. Mr. Stevens feels that he has been fortunate in that "Ever since I came to UPI, I've reported to the president and in essence have had everyone else reporting to me."

When asked about the goals of UPI, Mr. Stevens responded that, "As I see it, we have goals in in three major areas: profitability, sales level and personal relationships," In discussing his own personal goals, Hank explained that he hoped that the organization would grow and as a result he would be able to grow along with it. Since Mr. Stevens works so closely with Mr. Brown, he has given considerable thought to his boss's business philosophy:

I feel that George's business philosophy is unique. I guess the best way to describe it is to say that above all he is a businessman. Also, he has very high moral values, and as a result of that he is extremely honest and would never cheat anybody. Actually, the company would probably look better financially if it was run by someone who didn't operate with the same values as George.

When asked about the sales force at UPI, Mr. Stevens commented that "when a new salesman starts with the company, he does so with full salary. After a period of about two years, we change him over to a commission basis." As has always been the case, UPI concentrated its sales efforts on large customers. Mr. Stevens noted that "on the average the company processes approximately 105 orders per day, with an average dollar value per order of roughly $132. It's not that we won't write small orders, we just don't solicit business from small accounts. It just makes more sense to concentrate on the larger accounts."

Mr. Jim Hanes

Jim Hanes, 24, has been with UPI for over six years and during that time has worked his way up from assistant service manager to his current position as the number-three man in the company--manager of purchasing and shipping. Jim is responsible for the front office, repair work, and the warehouse. He feels that his reporting responsibility is approximately 60 percent to Mr. Stevens and 40 percent to Mr. Brown. "Since I have responsibility for all merchandise entering and leaving the company, I get involved with both Hank and George, and, therefore, I guess I report to both of them." In talking about where he would go from his present position, he explained that

I guess the next step is for me to become a salesman so that I can broaden my background and move up in the company. However, I am a little worried; I don't think the salesmen in our company are given the right sales training. As the system works now, a new man is assigned to work with an experienced salesman for about six weeks--after which time he is given his own territory. Perhaps if our sales manager had more experience as a salesman, then he would handle the training differently.

In commenting on his understanding of Mr. Brown's philosophy, Jim summed up his position thusly, "George is a very open person. I think he is too honest for a businessman. He certainly gives his people responsibility. He gives you the ball and lets you run with it. I don't think enough planning is done at UPI. At most, it appears that we look ahead one year, and even then what plans are developed are kept very flexible."

## UPI'S CORPORATE STRATEGY

When asked about UPI's current strategy, Mr. Brown responded that "the company is presently a distributor in the industrial packaging equipment, shipping supplies, and heavy duty stapling equipment business. In the past when we've wanted to grow, we have done one or both of the following: either add new lines of merchandise or additional salesmen. For example, this past year I got the idea of what I call a contract sales department. It is a simple concept. I took one man, put him in an office with a telephone and a listing of the Fortune top 1,000 companies, and told him to call and get new business. You would be surprised at how easy it was to pick up new accounts."

Mr. Stevens looks at UPI as being in the distribution and shipping of packaging supplies business. "In order for UPI to reach the goals that have been set we have to sell more products. That is, we can grow by adding new salesmen, adding more product lines, purchasing more effectively, and undertaking more aggressive sales promotion."

Mr. Brown believes that UPI should try to maximize the profit on every item sold. To do this the company tries to set its prices at a level which is approximately 10 percent above the competition. Mr. Brown explained his pricing philosophy:

I don't understand why people are afraid to raise prices. If you increase the price, you will pick up more business and make more money. That allows you to keep the volume low and still make more money. In addition, although the customer may pay more, he gets more. The higher price allows me to provide top-notch service to all my customers.

In his view, UPI is an innovative company. "Until very recently we were always innovating with new products and new applications. Now I think it's again time that we started to look for additional new and exciting products."

Brown was aware that UPI's strategic emphasis on service, together with his business philosophy, had resulted in UPI's organization being larger than it had to be, given the level of business. Mr. Brown explained the reasoning behind this condition, "I know the organization is bigger than it has to be. We probably could handle three times the present volume of business with our present staff and facility. I think it's because of my conservative attitude; I've always wanted the organization to stay a step ahead of what is really needed. I feel conforable with a built-in backup system and, therefore, I am willing to pay for it."

In December 1974, Mr. Brown talked optimistically about the future. He felt that sales should reach the $6-7 million range by 1978. "Looked at in another way, we should be able to grow at 20-25 percent per year without any particular effort." He went on to say:

I want to grow and, therefore, I am making a concerted effort. I am constantly looking for possible merger avenues or expansion possibilities. I do not want to expand geographically. I would rather control the market area we are now in.

I recently sent a letter to all competitors in New England offering to buy them out. Believe it or not, no one responded.

I do not see any problems in the future. The history has been good, therefore, why won't it continue to happen?

Growth is easy. All I have to do is pick up a new line and I've automatically increased sales and profits. Basically we are distributors, and we operate as middle-men between the manufacturers and users.

In light of what has been happening in the market, I feel that supply and demand will continue to be a problem. Therefore, I am giving serious thought to integrating vertically and becoming a manufacturer. This will guarantee our supply.[2]

Actually, I don't want to do the manufacturing. I think it would be better if I bought the manufacturing equipment and then had someone else use it to make my products.

--------------

[2] Refer to Exhibit 3 (at the end of the case) which contains minutes of a United Products sales meeting held at the end of 1973.

## THE FUTURE

Nevertheless, after reviewing with his accountant the results for the just-completed fiscal year, Mr. Brown was concerned about UPI's future course. " I know changes have to be made for next year as a result of this year, but I'm not sure what they should be." Mr Brown continued:

I think this next year is going to be a real bad year. Prices will probably fall like a rock from the levels they reached during 1974 and as a result those items that would have been profitable for the company aren't going to be, and we have much too large of a inventory as it is. It isn't easy to take away customers from the competition. As a result of this, I feel we have to step up our efforts to get new lines and new accounts. Recently, I've given some thought to laying off one or two people for economic reasons, but I'm not sure. I will probably give raises to all employees even though it's not a good business decision, but it's an ingrained part of my business philosophy.

When asked if he had informed his employees of his concern about the future, Mr. Brown referred to the minutes of a sales meeting that had been held in November 1974:

Mr. Brown then presided at the meeting, and announced that Al King had won the coveted award of "Salesman of the Month." This was a "first" for our Al and well deserved for his outstanding sales results in October. Congratulations and applause were extended him by all present. The balance of the meeting was then spent in a lengthy, detailed discussion, led by Mr. George Brown, of the general, overall picture of what the future portends in the sales area as a result of the current inflationary, recessionary, and complex competitive conditions prevailing in the economy.

The gist of the entire discussion can be best summarized as follows:

1. Everyone present must recognize the very real difficulties that lie ahead in these precarious economic times.
2. The only steps available to the salesmen and to the company for survival during the rough period ahead are as follows;
   a. Minimize the contacts with existing accounts.
   b. Spend the majority of time developing new accounts on the less competitive products and selling new products to established accounts.
3. Concentrate on and promote our new items.
4. Mr. Brown and inside management are making and will continue to make every concentrated effort to find new products and new lines for the coming year.

In preparation for his meeting with Hank Stevens, Mr. Brown had drawn up a list of activities to which Hank should address himself while running UPI during George's upcoming vacation. Mr. Brown believed that upon his return from Europe his activities at UPI would be increasing as a result of the problems caused by the uncertain economic conditions. The first item on the list was a possible redefinition of UPI's marketing strategy. Mr. Brown now believed that UPI would have to be much more liberal with respect to new products considered for sale. "I'm not saying we are going to get into the consumer goods business, but I think we need to give consideration to handling consumer products which require no service and which carry a high-profit-margin factor for the company."

As he sat at his desk thinking about possible changes which he could make in UPI's planning process, Mr. Brown was convinced that if he hadn't done some planning in the past, the situation would be more drastic than it was. Yet at the same time, he wasn't sure that a more structured and formalized planning process would put UPI in any better position to face the more difficult times that he saw ahead.

EXHIBIT 3    Minutes of UPI's Sales Meeting, December 5, 1973

Mr. Brown presided at the meeting. His opening remarks highlighted the extraordinary times our country and our company are going through as far as the general economy and the energy crisis are concerned, and the extraordinary effects of these unusual crises on people and businesses, including our company and our sources of supply.

He thanked all present for the many thoughful, considered, and excellent suggestions which they had offered in writing as to how best the salesmen and their company might handle the gasoline crisis without incurring an undue loss of sales and profits, and still maintaining the high standards of service to which UNITED PRODUCTS' thousands of satisfied customers are accustomed.

The whole situation, according to Mr. Brown, boils down to a question of supply and prices. Mr. Brown reported that on his recent trip to the Orient, there were very few companies who wanted to sell their merchandise to us--rather, THEY WANTED TO BUY FROM US MANY OF THE ITEMS WE NORMALLY BUY FROM FOREIGN COMPANIES, i.e., carton-closing staples, tape, gloves, et cetera . . . and at inflated prices!!! The Tokyo, Japan market is so great that they are using up everything they can produce--and the steel companies would rather make flat steel than the steel rods which are used for making staples. A very serious problem exists, as a result, in the carton-closing staple field, not only in Japan but also in Europe and America.

Mr. Brown advised that every year the conpany's costs of operating increase just as each individual's cost of living goes up and up yearly. Additional personnel, increased group and auto insurance premiums, increased social security payments, new office equipment and supplies, new catalogues, "Beeper systems" for more salesmen--all of these costs accumulate and result in large expenditures of money. Manufacturers cover their increased operating costs by pricing their products higher--but to date, UNITED PRODUCTS has never put into their prices the increased costs resulting from increased operating expenses. Last year, the 3 percent increase which the company needed then was put into effect by many of you. HOWEVER, in order for the company to realize that additional profit, this 3 percent price increase had to be put into effect ACROSS THE BOARD . . . all customers . . . all items!

THAT did not happen!!!

Mr. Brown advised that UNITED PRODUCTS got LAMBASTED when all of the sources of supply started to increase their prices. When SPOTNAILS, for example, went up 10 percent, the salesmen only increased their prices 7 percent, et cetera. We did not get the 3 percent price increase above the manufacturers' price increase--and we needed it then and need it even more NOW.

Eliminating the possibility of cutting commissions, there are three possible solutions for the problem of how to get this much needed and ABSOLUTELY IMPERATIVE additional 3 percent PRICE INCREASE ACROSS THE BOARD to cover the constantly growing operating costs for running a successful, progressive-minded and growing business whose high standards of service and performance are highly regarded by customers and sources of supply alike, namely:
  a. A 3 percent increase on all items to all customers across the board.
  b. A surcharge on all invoices or decrease in discounts allowed off LIST.
  c. A GCI charge (government cost increase) on all invoices.

Considerable discussion regarding these three possibilities resulted in the following conclusions concerning the best method for obtaining this special 3 percent ACROSS THE BOARD PRICE INCREASE, as follows:
  a. A new PRICE BOOK should be issued with all new prices to reflect not only the manufac-
  turers' new increased prices but in addition the 3 percent UNITED PRODUCTS PRICE INCREASE. All
  of the salesmen agreed that it would be easier to effect the additional 3 percent price increase if the
  3 percent was "Built in" on their price book sheets.
  b. This new PRICE BOOK will be set up in such a way that prices will be stipulated according
  to quantity of item purchased . . . with no variances allowed. WITH NO EXCEPTIONS, the price of

(Exhibit 3 continued)
any item will depend on the quantity a customer buys.

    c. Some items will continue to be handled on a discount basis--but lower discounts in order to ascertain that UNITED PRODUCTS is getting its 3 percent price increase.

    d. Until these new PRICE BOOKS are issued, all salesmen were instructed to proceed IMMEDIATELY to effect these 3 percent price increases.

## 10 NEW ACCOUNTS CONTEST

Seven of our 10 salesmen won a calculator as a result of opening up 10 new accounts each . . . a total of 70 NEW ACCOUNTS for our company!!! However, both Mr. Brown and Mr. Stevens confessed that the dollar volume amount stipulated in the contest had been set rediculously low, as a "feeler" to determine the success and effectiveness of such a contest. All the salesmen voiced their approval of all of the contests offered to them--and agreed that they had enjoyed many excellent opportunities of increasing their peronal exchecquers.

## NEW CUSTOMER LETTERS

Mr. Brown again remined all present that we have an excellent printed letter, which is available for sending to every new customer--and urged all to take advantage of this service by the office personnel by clearly indicating on their sales and order slips "NEW CUSTOMER." this procedure is but another step towards our goal of becoming more and more professional in our approach with our customers.

## NEW CATALOGS

Mr. Brown advised that by the first of the new year, hopefully, all our hard-cover catalogs with their new divider breakdowns will be ready for hand-delivering to large accounts. These catalogs cost the company over $5 and should only be distributed by hand to those customers who can and will make intelligent and effective use of them.

## EXCESSIVE ISSUANCE OF CREDITS

As a result of a detailed study made by Mr. Brown of the nature and reasons for the ever-increasing number of credits being issued, he instructed all of the salesmen to follow these procedures when requesting the issuing of CREDITS:

    a. Issue the CREDIT at the right time.
    b. Do not sell an item where it is not needed.
    c. NEVER PUT "NO COMMENT" for the reason why merchandise is being returned.
    EVERY CREDIT MUST HAVE A REASON FOR ITS ISSUANCE.

The ever-increasing number of CREDITS being issued is extremely costly to the company: (1) new merchandise comes back 90-plus days after it has been billed, and frequently, if not always, is returned by the customer FREIGHT COLLECT; (2) CREDIT 9-part forms, postage for mailing, and extra work for both the Bookkeeping and Billing and Order Processing Departments mean higher expenses for the Company. More intelligent, considered and selective selling, plus greater care on the part of the Order Processing personnel, according to Mr. Brown, could easily eliminate a large percentage of these CREDITS.

**NOTES:**

106

# CASE NO. 3    NEC CORPORATION'S ENTRY INTO EUROPEAN MICROCOMPUTERS*

In April 1985, nearly five years after the introduction of its first personal computer to the European market, NEC Corporation had not yet established a significant presence in Europe. Despite the vast commercial potential of microcomputers, and despite NEC's widely recognized technological leadership and considerable financial resources, the company had not transferred its phenomenal success in Japan, where it had captured 55 percent of the personal computer market, to Europe. The time had come for NEC to reevaluate its strategy for entry into the rapidly evolving European microcomputer market, to review its current position, and to consider its options for the future.

## EVOLUTION OF NEC CORPORATION

From its modest beginnings in 1899 as an importer and then manufacturer of telephone equipment, NEC, with 1984 sales of $8 billion, and net income of nearly $200 million, had become a leading international force in telecommunications, the world's third largest vendor of microchips, and Japan's number two computer maker (behind Fujitsu). Expertise in these three major areas of the information industry placed NEC in a unique and enviable position to challenge its rivals both at home and aboard. NEC's president noted that, *"IBM may be ahead in computers, AT&T has good capacity in communications, and Texas Instruments is strong in semiconductors. But no company has such a combination of businesses in all three areas."*

## PRODUCT AREAS

NEC is divided into four separate divisions for its main businesses: Communications, computers and industrial electronic systems, electric components, and home electronics.

### A. Communications

Sales of communications systems and equipment in fiscal 1984 rose to $2.55 billion and has been growing at a compounded annual rate of 15.3 percent since 1980. NEC is the largest Japanese telecommunications company and has had considerable success in export markets, including selling its digital public telephone exchange in 28 countries. The company is also the world's largest supplier of satellite earth stations and microwave communications equipment.

### B. Computers and Industrial Electronic Systems

Computer and industrial electronic systems recorded sales of $2.39 billion in fiscal 1984, sustaining a compounded annual growth rate of 26.7 percent since 1980. The division has an extensive product list. The major products are super computers, general-purpose ACOS series computers, minicomputers, control computers, personal computers and software, data communications equipment and software, peripheral and terminal equipment, etc.

Within Japan NEC lags behind Fujitsu and IBM in overall computer sales, the company leads the Japanese market in sales of personal computers with a 55 percent share. Computers now account for 31 percent of the companies revenues. According to company officials, the major reason for this success lies in NEC's strength in semiconductors.

------------

* This case was prepared by Michael Hergert and Robin Hergert, San Diego State University, published with permission. Editors note: Some background information has been deleted from the original case to comply with the limitations set for this text.

Although NEC is looking to overseas data-processing markets for growth, its penetration of international markets for computers is very limited. The Japanese company has garnered only a tiny share of the personal computer market in the United States, the largest of NEC's foreign markets.

Industry analysts attribute NEC's lack of significant international presence in computers in foreign markets to the company's refusal to produce IBM-compatible mainframes. Observers note that IBM's more aggressive stance and its dominance of the mainframe market has made it hard for other companies to succeed with different systems. NEC counters that companies that seek to poach on IBM's customers by offering technically compatible machines expose themselves to the threat of crippling retaliation by IBM. The vice-president of the computer division, feels that the battle with the U.S. giant is undergoing a shift in emphasis: *"IBM's profits will come increasingly from software, maintenance, and system communications rather than from the computer hardware itself. So we have to compete with IBM in software rather than hardware."*

NEC is putting huge resources into improving the production of its software--it has 13 wholly owned software subsidiaries and employs some 8,500 programmers--one company official indicated that Japan's social and educational system may be a handicap. By emphasizing highly organized group activity, he thinks it discourages the individualism that often sparks off innovation. The company aims to fill the gap by tapping outside talent.

Although NEC's management predicts that demand for computers and industrial electronic systems will continue to rise as harsh conditions force companies to rationalize and upgrade their operations, they also recognize that competition is certain to increase as computer manufacturers around the world move to capitalize on the wealth of opportunity at hand. Industry observers are less than enthusiastic about NEC's ability to capitalize on these international opportunities. One consultant noted that *"While they've done fine with printers and semiconductors, they are not very strong in computers."*

## C. Electronic Components

NEC's sales of electronic devices reached $1.89 billion in fiscal 1984 and had been growing at a compounded annual rate of 23.1 percent since 1980. The company leads the increasingly successful Japanese assault on the world's semiconductor markets, and it ranks among the worlds top four microchip suppliers.

## D. Home Electronics

This division posted sales of $755 million in 1984 and has grown at a rate of 11 percent since 1980. In this area NEC's activities are small when compared to producers of consumer electronics in Japan such as Matsushita, Sony, Sanyo, JVC, and Hitachi.

Despite the firm's modest showing in consumer electronics, NEC believes that the division, and particularly the personal computer, is very important. NEC's president explains, *"In 10 or 20 years' time, consumer products will be the largest single part of. . .our strategy."*

## NEC STRATEGY

NEC sees itself as a tree whose roots are firmly embedded in high technology. One product recently developed by the Tokyo-based company is an automatic software-development system that makes productivity 5 to 50 times more efficient. Yet management thinks it could do better, committing over 10 percent of sales to R & D, and engineering activities.

NEC's competitors are beginning to run out of adjectives to describe such relentless striving for higher performance. The Japanese multinational, however, has still bolder ambitions. It has set its sights on the twin goals of increasing consolidated annual sales at 18-20 percent for the rest of the decade and of becoming a world leader in high technology. To accomplish their growth goals they plan to raise overseas contribution to sales to 40 percent, half of it manufactured outside Japan.

If NEC's targets are bold, its operational style is even riskier. While arch-rivals Fujitsu and Hitachi have set up partnerships with computer manufacturers in the United States and Europe to gain a sizable penetration of information-processing markets, NEC has shunned such shortcuts in favor of developing its own brand name. The Chairman explains *"Our intention is simple: walking on our own feet."* The president elaborates on this point: " *We aim to establish real companies abroad that can design, make, and maintain the products that they sell on their own.''* He is convinced that this policy of decentralization is the most effective way to secure NEC's future in an increasingly volatile and treacherous business climate. Indeed, growing fears of a trade war with the United States and the European Economic Community (EEC) have heightened the sense of urgency.

As a result of this go-it-alone approach, coupled with the decision not to make computers that are compatible with those made by IBM, NEC's machines have not yet achieved significant penetration in the West. To compensate, NEC has resorted to aggressive marketing and ruthless price cutting. According to one analyst at Yamaichi Research Institute, *"NEC uses its profits in other areas to allow it to cut prices in computers."* A strategy based on price competition is not without risk. For example, the U.S. Commerce Department recently found NEC guilty of dumping $3 million worth of microwave components on the US market.

NEC departed from the firm's policy of developing largely through internal growth when they acquired Electronic Arrays a small California chip maker. NEC executives have indicated, however, that there are no plans to bolster international marketing operations through the purchase of other companies with strong marketing organizations.

NEC's driving ambition is symbolized in its slogan "C&C," standing for the convergence of computer and communications technologies that lies at the heart of the revolution in electronic information handling. Since Dr. Kobayashi, Chairman of NEC, first coined the term the company has been actively promoting C&C within the entire organization. This theme dominates NEC management and activities to an almost obsessive degree. No document or conversation is complete without some reference to C&C.

Despite NEC's technical achievements and strongly held belief in the convergence of computers and communications, the company has a long way to go in coordinating it's communications, computer, semiconductor, and consumer electronics divisions. To enhance cooperation, the company has set up occasional project teams that span the different divisions.

THE EUROPEAN MICROCOMPUTER INDUSTRY

In 1985 the microcomputer industry in Europe displayed many features typical of emerging markets. Great technological uncertainty, buyer confusion, and unclear market segments created an environment where strategy formulation was difficult. Current events left many industry observers puzzled; spectacular successes and failures were the norm, and some of the world's mightiest multinationals had proven unable to establish viable competitive positions. NEC was among this group having failed to capture a significant market share after five years of effort.

In this market, even a precise product description is controversial. Microcomputers span the range from simple machines costing a few hundred dollars and primarily used for playing games to sophisticated desktop units capable of supporting several hundred users simultaneously.

## MARKET SIZE AND SEGMENTATION

The European microcomputer industry is not a unified market of standard products or users. Rather, it is composed of many national markets, each with different requirements, levels of sophistication, and distribution channels. As a result, it is dangerous to generalize about competitive requirements for success using the whole of Europe as a reference point.

Many industry observers believe that the evolution of the European markets will parallel the development in the American market. In the 1970's, this seemed to be the case, as European markets were dominated by American multinationals exporting products they were already selling in the United States.

The largest market in Europe is the United Kingdom, with approximately 24 percent of the $2 billion industry in 1983. As shown in Table 1, Germany is a close second, and the four largest (United Kingdom, Germany, France, and Italy) account for 76 percent of European sales. The major market segments are as follows:

*   The home user/hobbyist whose demand is oriented toward smaller micros and leisure applications. This segment was especially well developed in England by Sinclair. A strong position in this market is thought to provide a basis for creating customer loyalty that can be exploited in tradeups to larger products.

*   The educational institution that purchases microcomputers to teach computer literacy. This segment has not proven very lucrative for producers because government purchasers are price sensitive and may use their purchasing power to promote a national champion. This segment has been used as a loss leader by some manufacturers to create brand visibility and preference.

*   The scientist user who relies on a microcomputer instead of a mainframe to perform very specific operations. Scientific applications typically require powerful micros with specialized software.

*   The business user who relies on a microcomputer for word processing, data analysis or administrative tasks. As shown in Table 1, this is the largest segment in Europe, accounting for nearly two thirds of all microcomputer revenues.

## DISTRIBUTION

Microcomputers in Europe are sold through a variety of channels. Although distribution networks differ somewhat across countries, the following channels generally exist to some extent in all European nations. A summary of the distribution channels of Europe appear in Table 2.

### Direct Sales Force

For large accounts, direct sales calls are common. Companies with an existing position in a related field, such as telecommunications, large computers, or office products, are most likely to emphasize this channel. This provides the advantage of being able to sell a bundle of related products as a customized system to corporate clients. The ability to provide such systems is thought to be a crucial capability for future success in large accounts.

## Table 1. EUROPEAN NATIONAL MARKETS, 1983

|  | Revenues | Percentage of European Market |
|---|---|---|
| United Kingdom | $ 480 million | 24% |
| Germany | 460 | 23 |
| France | 360 | 18 |
| Italy | 220 | 11 |
| Scandinavia | 160 | 8 |
| Benelux countries | 140 | 7 |
| Spain/Portugal | 100 | 5 |
| Switzerland/Austria | 80 | 4 |
| Total (approximately 300,000 units) | $ 2 billion | 100 % |

**European user segments by size:**

|  | Percentage of total market | |
|---|---|---|
|  | Units | Value |
| Home | 61% | 12% |
| Business | 26 | 63 |
| Education | 7 | 3 |
| Scientific | 6 | 22 |

Source: International Data Corporation

Retail Stores

Retail computer stores are the single most important channel of distribution accounting for over one third of all sales in Europe, and as much as 45 percent in the United Kingdom.

PRODUCTION

Manufacturing microcomputers is a relatively easy task. Components and subassembles are readily available on world markets, and many producers have adopted policies of purchasing nearly all inputs externally and simply assembling the product and attaching their brand name. Even IBM, with its great potential for vertical integration, has chosen to rely on outside vendors for nearly all the components of the PC.

**Table 2  EUROPEAN DISTRIBUTION NETWORKS FOR MICROCOMPUTERS**
(priced $1000 and above)

| | Retail outlets | System houses | Total network |
|---|---|---|---|
| United Kingdom | 832 | 350 | 1182 |
| Germany | 672 | 250 | 922 |
| France | 620 | 250 | 870 |
| Italy | 580 | 100 | 680 |
| Belgium | 144 | 100 | 244 |
| Netherlands | 145 | 70 | 215 |
| Spain | 130 | 70 | 200 |

Distribution network by type of outlet
(percentages based on 1983 volumns)

| | Mass outlets | Computer stores | Office equipment stores | System houses | Direct sales |
|---|---|---|---|---|---|
| United Kingdom | 7-10% | 42-45% | 2-4% | 23-25% | 20-22% |
| Germany | 3-4 | 26-29 | 22-24 | 24-26 | 20-22 |
| France | 1 | 38-40 | 4-5 | 32-34 | 22-25 |
| Italy | ---- | 31-35 | 19-21 | 28-32 | 16-18 |
| Spain | 4-6 | 33-35 | 16-18 | 29-31 | 13-15 |
| Belgium | 3-5 | 38-40 | 8-10 | 24-28 | 21-23 |
| Netherlands | 2-4 | 33-35 | 12-14 | 18-20 | 30-32 |
| USA | 28 | 33 | 6 | 13 | 15 |

Source: Electronics Business and Electronics Intelligence.

## BASES OF COMPETITIVE ADVANTAGE

In choosing a competitive strategy in microcomputers, there are numberous bases for competitive advantage. The strategies of many competitors are derived from their strategies in related markets. Because the microcomputer is at the intersection of several technologies, firms have been attracted to the industry from many directions. This pattern of gateways is summarized in Table 3. For example, as producers of typewriters, such as Olivetti and Triumph-Adler, saw their products increasingly being replaced by word processors, they were induced into offering their own microcomputers. Similarly, as microcomputers became more powerful and better substitutes for larger computers, integrated computer companies were motivated to introduce their own products. On the technology side, the trend toward a convergence of data processing and telecommunications brought the entry of AT&T, ITT, and NEC. Similarly, consumer electronics companies (Panasonic, Sharp, Tandy), toy producers (Atari, Mattel, Coleco), and start-ups (Apple, Fortune) all entered the market with distinctive motivations, resources, and ways of doing business.

This variety of perspectives has manifested itself in different competitive postures. It is possible to strive for competitive advantage in any of the following (not necessarily mutually exclusive) ways.

---

Table 3   MICROCOMPUTER   ENTRY   GATEWAYS

---

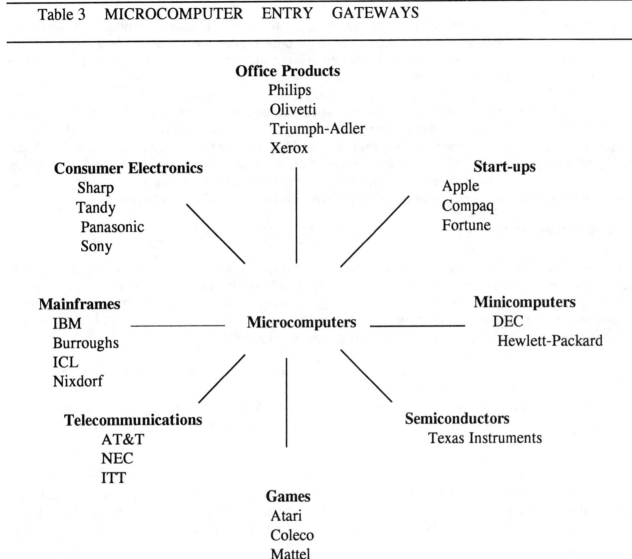

**Office Products**
Philips
Olivetti
Triumph-Adler
Xerox

**Consumer Electronics**
Sharp
Tandy
Panasonic
Sony

**Start-ups**
Apple
Compaq
Fortune

**Mainframes**
IBM
Burroughs
ICL
Nixdorf

Microcomputers

**Minicomputers**
DEC
Hewlett-Packard

**Telecommunications**
AT&T
NEC
ITT

**Semiconductors**
Texas Instruments

**Games**
Atari
Coleco
Mattel

a). Cost Leadership - In its announcements and in its actions IBM has indicated that it intends to be the low-cost producer of microcomputers. It has even deviated substantially from corporate tradition to attain this goal. For example, despite its strong existing capabilities in many aspects of microcomputer technology, IBM has declined to vertically integrate for fear of increasing costs. In the case of printers IBM selected Epson over its own printer manufacturing division because of costs. IBM's large market share allows it to receive volume purchasing discounts and scale economies in assembly and marketing. Although it has yet to occur, industry analysts look to Asia for significant future challengers to IBM's cost position.

b) Full-Line Complementarity - This approach is to view the microcomputer not as a stand-alone product but as a part of an office system. Producers who sell a full line of office products can sell their microcomputers as part of an integrated system. DEC and Xerox have been leaders in pursuing this strategy.

b) Full-Line Complementary - Another approach is to view the microcomputer not as a stand-alone product but as a part of an office system. Producers who sell a full line of office products, such as PABXs, local area networks, telex machines, terminals, large computers, and word processors, can sell their microcomputers as part of an integrated system. This overcomes the problems of incompatibility between individual products supplied by different vendors. DEC and Xerox have been leaders in pursuing this strategy.

c) Proprietary Closed System - As an alternative to conforming to industry standards in hardware and software, a microcomputer producer may elect to introduce its own unique computer architecture and operating system. Here the benefit of differentiation must be weighed against the risk of the market not accepting the new system.

d) "Me-Too"- The single most common competitive strategy in microcomputers is to offer a clone or look-alike product that emulates the industry standard (generally IBM). There are currently hundreds of companies that produce microcomputers that are physical and electronic copies of IBM's PC. Such products generally sell for discounts of 15-40 percent off the IBM price. This strategy is not limited to small firms: ITT, Siemens, Ericsson, Olivetti, and Tandy have joined ranks with the many start-up firms that offer products with little or no enhancement to the basic IBM model.

NEC'S ENTRY INTO THE EUROPEAN MICROCOMPUTER MARKET

In 1985 NEC was struggling to find a way to transfer its success in the Japanese microcomputer market to Europe. At home, NEC enjoyed a market share of over 55 percent in personal computers. In addition to systems, they offered a full line of peripherals such as printers, screens, and modems. Their position in the Japanese market was similar to the role of IBM in America and Europe. A majority of personal computer software developed in Japan was written for NEC machines.

NEC was best known in Europe for its computer peripherals. Obtaining distribution for microcomputers was extremely difficult as a result of the practice of handling only three brands in each store. For peripherals, however, distribution was far easier. Although it was widely suspected that few microcomputer companies were making a profit on their computers, NEC acknowledged that the peripherals business was very lucrative.

NEC produced all of its microcomputers in Japan. The freight to Europe was approximately 10 percent of the product's cost, and an additional 5.4 percent duty was paid on entry. NEC stated that it would continue to produce exclusively in Japan as long as delivered costs were minimized. If volume in Europe became sufficient, or EEC policy dictated import penalties, NEC would consider local production.

As NEC contemplated its strategy for the European markets in early 1985, events gave cause for concern. Persistent rumors of an imminent shake-out made NEC executives wonder if the time for a major commitment to this market had already passed. However, their management felt that its outstanding technological skills in computers and related markets and its competitive cost structure should provide the basis for success. Making the concept of C&C a reality was proving for more elusive than NEC had anticipated.

# CASE NO. 4          CRISIS IN GENEVA*

BACKGROUND

At 9:00 A.M. Mr. Lansing, Vice-President Europe, is busy already in his Geneva, Switzerland, office, with a sweeping view of the lake and distant mountains. This is the European central office for the Allen Corporation of Chicago, a major producer of over the counter (OTC) pharmaceutical and nutritional products. He is preparing himself to call the Chicago headquarters at 4:00 P.M., which is the start of the business day in the Midwest.

Last week he had received an urgent call from Mr. Davidson, President and CEO of the Allen Corporation, who was concerned about the under-plan performance of his European operations for the first quarter. The profit shortfall for this period is estimated to reach $65,000 because of slower than expected sales, operating expenses that were higher than had been planned, and a constantly rising exchange rate for the dollar. The president seemed well briefed about business details. The rather one-sided conversation emphasized his deep concern for the present situation and its likely impact on the rest of the year. He accused Mr. Lansing of not having a viable business plan to effectively reverse the under-plan performance of his major affiliates in local currency. This would help to minimize the exchange rate problem, which was otherwise accepted as being outside the sphere of influence of both executives.

Mr. Davidson had demanded a return call first thing this morning and specific answers the following questions:

1. What accounted for the soft sales in almost all of the major affiliate markets, and why were sales 5%-9% under local budgets for France, the U.K., and Germany, which together accounted for 72% of all European sales?

2. What is being done to reduce the operating expenses, which were both in excess of local budgets and, because of the low sales, far above approved company guidelines? Mr. Davidson had sarcastically accused Lansing of not being in control of his business at this point.

3. What were the new sales and profits forecasts for the next quarter and the rest of the year, following the first quarter disaster? Could new product introductions, marketing strategies, or customer groups be expected to compensate for the loss of the first three months? If not, where was he proposing to cut expenses without further hurting business development?

Mr. Lansing had prepared himself for the afternoon's teleconference with headquarters. In addition to Mr. Davidson, the corporate Vice-President of Finance, the Treasurer, and the Vice-President of Marketing would most likely attend the meeting and have a whole array of uncomfortable questions.

------------------

*This case was prepared by Professor Rolf Hackmann of Western Illinois University, published with permission.

During the past week Mr Lansing had called in the national managers, with their finance directors and marketing managers, for a business and budget review. After thorough discussions of all related aspects he was confident that he could address the issues in a very constructive manner.

The first two questions could be handled in a very straightforward and factual way that would help defuse the potentially explosive atmosphere. It was the last one that had caused him quite some difficulty, not so much because he and his associates had suffered from a lack of ideas about the revival of the business, but because certain aspects of their implementation were delicate.

He hoped that against the background of his dismal profit record -- his first actually since he had been appointed to his present position -- his proposal would be accepted even though it was rather innovative by the standards of his fundamentally conservative company. Actually, it presented the only workable solution to his present predicament as he saw it.

His response to the first question could be that it had been the consensus in hindsight of his European colleagues that the sales budget had been overly optimistic for the first quarter. Everyone from public health authorities to industry sources and retailers had anticipated a recurrence of the strong flu of three years ago. So far it had not materialized and it was unlikely to occur this spring.

Allen's European sales thus were affected by the heavy stocking of cough and cold products with wholesalers and retailers at the end of last year, in anticipation of a strong first-quarter demand. This had helped to produce a record profit performance for the prior year but was now haunting the next budget period.

Another factor depressing to Lansing was the recent increase in interest rates across Europe, which led to tighter inventory policies by the trade. This tightening of inventories could actually provoke product returns, as the channels were grasping for any chance to improve their working capital situation. According to the affiliate managers, the likelihood of actual and sizable returns looked remote despite the company's liberal returns policy. However, they all agreed that the high trade inventories could not be worked off until the middle of the second quarter and so would lead to another poor sales picture for the next three months. After June, sales were expected to return to normal and meet the plan for the rest of the year. The second quarter was expected to produce another profit shortfall which, under the best of circumstances, could be as low as $40,000 and, in the worst-case scenario, might go as high as $54,000.

Expenses in excess of the first-quarter's plan could be defended with effects of the high sales expectations for that period. The overperformance was mainly due to heavy advertising and forty-five percent of the promotion budget had been concentrated in the first three months, to give maximum push to all OTC (non-perscription) health products. The contracting policies of Europe's state-owned T.V. and radio stations required advertisers to prepay air time and did not grant them the right to quick cancellation as was done in the U.S. These funds thus had been committed and were spent. The remaining advertising/ promotion budgets offered very little room for significant expense cuts. An area that would allow immediate and substantial corrective action, through, was selling expenses.

The U.K. had hired five new reps plus one district manager on the first of January at a total annual budgeted expense of $193,000 (U.S.), including salary, training, and operating expenses. France had added seven salespeople at the cost of $241,630 (U.S.) and Germany had expanded its sales force by five reps and one district manager at a total of $242,900 (U.S.). All dollar figures calculated at the budgeted exchange rates for each currency. The other European affiliates had also increased their sales forces with a combined expense of only $150,000 for the full year. All positions had been approved in the budget.

In accordance with local labor laws, any or all of the new salespeople in the three big countries could be terminated without cause during a 90-day probation period. Sizable amounts of profit could be produced immediately by slashing salesforce budgets if headquarters really pressed for economy now. Compensating for the projected profit loss of the first half would require the termination of five or six salespeople. This would be only a minor cosmetic surgery if the firings were distributed among the three markets, but Mr. Lansing disliked the idea of even such a small setback for his organizational development plans.

After four weeks of training and a six-month break-in period these people would finally become productive and within two years should contribute average sales of $280,000 per year and a total of roughly $42,000 in operating profit. Cutting manpower now, after only three months, would not only waste all the money invested so far, but would also make it difficult to reverse the consequences of such a decision if business improved later in the year. Most firms are on annual bonus plans that make salespeople reluctant to change jobs before year-end and forfeit the accured bonus. One way to overcome this obstacle would be to offer reimbursement of the lost bonus to potential recruits but under present business conditions this did not seem very practical.

DEVELOPING A NEW BUSINESS PLAN

During the discussions with his managers, a line of action had surfaced that would allow Mr. Lansing to retain the sales force expansion and still meet his profit goals for the year, should Mr. Davidson immediately approve the plan that he intended to submit this afternoon.

Over the last couple of years Allen Corporation had successfully introduced a diet product under the trade name Figurella ™ in most European markets except France. The French introduction was subject to government approval, a lengthy process required for all drugs and dietary products. Approval was not expected to come before the end of the year. This arrival would be far too late for the all-important summer demand peak for this highly seasonal product, and thus it had not been included in the French budget for the year.

It was Mr. Dedieu, the French manager of Laboratoires Berliot (the Allen subsidiary in Paris), who had come up with a novel and timely solution to the profit problem. He suggested that they proceed with the marketing of Figurella even before the summer. In support of his proposal, he had pointed out that sales of the product as a simple food supplement or a quick meal would not require formal government registration procedures.

Although this was a welcome suggestion, he admitted that a problem could arise with trying to position the product in the dietary market without a clear-cut promotional message for weight control. That vital message would, under this plan, not be approved by the authorities. But, according to Mr. Dedieu, this was a minor problem in view of the proposal's advantages, and could be overcome if the product were sold only through pharmacies. Market research had shown that in France, like in other markets of Europe, pharmacists played a significant role in counseling people concerned about their weight but overwhelmed by the multitude of products in the market.

This was also the reason why pharmacies accounted for two thirds of the sales of all diet products in France. Heavily promoting the weight-control aspects of Figurella to French pharmacists would help in overcoming or at least minimizing the lack of the diet theme in advertising and promotion. Marketing the product this way would also allow maintenance of better margins and higher retail prices than would result from mass-marketing outlets. These outlets were notoriously unsuited for direct and personal customer counseling. Besides, they tried to attract business strictly on a price basis.

Excluding other channels from the marketing strategy would be unique in this very competitive market, but it would appeal very strongly to the ultraconservative pharmacists who were always jealously protective of their professional status and business interests. Obtaining their full support in the early phases of the marketing program made good business sense by also being consistent with Allen's overall business strategy. Over the years, Laboratoires Berliot had established very close ties with the French pharmacies because of its health-related product lines, and this new product could certainly help to deepen the friendly relations.

Withdrawal of the application for product approval now before the French authorities would thus clear the way for immediate product introduction.

The plan delighted Mr. Lansing because it not only offered a seemingly perfect solution to his present profit crunch, but also presented a legitimate defense of his salesforce expansion in France. Monsieur Dedieu had come prepared with a complete marketing plan for Figurella. Proposing a May 15 introduction date, which would be right in time for the summer season, he was confident that he could sell 125,000 cans of 500 grams each for the season, at a wholesale unit price of FF 44.70 ($5.87) excluding VAT (Value Added Tax). This volume would generate sales of FF 5,587,500. Germany as well as the U.K. would be potential supply sources since both countries manufactured the product. Assuming that production costs would be lower in the U.K. than in Germany, he had indicated a preference for English supplies. He had further assumed transportation charges, based on truck delivery, London-Paris or Frankfurt-Paris, to be about the same. As members of the European Community, both countries were exempt from French import tariff levies.

PRODUCT INFORMATION

Figurella is basically a variation of a nutritional supplement developed by Allen Corporation for use by persons debilitated by inadequate food intake because of disease or other medical reasons. The original product is sold under a different trademark and provides accurately measured supplementation of daily nutritional requirements. It is supplied in 500-gram cans and three different flavors--chocolate, vanilla, and strawberry--to prevent product fatigue in users. Basically the product is milkpowder formulated with added carbohydrates for taste improvement and nutritional balance. One of the three variants presently on the market in the U.K. and Germany, the strawberry formula cannot be sold in France because the coloring agent FDC Red #2 has been banned for some time in the EC (European Community) because of its potentially mutagenic properties.

MANUFACTURING COST INFORMATION

According to data from the finance department, production costs for the chocolate and vanilla product in the U.K. amount to $1.48 per can for the chocolate and $1.34 for the vanilla flavor. Production costs are 2.5% higher in Germany than in the U.K. for both flavors.

Based on this information and a 50/50 sales split (based on number of cans) between the two flavors, the average cost per finished and French-labeled can is $1.41 from the U.K. and $1.445 from Germany. If there is an average net wholesale price of $5.87 per can in France, the gross margin amounts to $4.46 per can for the U.K. and $4.43 per can for German-produced material, before allocation of freight, handling and storage charges. All three countries are EC members and therefore, no import duties apply.

TRANSPORTATION CHARGES

Transportation expenses for U.K. and German-produced materials vary only slightly. Based on a standard shipment of 20,000 cans--3333 cartons of six cans each--and a total estimated shipping weight of 15,000 kilograms, these are the estimated total handling and freight charges supplied by freight forwarders, for carriage to Paris.

| | |
|---|---|
| Inland freight (truck) from Frankfurt | $1,199 |
| Barge and inland freight (truck) from London | $1,593 |

The charges translate to $.06 per can for German supplies and $.08 per can for U.K. Figurella materials.

PROFITABILITY PROJECTIONS

The sales forecast of 125,000 cans for France looks realistic and fully in line with introductory sales volumes generated in other markets.

Checking with pharmacists in major population centers indicated a high level of enthusiasm for the new product because of its exclusive sale through pharmacies and the very good profit margin for this type of product. No big difficulties were anticipated for promotion of an official food supplement as a weight-control product.

The consolidated profit picture looks very good and would allow Mr. Lansing to more than compensate for the expected shortfall in the first half. If U.K. supplies were used, unadjusted gross profits of $557,500 would be generated from the sale of 125,000 cans of Figurella, while German supplies would contribute the slightly lower amount of $553,125.

TAX CONSIDERATIONS

With an effective rate of 50% on reported profits, corporate taxes are practically identical for all three nations. (Germany's rate may go up to 56% but that would apply to undistributed profits only and would not apply in this case.) Shifting profits among the three countries, therefore, through intracorporate pricing manipulations would ordinarily only have neutral effects on the overall corporate-tax liability. But Allen Corporation has honed its tax management skills during many years of transfer pricing, involving Swiss corporate intermediaries.

To minimize the impact that high taxes within some countries would have on consolidated corporate profits, the Allen Corporation has set up three trading companies in Switzerland. Each of them is run under a different name, that is not readily identified with its owner, and is located in a different city with a different tax structure. The companies are practically one-man organizations (small offices, a manager and a few secretaries, telephones, Telex equipment) and serve the sole purpose of shifting profits among Allen Corporation and its subsidiaries. Some third-party business is occasionally added for window-dressing.

For the purpose of selling Figurella to France, Mr. Lansing has selected Flueli GmbH. in Zug to act as the pro-forma purchaser of the British product. After consulting with his financial director, Mr. Lombardi, he will propose to headquarters that the U.K. subsidiary sell a finished can of Figurella at $1.54 to Flueli and Flueli in turn sell the can for $5.28 to the French subsidiary, with a profit of $3.74 per can going into the Swiss account. Transportation and related charges do not affect this part of the transaction. The French gross profit of $.51 per can (adjusted for transportation charges) will have to cover product introduction and marketing expenses but is not expected to produce a profit for the French operation.

This tax maneuver is going to net $126,412 in extra profit, because the maximum corporate tax rate in Zug is only 22.96%. That portion of the consolidated profits alone more than offsets the profit underperformance forecasted for the first half of the year for all European operations.

Mr. Lansing expects to get quick approval from headquarters for this part of his plan, partly because it promises a substantial and quick recovery of the profit picture, and partly because the payoff depends entirely on the introduction of the product by mid-May, which is only two months away. It presents no unusual business risks and there was unanimous support for it by his European associates.

Sourcing and transfer-pricing decisions invariably lead to resistance by his country's managers who are always quick in suspecting that they are getting an unfair deal. He thus is hearing complaints from the managers in U.K. and Germany, as well as France. Their bonus plan rests on profit performance and any over-plan operating results yield very substantial pay-offs over the above base salary.

The German manager resents not having been chosen at least as a partial supplier. His contention is that the minimal production-cost advantage of the British material is more than offset by the stability of German labor relations--the U.K. plant has been the target of wildcat strikes in the past--plus the lower transportation charges.

The English manager wants to have an "arm's length" price, equal to his average local net wholesale price of $4.71. Under the proposed pricing, he stands to lose a local profit of $3.30 per can and claims that the arbitrarily low export price will lead to inquiries by the tax authorities who are always suspecting tax evasion maneuvers by the multinationals.

The French manager, finally, argues that his purchase price is too high to make the product profitable locally, because of the high launching expenses required for salesforce training, distribution, selling, and promotion. He points to the corporate profit guidelines whereby no new product should be introduced with pretax profit margins of less than 25%, which in this case is not going to be realized initially or eventually, because of the high landed (delivered) cost in France.

Mr. Lansing will have to address the issue at some time in the near future because management unrest about bonus prospects can be disruptive. But he does not intend to raise the subject with Chicago today unless specifically asked. If asked, he is prepared to propose allocation of profits on a management basis by splitting the Swiss profits equally between France and the U.K.

While the Figurella plans for France were being discussed, an interesting and tempting piece of information came up. According to Mr. Dedieu, exports of agricultural surplus products from the European Community (EC) are subsidized by Brussels (the EC headquarters). In the Figurella case, both the milk powder and the sucrose are eligible for export-support payments based on a rate of ECU 85.86 per 100 kilograms of spray-dried milk power and ECU 37.78 per 100 kilograms of sugar. (ECU stands for European Currency Unit, which is comprised of a currency basket of the 10-member currencies.)

The sale of 125,000 cans could thus result in subsidies amounting to:

```
    35.94 tons of milk power  =  ECU 30,858
      26.56 tons of sugar     =  ECU 10,034
   Total subsidy payment       =  ECU 40,892
```

Converted at the green (agricultural) rate this is equivalent to $38,348. This would be a tidy extra profit that promises to expand with growing sales of Figurella but there are some caveats. In order for the sale to Flueli GmbH., to qualify Allen Ltd. for payment of the EC subsidy, the merchandise itself should become a bona fide EC export. But in order to save transportation and handling charges, plus time, Allen Ltd. sells the merchandise to Flueli GmbH. and in a simultaneous transaction Flueli sells the same shipment to Laboratoires Berliot. With two sets of the necessary shipping and insurance documents, commercial invoices, and certificates of origin prepared in the U.K., the shipment does not need to be detoured to Switzerland but goes straight from London to Paris.

From many similar transactions between Allen Ltd. and Flueli GmbH. in the past, a very efficient order-handling procedure has been developed. This allows the use of Flueli GmbH. letterhead stationery and invoice forms by Allen Ltd. order-processing personnel in the London offices. Thus unnecessary mailing delays and transportation expenses are avoided. The blank forms have already been signed before by an authorized Flueli GmbH. official and copies of the whole process are sent to Zug for filing. Without violating any customs procedures, the documents will be processed and stamped at the respective border-crossings and thus ligitimate the merchandise so the merchandise has both proof of export from the U.K. to Switzerland--which makes it eligible for the subsidies--and entry as Swiss-owned but EC-produced merchandise into France--which eliminates any import levies.

These "triangle" business transactions are known to be widely practiced as the rewards are so tempting, but they obviously violate ethical and legal norms and are thus subject to the EC penal code. Nonetheless, Mr. Lansing intends to ask for headquarter's authorization for this particular aspect of the plan this afternoon, and he will plead that the chances for embarrassment are practically nil.

PROFIT CONSOLIDATION

For the afternoon's discussion Mr. Lansing has prepared the following profit and loss consolidation (Exhibit 1) which summarizes the effect of the various transactions he will propose. The data look extremely favorable and should present a pleasant surprise even to Mr. Davidson. They are, above all, very realistic, and Mr. Lansing is confident that approval from Chicago will be forthcoming during his afternoon's business review. After all, the realization of these figures rests entirely on top management's authorization today, as time for the implementation of the whole plan is already running very short.

## EXHIBIT 1 Figurella P&L Consolidation (based on U.K. production)
[in U.S. Dollars]

| | | AMOUNT |
|---|---|---|
| Sales | | $733,750 |
| Cost of Goods Sold (COG) | | 186,250 |
| Gross Margin | | 547,500 |
| Total operating expenses | | 63,750 |
| Corporate taxes: | | |
| U.K. (50%) | 8125 | |
| France (50%) | 0 | |
| Switzerland (22.96%) | 107,338 | |
| Total tax liability | | 115,463 |
| Other income: | | |
| EC export refund | | 38,348 |
| Net profit adjusted | | $406,635 |

To be ready for any question that might come up during his presentation, Mr. Lansing has also prepared local P&L data for each country in support of the consolidated P&L figures. These are presented in Exhibit 2 below. A copy of all financial data has been Telexed to Chicago to be in the hands of all participants for this purpose.

The French operating expenses were deliberately set at a level equal to the local gross margin of the product. This neutralizes tax aspects and simplifies the calculation, though it does not account for realistic levels of introductory expenses. Mr. Davidson would probably not be overly interested in precise data on this point as the total package assures him of an extremely positive consolidated profit recovery for Europe. This success will hold true even if he should not approve all parts of the plan as presented.

## EXHIBIT 2. LOCAL P&L DATA FOR FIGURELLA
[In U.S. Dollars]

| | UNITED KINGDOM | SWITZERLAND | FRANCE |
|---|---|---|---|
| Price per can | $ 1.54 | $ 5.28 | $ 5.87 |
| Cost of Good per can | 1.41 | 1.54 | 5.36 |
| Gross Margin per can | .13 | 3.74 | .51 |
| Gross Margin per dollars | 16,250 | 467,500 | 63,750 |
| Operating Expenses | 0 | 0 | 63,750 |
| Direct Operating Profits | 16,250 | 467,500 | 0 |
| Taxes | 8,125 | 107,338 | 0 |
| Other Income | 38,348 | 0 | 0 |
| Net Profit | 46,473 | 360,162 | 0 |

# CASE NO .5     CAMBRIDGE PRODUCTS, LTD. (A)*

Seated in his Waterloo, Ontario, office one morning in June 1982, Bill Spencer picked up one of his recently printed business cards. On one side, above his name, address, title (Vice President, Corporate Relations) and the "Cambridge Products, Ltd." logo, a bright red Canadian Maple leaf stood out prominently against a silver background; on the other side the same information was printed in Japanese were just the latest (and relatively minor) expense item in CPL's bid to export its conventional top of the range cookware products to Japan.

A week earlier, in Tokyo, Spencer had met with Jiro Hattori, president of the Kuwahara Co., one of the largest manufacturers of cookware in Japan. Hattori had proposed that Kuwahara would distribute 1,500 sets of CPL cookware a month in the Japanese market starting in October, if CPL could produce an exclusive cookware product, with whistling knobs and specially designed handles. In a few hours' time, Bill would be meeting with Jack Nolin, executive vice president, to discuss whether CPL should begin a crash development program to modify CPL's existing product at an anticipated cost of over $140,000, and place orders for steel and other raw materials worth over $100,000 by the end of the week, to prepare for the expected October delivery. For CPL, with 1981 sales of $6.3 million and net profits of $500,000, this represented a substantial investment.

As he gazed at the Japanese print on his business card, Bill Spencer wondered what he should recommend to Jack Nolin. Should CPL be better off concentrating on familiar markets in which it was already quite successful, rather than attempting to penetrate that notoriously difficult market in a far corner of the world?

## THE COMPANY

CPL's origins can be traced back to 1944, when Brian Wilson, a young entrepreneur, started up a small metal finishing plant that polished "anything in metal." Sales in that first year were $4,000. The company specialized in custom metal-working jobs that included polishing of cookware for other manufacturers. In 1952 Wear Ever, one of CPL's U.S. customers, went bankrupt and left CPL holding a substantial quantity of cookware; CPL inadvertently entered the cookware business.

Initially, CPL marketed aluminum cookware manufactured for the company by others. By the early 1960s, the company brought in new equipment and began to manufacture its own cookware products. Cookware sales in the early 1960s reached $1 million. CPL, which until then sold only aluminum cookware, began to experiment with stainless steel, and by 1963, introduced stainless steel cookware in the market. It soon discovered that stainless steel cookware was a market whose time had come.

By 1967 CPL had acquired major department store accounts and sales had risen to $200,000 a month. Throughout this period the company maintained its original industrial sales business, which provided a fall-back position when problems arose in the cookware industry. In the 1970s, the Canadian market for cookware began to mature, and over the decade, the number of distributors declined. Competition was strong and included Canadian companies such as Supreme Aluminum Ltd., Soren, Paderno and foreign competitors such as Regal, Culinaire, Westbend, Ekco, and Lagostina.

Yet CPL performed well in this market, managing to capture a market share of approximately 50 percent in the segments in which it competed. It had manageed to accomplish this by constant product innovation and efficient, low-cost production. In fact, CPL had, at one time or another, supplied parts directly to its competitors at prices lower than the competitors could produce for themselves, while still making a profit. In 1981 CPL operated an 80,000 square-foot manufacturing facility in Waterloo, Ontario (where it also conducted its R & D activities) and a sales office in Newark, New Jersey.

---

* This case was prepared by Ken Coelho under the direction of Donald Lecraw, Univ.of Western Ontario, published with permission.

## PRODUCT DEVELOPMENT

In the late 1960s, CPL was the first developer (at a cost of $1 million) in five-ply cookware, which is marketed under the brand name Ultraware. Five-ply construction bonded a three-layered aluminum's core between two layers of stainless steel. Because of aluminum's exceptionally good capacity to store and conduct heat, the multilayered construction resulted in quick and even heat distribution across the bottom and sides of the utensil, reducing cooking time and saving energy. CPL also experimented and designed specially weighted covers, knobs, and handles--innovations that paid off well in sales.

In the 1980s CPL began experimenting with seven-ply cookware and magnetic steel which, in the future, could be used with magnetic stoves then being developed in Japan. The use of magnetic stoves and utensils would result in energy savings of up to 30 percent, which was of far greater significance in energy-poor Japan than in North America. (Three-ply cookware sold better in Canada and the United States than the five-ply variety, which, although more expensive, was more efficient.)

## EXPORTS

When CPL first started in the cookware business in the early 1950s, it realized (as had other cookware manufacturers who had set up plants for the British Common-wealth preference rather than just the Canadian market) that the Canadian market was not large enough to support an efficient scale operation. CPL found it convenient to do business through Wear Ever distributors in the United States, and to promote its products through trade shows. CPL's industrial sales division also sold its products in the United States. (The industrial sales product list included fire extinguisher shells, nonpressure brake housings, heat lamp reflectors, lamp bases, barbecue bowls, ashtrays, hospital equipment, kettle bodies, motor housings, meat hooks, venturi collars, animal feeding and stainless steel dishes. The company had, at one time, even supplied missile launching shell casings to the U.S. government.)

By 1979 exports constituted $2 million of $4.8 million in total sales, U.S. exports made up 40-49 percent of total exports. The other countries to which CPL exported included Italy, Australia, and South Africa. Exports to EEC countries were especially difficult, since EEC had imposed tariffs of up to 22.5 percent on cookware. In the 1980s CPL put sales to the United States on the back burner, while it concentrated on markets in Japan, Australia, and Europe.

In 1981 CPL exports were $3.5 million of total company sales of $6.3 million (Exhibit 1). Of total exports, $1 million were to the United States, $800,000 to Australia, and the remainder ($1.7 Million) to Europe, Hong Kong, Singapore, and Japan. Sales to Japan, however, were very small and sporadic. Every once in a while CPL received an order, but there was little on-going business.

## ENTRY INTO THE JAPANESE MARKET

CPL's entry into the Japanese market was almost accidental. An earlier routine introductory letter to the Canadian embassy in Japan had elicited the reply that the Japanese market was too difficult for CPL to successfully penetrate--they should not even try, the Canadian embassy advised. CPL did have one customer in Japan Prior to 1981, who had seen CPL cookware at a trade show and ordered about 100 sets (worth approximately $20,000) sporadically every two or three months.

In early 1981, David Taylor, Vice President of CPL's U.S. subsidiary, showed samples of CPL cookware to an acquaintance, Izu Tsukamoto. Tsukamoto, born of Japanese parents in China, had moved to Japan with his parents as a child. Shortly after World War II, the Tsukamoto's migrated to the United States. Izu Tsukamoto spoke Japanese, and was familiar with Japanese customs. In 1981 Izu Tsukamoto worked as a California-based distributor of cookware (for Ecko and others) on a 5 percent commission basis. Tsukamoto felt that CPL's product would sell well in Japan, and sent samples by Federal Express to distributors in Japan.

## EXHIBIT 1 CAMBRIDGE PRODUCTS, LTD. (A), 1982 FINANCIAL SUMMARY

**Income data**

| | |
|---|---|
| Total sales | $6,300,000 |
| Total exports | $3,500,000 |
| Profit before taxes | $ 800,000 |
| Net profit | $ 500,000 |

| Financial data* | Net book value | Realizable value |
|---|---|---|
| Inventory | $3,000,000 | $3,000,000 |
| Building | 500,000 | 2,000,000 |
| Machinery & equip (10% straight line) | 800,000 | 2,500,000 |
| Dies, tools | 0 | 500,000 |
| Retained earnings | $1,400,000 | |

\* As of September 1982

Tsukamoto's first contact was Jiro Hattori, president of Kuwahara Company, a Japanese import-export firm specializing in cookware and related items such as china and cutlery. Kuwahara was 50 percent owned by Hattori, and 50 percent by Ohto Overseas Corp., one of the largest pen manufacturers in the world, with assets of over 2 billion yen ($100 million U.S.). Kuwahara in 1981 distributed approximately 100,000 sets of Regal and Westbend cookware imported from the United States and one product line of Japanese make, to six or seven direct sales organizations.

CPL's five-ply cookware, relatively new to Japan, was so well received by Jiro Hattori, that Tsukamoto decided to travel personally to Japan. Thus began a series of trips to Japan by Tsukamoto, Taylor, Nolin, and Spencer which culminated in Jiro Hattori's proposal to CPL in June 1981.

Hattori's Proposal

Jiro Hattori expressed an interest in distributing 3 of CPL's 20 styles of cookware. However, he wanted exclusive products and two major modifications--a whistling knob and specially designed wraparound flameguards. These flameguards around the handles were desirable, said Hattori, because most Japanese consumers used liquid propane gas (LPG) for cooking ( even though the existing cookware did have heat resistant handles). If CPL could have satisfactory samples of the redesigned cookware ready by the end of August, Hattori would accept deliveries of 1,500 sets a month for four months and more thereafter. The exact price would be negotiated later, but Hattori and Spencer tentatively agreed on a price of (U.S.) $125 a set.

Bill Spencer gathered all the notes on the Japanese market that he had made during his trips--the useful information provided by the Ontario government trade office in Japan (the Canadian government office in Japan, in contrast was useless, Bill felt), and his analysis of the development costs. There were several factors he would have to consider before making his recommendations to Jack Nolin.

The Market

The Japanese consumed more cookware per capita than any other country in the world. The market for cookware in Japan was estimated to be about $100 million. It was (as the market for more consumer goods in Japan appeared to be) very competitive. The high end in which CPL would be competing was approximately $60 million and was dominated by imports (97 percent).

Regal, which had just introduced five-ply cookware, had developed a whistle knob (which was probably the reason for Hattori's haste). Westbend, and Ekco, which produced bonded bottom cookware, were already well entrenced in the market. Two local Japanese manufacturers served the low end of the market.

The Japanese Consumer

The cliches about a Japanese consumer--"very knowledgeable, extremely quality conscious, and willing to pay high prices for exclusive, prestegious products," appeared to be quite true, Bill Spencer reflected. He recalled conversations with other executives doing business in Japan:

*"The Japanese market is the toughest in the world. I would prefer to deal in Taiwan or South Korea."*

*" The Japanese customer is very knowledgeable, very demanding, and the market is extremely competitive. Understanding Japanese customs and preferences is a necessary prerequisite for doing business in Japan."*

*" The Japanese are very thrifty--as individuals they are among the highest savers in the world. They are willing to spend money only on high-quality goods. In Canada there are three criteria by which consumers select cookware: (1) Price, (2) Quality, (3) Appearance. In Japan it is (1) Quality, (2) Quality, (3) Quality! They are so quality conscious, it is almost revolting; there are customers who check cookware handles using a screwdriver! It is not unusual to see a car buyer underneath a car in a showroom, checking it out."*

*"Japanese consumers are very knowledgeable. They read every word in a brochure (you must have literature in Japanese) and ask pointed questions. The distributors are also extremely knowledgeable--the typical distributor knows as much about a product's characteristics as a manufacturer in North America."*

*" The Japanese are also very fond of exclusivity--and designer names--this appears to be the only exception to the quality rule. We know this from experience. A line of cheap yellow-colored pans sold a million sets in an extremely short time--because they bore the designers name--Pierre Cardin!"*

*"It is important to understand Japanese customs--because the islands are so crowded and houses are so small (it is common for a family of four to occupy a one-bedroom apartment), cookware is hung on the wall--it is therefore important for the cookware to look good (and to be exclusive)."*

*"Understanding Japanese customs is also important when negotiating--they use a lot of euphemisms--if they say they will 'think about it' more than three times, most likely they are politely saying 'no'. If they do say 'no' directly--you had better leave quickly."*

*"They can take very long to make decisions. When negotiating with a team it is difficult to identify the decision maker--his is usually silent. The person you do most of your talking to is not usually the decision maker. When negotiating with the Japanese, you have to be very well prepared--know precisely what your costs are, and what potential modifications will cost you."*

Method of Entry

Given the potential in the Japanese market, there were other possible means of entry besides sales through the Kuwahara Company. CPL had ruled out a wholly owned subsidiary or a joint venture in Japan, since CPL did not have the necessary resources. Even a sales office would be too expensive to maintain, for a company with sales of $6 million, and net profits of $500,000. Bill estimated that it would cost (U.S.) $50,000 in salary and $150,000 in expenses for a one-person operation. Licensing was a poor option--patents were, for all practical purposes, ineffective in protecting cookware design; and in addition, the prestige associated with imported goods was an important buying criterion for the Japanese consumer.

The choice of the appropriate distribution system in Japan often posed a serious problem to many companies trying to penetrate the Japanese market. There were three broad patterns of distribution for consumer goods (Exhibit 2). Distribution varied depending on the type of product. (Distinction is made between the three routes for illustrative purposes only; in actual fact, the distribution routes could be very complex.)

1. **The Open Distribution Route**, used for distributing merchandise over extremely broad areas and involving many intermediate distributors, such as primary and secondary wholesalers. Manufacturers who sold products through this route, usually entrusted ensuing sales to the wholesaler, not knowing clearly where or how their merchandise would be sold from then on, and having little direct contact with the secondary wholesalers or retailers. This form of distribution was adopted primarily for basic essential products with a wide demand, such as fresh and processed foods.

2. **The Restricted Distribution Route** in which distribution was restricted to certain licensed retail stores, with the products going through specialized distribution channels. This form of distribution was common for specialty items such as pharmaceuticals and cosmetics.

3. **The Direct Distribution Route** involved direct transactions between the producer and retailer, or the producer and consumers via door-to-door salespersons. The Kuwahara Company employed a form of this method of direct sales, which was common for imported products in the cookware category, where the originality and specific features of the foreign merchandise had to be directly conveyed to consumers;

---

**EXHIBIT 2 DISTRIBUTION ROUTES FOR CONSUMER GOODS IN JAPAN**

**Open distribution route**

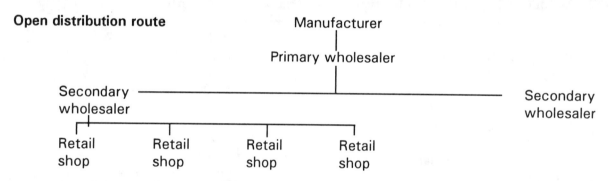

**Restricted distribution route**

**Direct distribution route**

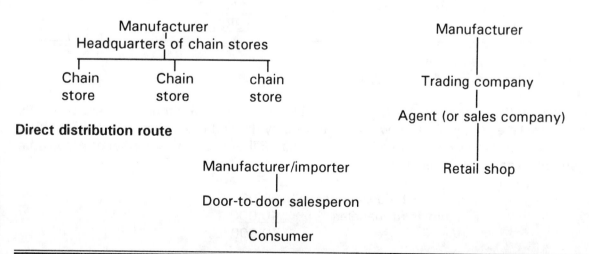

---

While in Japan, the CPL executives had contacted several distributors besides Kuwahara--Basic Japan, Silverware, Noah, Zeny, Prima, Magry Systems, Royal Cookware, and Sunware. These were operations similar to the Kuwahara Co., which was one of the largest and most established (distributing 8,000 cookware sets a month, besides other kitchenware products).

The direct sales organizations that Kuwahara had connections with comprised several hundred door-to-door salespersons, who underwent a six-to-eight week training program organized by Kuwahara. Each sales organization serviced a certain region, such as Osaka. The selling techniques emphasized getting in the door--once that was accomplished, there was usually an 80 percent chance of getting a sale. Part of the selling job included lessons on how to use the cookware. Some distributors had even set up test kitchens to teach women how to cook, and to display cookware. This tactic proved very effective. It was estimated that approximately 80 percent of Japanese women learned to cook outside their homes. The average salesperson sold two to three cookware sets a week, in addition to related items such as china and cutlery.

Pricing

The tentative price that CPL and Hattori agreed on ($125 U.S.) would enable CPL to earn a margin of 15 percent, which was normal for a volume of 1,500 to 2,000 sets a month. CPL would charge up to 35 percent more for smaller volumes. Izu Tsukamoto would earn a 5 percent commission and David Taylor would get 5 percent after Tsukamoto's commission. The cookware would be subjected to a 20 percent tariff, and Kuwahara would usually sell at a 30 percent markup over landed costs. The door-to-door saleperson would sell at a 75 percent markup over the Kuwahara price. Payment would be made by letters of credit. Table 1 illustrates the margins involved.

### Table 1  PROJECTED COSTS AND MARGINS ON THE JAPANESE DEAL

| | |
|---|---|
| CPL cost | $100.00 |
| CPL price (from factory) | 115.00 |
| Freight and insurance | 15.00 |
| | 130.00 |
| | |
| Tsukamoto's commission | 5.75 |
| Taylor's commission | 5.45 |
| CPL's price to Kuwahara (cost, ins., freight) | 141.20 |
| Tariffs | 28.24 |
| Kuwahara's landed costs | 169.44 |
| Kuwahara's price to sales organization | 220.27 |
| Price to final consumer | $385.50 |

Development Costs

The modifications that Jiro Hattori requested would, under normal circumstances, take CPL about five months to develop; but Hattori wanted samples by the end of August, and that left CPL only 10 weeks in which to redesign the handles and knobs. Bill Spencer was confident it could be done. The costs involved would be as follows:

| | |
|---|---|
| Whistle knob development | $100,000 |
| Two molds for handles | 40,000 |
| | $140,000 |

128

In addition, at $5,000 per trip to Japan for travel and the traditional Japanese after-hours business entertainment, CPL had already spent $25,000 on exploring the market; and travel costs could be expected to total at least $50,000 more if the decision to begin product development was made.

## Capacity

1981 and 1982 were boom years for the cookware industry. Manufacturers in the industry were usually affected by downturns in the economy with a six-month lag, being cushioned by retailer's preplanned orders. CPL was working at full normal capacity, which involved 10-hour shifts, four days a week, producing approximately 3,125 sets a month. The machines could be worked up to 18 hours a day (one 8-hour shift five days a week, and one 10-hour shift four days a week) or the work week could be extended to accommodate extra sales to Japan if necessary, but such a pace could not be maintained in the long run (over a year) without adversely affecting machine maintenance. Also, CPL's planned four-year $2 million machine upgrading program might have to be speeded up, should capacity utilization be increased.

CPL currently employed approximately 60 production workers, and an increase in capacity utilization would necessitate hiring about 30 to 40 new employees. To begin deliveries in October, CPL would have to begin hiring and training workers by July. In addition, because of the long lead times involved, steel and other raw materials worth over $100,000 would have to be ordered by the end of the week. By the end of August, orders for a further $200,000 in steel (which constituted 50 percent of the direct cost of sales) would have to be placed, for a total investment of $300,000 in raw materials, $140,000 in product development and $75,000 in travel costs, before a firm order could be obtained. Because of CPL's good relationship with its banks, Bill Spencer foresaw no problem in obtaining an extension in its line of credit to cover the increased working capital.

As he reviewed his notes, Bill Spencer wondered what recommendations he should make to Jack Nolin. Could CPL compete in the Japanese market? The risks were enormous. As yet CPL had no written contract with Jiro Hattori, and once the product development was started and the steel was ordered, these costs were sunk. The decision that the CPL managers would make that day would indeed be critical to CPL's future operations.

**NOTES:**

# CASE  NO. 6  CAMBRIDGE PRODUCTS,  LTD. (B)*

Bill Spencer shook his head in exasperation as he gathered up his papers at the end of a long day of negotiations.  Outside the Cambridge Products, Ltd. (CPL) office in Waterloo, Ontario, in late September 1982,  the first snowflakes of what promised to be a cold winter were drifting to the ground; but inside, no one even noticed.  Present at the meeting which had just ended were Jiro Hattori, president of the Kuwahara Company, one of the largest wholesalers of cookware in Japan; Jack Nolin, executive vice president of CPL, Canada's leading manufacturer of conventional, top of the range cookware; David Taylor, vice president, CPL U.S.; Izu Tsukamoto, CPL's California-based distributor; and Bill Spencer, vice president, corporate relations.

The CPL executives had entered the meeting expecting to reach a final agreement with Jiro Hattori to commence shipping 2,000 sets of cookware a month at (U.S.) $125 per set in late October.  Three weeks earlier, after a 10-week crash development program, CPL had sent Hattori 150 sample sets of high quality, 3- and 5-ply cookware that sported whistling knobs and handles with wraparound flameguards (ferrules)--modifications that Hattori had specifically requested.  CPL had spent nearly $225,000 on product development and travel to date on this project.  Taylor and Tsukamoto had verbally negotiated price and delivery terms with Hattori in Japan, although no written contract had been drawn.  Steel and other components had been ordered, at a cost of $400,000, and 40 new employees hired to prepare for the expected October delivery.

Therefore, CPL executives were flabbergased when Jiro Hattori,  on this first day's meeting, announced that more modifications were required--a higher gloss on the outside and more polish on the inside.  Doing a quick calculation,  Bill Spencer figured it would cost CPL $3.00 more per set, lowering CPL's 15 percent margin.  But even more disturbing was the possibility that this new demand by Hattori was just the tip of the iceberg--would more demands follow?  Bill wondered if the Japanese would ever be satisfied.  Had CPL miscalculated in investing nearly a quarter of a million dollars developing a product for the Japanese market without a written contract?  And what should CPL do now--cancel the deal?  Or try to negotiate more favorable price and volume terms?  The CPL executives knew they would have to consider their options carefully and come up with some answers before negotiations resumed the next day.

Bill Spencer thought back to that warm summer day in June,  when he and Jack Nolin had discussed Jiro Hattori's proposal to distribute 1,500 sets a month if CPL could come up with a satisfactory product by August  The two executives had considered several factors--the development costs, capacity expansion, and pricing; had analyzed the information they had available on the Japanese market; and finally decided to go ahead with the product development.

A crash program was instituted and the modifications were developed in 10 weeks instead of the normal five months required for such a job.  And they were heartened by Hattori's subsequent offer to take 2,000 sets a month instead of the 1,500 he had proposed earlier--the increased production would not add to overhead significantly.  In early September, Tsukamoto and Taylor took 150 sample sets to Japan.  The product was superior to anything on the market, the CPL executives felt;  although no formal contract had been signed, preparations were made for deliveries of 2,000 sets a month by late October.  Steel and other components worth $400,000 were ordered.  Hiring and training of new employees began in July and, by September, employees totaled 100, up from 60 in June.

With price and delivery terms already settled in principle, CPL executives had looked forward to Jiro Hattori's first trip to Canada.  The Japanese executive came alone, Izu Tsukamoto acted as translator.  The CPL executives expected the meeting to end with a formal ratification of the earlier agreement, and the discussions began amicably.  Hattori's latest demand for more polish and a

---

*This case was prepared by Ken Coelho under the direction of Donald Lecraw, Univ. of Western Ontario, published with permission.

"sungloss" finish therefore took them by surprise, expecially since they believed they had achieved the ultimate in quality.

They had few options:

1. **Drop Hattori and switch to another distributor.** On their trips to Japan, Bill Spencer had talked to other distributors besides Hatori. They had all appeared to be willing, even eager, to carry CPL's cookware line. In the end, however, CPL had decided to go with Hattori, one of the largest and most powerful distributors in Japan, and their agent Izu Tsukamoto's initial contact there. Spencer was uncertain about the implications of switching agents at this late date in terms of credibility, volume, price, redesign, and delays. But at least there were other distributors besides Hattori. Spencer was also uncertain of whether CPL should try to raise this option with Jiro Hattori to try to gain leverage in the negotiations.

2. **Forget the Japanese market.** CPL could not cancel its steel orders without facing price penalties in the future. If steel was stored for use in normal production for the North American market, it could take well over a year to use up since cookware manufacturers were now beginning to feel the effects of the recession. Bill Spencer calculated that it would cost CPL roughly $150,000 in inventory costs and penalties if such a course of action were followed. Also, 40 of the new employees would probably have to be terminated, with at least two weeks' notice.

3. **Accept Hattori's terms and try to negotiate a better price/volume.** CPL had no written contract. Acceding to Hattori's request would lower margins by $3 per set, and a further investment of $20,000 in equipment and $25,000 in buffs and compounds. And even more worrying was the thought--was this the final demand, or were there more to follow? An increase in volume from 2,000 to 3,000 would lower direct costs by $5 per set, just covering the added costs of the modifications and additional investment. At this volume, sales to Japan would represent almost 50 percent of total sales.

As he politely shook hands with Jiro Hattori, Bill Spencer wondered what was in store for CPL.

# APPENDICES - RESOURCE MATERIAL FOR CASE ANALYSIS

## CONTENTS

A. FUNDAMENTALS OF EFFECTIVE BUSINESS WRITING
B. KEY BUSINESS RATIOS
C. HOW TO USE THE LIBRARY FOR CASE ANALYSIS

## APPENDIX A.  FUNDAMENTALS OF EFFECTIVE BUSINESS WRITING

This  section is designed to produce an immediate improvement  in the  writing skills of the careful reader. It cannot make the  reader an  expert on correct written English; however, it does offer a  quick tune-up  in effective usage of English for business  reports.   Should the reader wish a more intensive review of effective English usage, we heartily  recommend the 78-page paperback by William Strunk and E. B. White, The Elements of Style. We have borrowed frequently from this excellent monograph.

The  readers already have a vast store of writing  knowledge  and technique.  The rules of punctuation, grammar, and spelling have  been taught during elementary school. High school and college reports  have taught the  principles  of composition and  style.   Conversations, reading,  television, etc., have given readers  a  considerable vocabulary.  The  problem tackled by this section is to  direct  this collection of the readers' abilities toward clear, forceful,  concise writing.

How  can this section quickly improve the writing skills  of  the reader? We have observed that the same errors and weaknesses occur in the  writing  of  many students. Hence,  by  concentrating  on  these frequently  occurring weaknesses, many students can eliminate a  large percentage of  their weaknesses.  In addition, stylistic  goals  for effective business writing often have not been clearly  presented to students. A careful reading of the compositional principles and goals stated  in  this  section will result in a  handsome pay-off  to  the reader.

This section is divided into three parts:

* Checklist A.a:  Common Errors in Writing.
* Checklist A.b:  Minor Oversights in Writing.
* Checklist A.c:  Stylistic Goals in Writing

Each section contains a number of points which describe a  common error  or useful principle.  The points are coded a.l, a.2, etc., and b.l,  b.2, etc. Readers wishing review work will  benefit  from  the basic material  in  Checklists A.a and A.b,  before  reviewing  the compositional principles in Checklist A.c.

A  useful  exercise for serious students is to  exchange  writing samples with a friend. Each person care-fully reads the other's  piece and writes on the paper the code for any error or principle  violated.  For example, if one essay had three terms not separated correctly  by commas, the friend would pencil "a.2" over the infraction. The  papers are  each returned and each author reviews errors.  The practice  both in  editing another's  work  and having one's  own  work  edited  is invaluable.  This  is an effective way to put a term paper  or  case report in final shape.

## CHECKLIST A.a:  COMMON ERRORS IN WRITING

This  checklist enumerates frequently made errors in  business  writing.  These  errors are caused both by carelessness  and  by  the writer's ignorance in the basics of English grammar and usage.

## a.1 Write in Sentences

The basic building block of written expression in the English language is the sentence. If a writer wishes to express complicated, interrelated data, then a table, graph, or picture may prove useful. If several related contributory thoughts are expressed but not developed, then the point form listing (often referred to as "bullets", see checklist item c.6) is often advantageous. Nevertheless, the development of ideas in prose is correctly done through sentences.

It is difficult to explain rules to distinguish sentences from collections of words. In general terms, a sentence expresses a complete thought and contains a subject, verb, and predicate. Ultimately, writers must rely on their experience and intuition ("ear") to distinguish sentences from groups of words. However, the following two examples illustrate two common errors in constructing sentences.

Incorrect:    The first quarter's sales effort was abandoned, there were no profits in the second quarter.

Correct:    The first quarter's sales effort was abandoned. There were no profits in the second quarter.

Correct:    There were no profits in the second quarter, because the first quarter's sales effort was abandoned.

In the first example, two independent clauses are improperly joined by a comma. This situation is corrected by making two sentences in the second example. The third example shows the relationship between the two ideas by using a conjunction to join the clauses.

Incorrect:    The accountant was a clever estimator. A person who had studied market conditions and trends for years.

Correct:    The accountant was a clever estimator who had studied market conditions and trends for years.

In the incorrect example above, a period has been incorrectly used in place of a comma. The second phrase cannot stand alone. A sentence must express a complete thought.

## a.2 Separate a Series of Three or More Terms by Commas

Weak:    newspapers, tabloids and magazines

Preferred:    newspapers, tabloids, and magazines

Correct:    The computer calculates the interest, debits the account, and prints the ending balance.

The rule is to separate by commas three or more terms in a list. In the incorrect example, the second comma has been omitted. It has become common to omit the comma before the "and"; nevertheless, lists are easier to read when the comma is retained. Notice how the commas clarify the reading of the following sentence.

Correct:    The warehouse stores paper, painting and photography supplies, and typewriters.

## a.3 Comma Before a Conjunction Introducing an Independent Clause

Incorrect:    The inflation rate is high this year but wage settlements promise to be favorable.

Correct:    The inflation rate is high this year, but wage settlements promise to be favorable.

An independent clause is a group of words with a subject and predicate which can stand alone as a sentence. In the above example, the parts of the sentence before and after the "but" are each independent clauses (e.g., "and", "or", "if", "when", and "because"). In all such instances except one, place a comma before the conjunction. The exception is when the subject is expressed only once and the connective is "and", then the comma is usually omitted.

Correct:    The foul weather prevented shipment and delayed production.

## a.4  Show the Possessive Form of Nouns

Singular nouns form the possessive by adding  's.

Correct:    customer's liability

Correct:    the business's responsibility

The possessive forms of ancient proper names ending in "-es" and "-is" and "Jesus" are exceptions to this rule.

Also, the pronominal possessives (e.g., "hers", "his", "theirs", etc.) have no apostrophe. These are to be distinguished from the possessive of the indefinite pronoun, "one's".  The possessive of plural nouns is formed by adding an apostrophe.

Correct:    several customers' orders

## a.5  The Possessive of "It"

Correct:    It's a shrewd business that ages its accounts receivable.   The form "it's" is a contraction for "it is". The form "its" is the possessive of "it".

## a.6  Refer Participial Phrases at the Start of Sentences to the Subject

Incorrect:  Running rapidly down the corridor, the new computer was seen by the loan officer's children.

Correct:    Running rapidly down the corridor, the loan officer's children saw the new computer.

A participial phrase contains a participle (a word derived from a verb having the qualities of both verb and adjective) and cannot stand alone as an independent clause. When used at the beginning of a sentence, a participial phrase refers to the subject of the sentence - whether or not this is the writer's intent. The consequence is often not as ridiculous as the above example, but may result in ambiguity. Who is arriving?

Incorrect:  On disembarking in Los Angeles, the sales manager will meet the new customers.

Correct:    After the new customers disembark in Los Angeles, they will be met by the sales manager.

## CHECKLIST   A.b  MINOR OVERSIGHTS IN WRITING

Editing is the important and "never quite finished" task of making corrections and improvements to text. Depending on the habits and skills of the writer, first drafts often contain many small punctuation errors, awkward word combinations, and sterile sentences. Some superb writers produce first drafts which are very weak; however, after several careful editings, their products turn into fine compositions. Although experienced writers edit as much by "ear" and intuition as by specific rules, specific enumeration of common weaknesses in writing can expedite the editing process.

The punctuation and compositional directives here are useful considerations in editing. We emphasize that some of the points here are matters of taste, not ironclad rules. Although the points in Checklist A.a are generally recognized rules, many points here depend on the stylistic goal of the author; they need not be resolved in the manner suggested.

## b.1 Avoid Double Negatives

Weak:     We find it not unreasonable to expect that the recent sales increase will not discontinue.

Strong:   We expect that the recent sales increase will continue.

Weak:     We may conclude from the consultant's report that the Parks Department does not have inadequate safety standards.

Strong:   We may conclude from the consultant's report that the Parks Department has adequate safety standards.

The objective of business writing is effective and efficient communication to the reader. Only skilled readers can grasp double negatives without a quick second glance. Even for these readers, double negatives waste words and weaken sentences.

## b.2 Use the Active Voice

Weak:     My first stockmarket gain will always be remembered by me.

Strong:   I shall always remember my first stockmarket gain.

In the active voice, the subject of the sentence performs the action of the verb, for example, "Man bites dog." In the passive voice, the subject of the sentence is the receiver of the action of the verb, for example, "Dog was bitten by man." The active voice is usually less wordy and frequently more clear and forceful than the passive. Consider the following examples.

Weak:     It would appear that chances for a special order are good.

Strong:   Chances for a special order appear good.

Weak:     There were many empty slots on the warehouse shelves.

Strong:   Empty slots dominated the warehouse shelves.

Do not exclude the passive voice from writing; a few sentences are more effective with a passive verb. For example, the passive is useful when the writer wishes to place emphasis on a particular item by making it the subject of the sentence. In the last example above, a report on the compensation provisions of the union contract would benefit by the passive form - particularly if this were the topic sentence of a paragraph.

## b.3 Be Wary of Adverbs Modifying Adjectives

Weak:     exceedingly inappropriate response

Weak:     very large contract

Weak:     very inaccurate forecast

Weak:     seriously large loss

The adverbs at the start of each of the above examples add little to the message. If the terms are important, there will be further analysis to explain or quantify the impropriety of the response or the inaccuracy of the forecast. If the terms are not used again, little substance is lost by deleting the adverbs.

## b.4 Principles of Commas

The comma easily wins top honors as the most frustrating punctuation mark. A prerequisite to learning all the rules for commas is the ability to identify subordinate clauses, coordinating conjunctions, complex-compound sentences, etc. Students who have mastered all these rules are unpleasantly surprised to find that writing is often improved by violating these rules. It is no wonder that grammar books complain that many students punctuate with the comma by intuition.

The purpose of the comma is to make a sentence easier for the reader to understand. This has resulted in a number of conventional and easily defined uses of the comma (see Checklist A.a). There are many other identifiable rules for punctuation with commas; however, few people can take the time to learn them. Thus, we suggest that the reader carefully observe the comma rules in the previous subsection, continue to comma intuitively, and consider the comma guidelines that follow here.

A fundamental principle is to enclose parenthetic expressions between commas. In general terms an expression is parenthetic if it contributes extra information which is not vital to the meaning of the sentence. Parenthetic expressions interrupt the flow of the sentence with additional, although interesting or important, information.

The following are common examples of parenthetic (or "extra") expressions.

Incorrect:   The new vice-president Chris Single will chair the planning committee meeting.

Incorrect:   The new vice-president Chris Single, will chair the planning committee meeting.

Correct:   The new vice-president, Chris Single, will chair the planning committee meeting.

The above examples illustrate a parenthetical expression called an appositive - an identifying phrase equivalent to the noun or pronoun identified. In the first incorrect example above, both commas have been omitted. In the second incorrect example, only one comma has been used.

If an expression is nonrestrictive, it is parenthetic and is set off by commas. If an expression is restrictive (i.e., is necessary to define the particular part of the subject modified by the expression), then it is not set off by commas. Notice how the meaning of the following sentence is changed by the use of commas:

Example:   The employees, who are dedicated workers, have recently donated enough money
to put the United Appeal Fund over target.

When the commas are included in the above example, the sentence means that all the employees have donated money. When the commas are omitted, the phrase is restrictive and means that those of the employees who are dedicated workers have donated the money. Thus, for example, the following sentence indicates that only the employees in the training program have shown improved attendance:

Example:   The employees who are enrolled in the management training program have shown
improved attendance.

## b.5 Avoid These Weak, Wordy Expressions

Many lackluster, wordy expressions reappear in business writing. Even though these expressions are technically sound, they drain vitality from sentences. Consider the following wordy expressions. The president decides the question as to whether we enter the market. (The president decides whether we enter the market.)

She is a person who wins respect.   (She)

The strategy is an effective one.   (The strategy  is effective.)

used for advertising purposes   (used for advertising)

it is necessary to first have interest rates calculated.  (first, have interest rates calculated)

It is possible for the company to increase profits.  (The company can increase profits.)

In order to reduce costs, reorder points were changed.  (Reorder points were change
to reduce costs.)

the fact that profits were down   (the decrease in profits)

in spite of the fact that costs have risen  (since costs have risen)

Strunk and White find "the fact that" to be the most debilitating of these expressions.  We agree.  The rewording necessary to eliminate this expression improves clarity and adds vigor.

## b.6  The Length of Sentences

An interesting variety of sentence structure and length  is  an important aspect of writing that becomes of increasing importance with the increasing length of a text.  However, there are no firm rules  on the effective composition of sentences. For almost  any  rule  that seems  to correspond with good practice, one can find  famous  authors who  achieve  their effects by repeatedly violating  the rule.   This discussion is of little comfort to the writer who wants guidance.

We suggest that for effective business communication sentences be between  10  and 40 words - unless there is  good  reason.   Sentences longer  than  40 words are imposing and often hard for the  reader to follow.   Many  people mistakenly think that long  sentences  indicate deep,  complex  thoughts and demonstrate literary ability.   However, clear  thinkers  with  writing skills will be able  to  convey  their thoughts  in a readable fashion. This typically results in  sentences less  than 40 words.  On the other hand, frequent use of sentences  of less than 10 words may indicate a lack of care in the composition, the syn-drome: "Run, Spot, run.  See Spot run".

## b.7  Use Parallel Constructions for Related Ideas

Weak:      the marketing department, production control group, and   the management committee.

Strong:      the marketing department, the production control group, and the management committee.

The weak example has been improved by the addition of a "the"  to correct  the imbalance in the enu-meration. The form of construction for related ideas should usually be the same. The addition of  "the" gives the above construction an artistic balance not found in the weak version.

In  the following examples, notice how the equivalent use of  the preposition  balances  the  three items in the  list  for  the  strong versions.

Weak:      The new plant will have improved  facilities  for  order assembly packaging,
            and for order shipping.

Strong:     The new plant will have improved facilities for order assembly, for order
            packaging, and for order shipping.

Strong:     The new plant will have improved facilities for order assembly,  packaging, and shipping.

## CHECKLIST A.c   STYLISTIC GOALS IN WRITING

Good style in writing includes coordinated choice of words, phrases, sentence structures, paragraphs, and overall organization to effectively convey ideas, stories, theses, and emotions to readers. In general literature, good style is an art that is only achieved by exceptional writers. Fortunately, much business writing is judged only on how efficiently and effectively the descriptions, ideas, and theses of the writer are conveyed to the reader. The less ambitious goals of business writing and more clearly defined criteria for evaluation mean that acceptable style in business writing is easier to achieve than acceptable style in general writing.

This subsection contains guidelines for achieving acceptable style in business writing. These are only guidelines; effective writers regularly find good cause to violate them.

We emphasize that good style in business writing can only be achieved if the writer is in tune with the objectives and capabilities of the readers. If the reader is a technical expert in the area of correspondence, then the message is fashioned quite differently than if the reader is a general manager.

### c.1 Paragraphs are Building Blocks of Composition

The paragraph is the basic unit of written, logically coherent theme development. The objective of business writing is to efficiently convey the thoughts of the writer. Correct word choice and sentence structure can be useless in the hands of writers who do not know how to combine sentences for clear, convincing compositions. If the problem is that the writer has done no clear, logical thinking, then little can be done to improve the composition. However, even carefully reasoned arguments can be lost if the basic points of the author are not developed in paragraph units.

A paragraph contains one central idea or topic. If the idea is brief, then the paragraph is short. If the idea needs extended development, the paragraph is long. If the resulting paragraph is too long - most readers are intimidated by large blocks of writing - then the idea is broken down into parts and each is developed in its own paragraph. In this way, writers match the topic by topic development of themes with paragraphs.

### c.2 Begin Paragraphs with Topic Sentences

Correct:    The effect of the promotion campaign on repeat purchases is difficult to predict.

Correct:    In summary, there are several clear benefits from the test market experiment.

Since written messages are developed by topics, one to a paragraph, the reader is well served by sentences introducing the topic for each paragraph. These sentences allow the reader to rapidly gain understanding of the content of the paragraph. The sentences give hurried readers the opportunity to skim the entire composition and, if required, to carefully read a few key paragraphs.

### c.3 Be Wary of One Sentence Paragraphs

Weak:    The room ventilation worked well.

Weak:    The office staff was pleased with the new equipment.

In the first example, if there is no consequence to the ventilator's performance, then the sentence may well be discarded from the text. In the second example, the reader would probably benefit from more explanation about why the office staff liked the new equipment.

One sentence paragraphs appear infrequently in effective business writing. They are most often used as transition paragraphs in composition. In business writing, transitions are often indicated by new sections, so that many one sentence paragraphs are symptomatic of ineffective composition.

A one sentence paragraph does not have sufficient space to develop an important idea for the reader. Writers with many one sentence paragraphs are like hunters who try to shoot elephants with BBs instead of bullets. The writer should take the idea in the sentence and ask: Is the idea important enough to include in the writing? Is the idea part of the development of the topic of another paragraph? Is the idea important enough to deserve more complete development?

## c.4 Omit Needless Words

There is a tendency in business writing to include many needless words and awkward constructions. The demands of business can force writers to write about themes not of their choosing. Under these conditions writers are prone to verbosity.

In the preface to the second edition of The Elements of Style, E. B. White forcefully demonstrates this theme:

"Vigorous writing is concise. A sentence should contain no unnecessary words, a paragraph no unnecessary sentences, for the same reason that a drawing should have no unnecessary lines and a machine no unnecessary parts. This requires not that the writer make all his sentences short, or that he avoid all detail and treat his subject only in outline, but that every word tell."

## c.5 Be Concrete and Positive

Weak:    The sales picture has shown definite improvement over the past three months when compared to the comparable period last year.

Strong:    Third quarter sales in '81 are 20 per cent above third quarter sales in '80.

Business writing demands the communication of facts, summaries, generalizations, and speculations. The choice of language and use of examples vary according to the content of the particular part. The use of concrete data is often effective in conveying information a manager needs for the assessment of a situation and the determination of appropriate action. Vague descriptive adjectives and adverbs are poor substitutes for the concrete data and descriptions needed.

Consider the following examples:

Weak:    The cumulative effect of the low volume items on inventory carrying costs is significant.

Strong:    The slowest-selling items, which account for 10% of sales, account for 20% of the inventory carrying costs.

Weak:    There have clearly been too many cases of billing errors, and these are having an adverse effect on customer relations.

Strong:    The 30 billing errors so far this year have resulted in written complaints from good customers.

## c.6 Consider Using Point Form

Weak:    The new computer model can be used for planning adequate staffing for future years, mediating the trade-off between arrival times and room congestion, and designing efficient building facilities.

Strong:    The new computer model can be used for:

* Planning adequate staffing for future years.
* Mediating the trade-off between arrival times and room congestion.

140

*   Designing efficient building facilities.

The point form method of expressing enumerated items, often called "bullets," communicates lists effectively to the readers. The bullets visually present the information for rapid comprehension and convenient review. Notice the use of a "bullet" (asterisk, or equivalent typewriter symbol) rather than a number preceding each point. The first word of each bullet is usually capitalized and the bullet is followed by a period. Even though the bullet is not a grammatically complete sentence, it expresses an important idea that deserves the emphasis indicated by a period. If the writer is going to later refer back to the items individually, then numbering is appropriate; otherwise, the number only presents unnecessary information.

## c.7 Do Not Overstate

Example:   GMI's cash discount is the best in the industry...delivery schedules are prompt and never fall behind schedule.

The objective of business writing is frequently to convince or impress the reader. In the above example, if a prospective customer knows of a vendor with a better cash discount than GMI, this fact will cause doubt about the sincerity of the delivery schedule claims. A single overstatement may cast doubts on other statements that are not directly verifiable.

# APPENDIX B    KEY BUSINESS RATIOS[1]

## THE RATIOS

To the economist and the statistician, terms like "median" and "quartile" are everyday working language, but their precise meaning is foggy at best to the typical business person.

In the ratio tables that appear on the next few pages, three figures appear under each ratio heading for each line. The center figure, in bold type, is the **median**; the figure immediately above and below the median are, respectively, the **upper** and **lower quartiles**. The biggest ratio figure is at the top, the lowest at the bottom. The figure that falls just in the middle of this series becomes the median for the ratio in that line of business. The figure halfway between the median and the highest terms of the series is the upper quartile; the term halfway between the median and the bottom of the series is the lower quartile. In a strictly statistical sense, then, each median is the typical ratio figure for all the concerns studied in a given line. The upper and lower quartiles, in turn, typify the experience of the firms in the top half and the bottom half of the sample respectively.

The following industry ratios (retailing, wholesaling and mfg.) were compiled in 1980, more recent data is unavailable since Dun's Review no longer publishes this information.

## DEFINITION OF TERMS

**Collection Period:** The number of days that the total of trade accounts and notes receivable, less reserves for bad debts, represents when compared with the annual net credit sales.

**Current Assets:** Total of cash, accounts and notes receivable for the sale of merchandise in regular trade quarters, less any reserves for bad debt, advances on merchandise, inventory less any reserves, listed securities, state and municipal bonds, and United States government securities.

**Current Debt:** Total of all liabilities due within one year from statement date including serial notes, mortgages, debentures, or other funded debt.

**Fixed Assets:** The sum of the cost value of land and the depreciated book values of buildings, leasehold improvements, fixtures, furniture, machinery, tools and equipment.

**Funded Debt:** Mortgages, bonds, debentures, gold notes, serial notes, or other obligations with maturity of more than one year from the statement date.

**Inventory:** The sum of raw material, material in process and finished merchandise. It does not include supplies.

**Net profits:** Profits after full depreciation on buildings, machinery, equipment, furniture, and other assets of a fixed nature; after reserves for federal income and excess profit taxes; after reduction in the value of inventory; after charge-offs for bad debts; after miscellaneous reserves and adjustments; but before dividends or withdrawals.

**Net Sales:** The dollar volume of business transactions for 365 days net after deductions for returns, allowances and discounts from gross sales.

**Net Sales to Inventory:** The quotient obtained by dividing the annual net sales by inventory.

**Net Working Capital:** The excess of the current assets over the current debt.

**Turnover of Net Working Capital:** The quotient obtained by dividing annual net sales by net working capital.

**Turnover of Tangible Net Worth:** The quotient obtained by dividing annual net sales by tangible net worth.

---

[1] Reprinted with the special permission of Dun's Review, November 1980, copyright 1980, Dun & Bradstreet Publications Corp.

# RETAILING

| Line of Business (and number of concerns reporting) | Current assets to current debt | Net profits on net sales | Net profits on tangible net worth | Net profits on net working capital | Net sales to tangible net worth | Net sales to net working capital | Collection period | Net sales to inventory | Fixed assets to tangible net worth | Current debt to tangible net worth | Total debt to tangible net worth | Inventory to net working capital | Current debt to inventory | Funded debts to net working capital |
|---|---|---|---|---|---|---|---|---|---|---|---|---|---|---|
| | Times | Per cent | Per cent | Per cent | Times | Times | Days | Times | Per cent | Per cent | Per cent | Per cent | Per cent | Per cent |
| **5531 Auto & Home Supply Stores (3,072)** | 4.96 | 8.54 | 39.91 | 47.81 | 8.47 | 9.07 | 40 | 7.8 | 63.7 | 149.3 | 216.5 | 143.5 | 112.4 | 111.7 |
| | 2.41 | 4.35 | 20.33 | 23.96 | 4.82 | 4.94 | 21 | 5.0 | 28.8 | 63.7 | 94.3 | 96.4 | 66.4 | 56.2 |
| | 1.52 | 1.08 | 8.65 | 9.09 | 2.61 | 2.78 | 9 | 3.4 | 12.0 | 22.1 | 33.3 | 65.5 | 31.8 | 19.2 |
| **5641 Children's & Infants' Wear Stores (1,912)** | 7.44 | 11.26 | 44.45 | 46.67 | 6.05 | 5.92 | 19 | 5.3 | 40.0 | 89.6 | 140.6 | 140.5 | 75.9 | 101.8 |
| | 3.33 | 5.45 | 21.48 | 21.71 | 3.53 | 3.57 | 7 | 3.7 | 16.8 | 35.9 | 58.8 | 97.2 | 41.5 | 57.0 |
| | 1.83 | 1.75 | 7.02 | 7.06 | 1.98 | 2.17 | 2 | 2.6 | 6.8 | 11.5 | 17.7 | 69.4 | 19.5 | 23.6 |
| **5611 Clothing & Furnishings, Men's & Boys' (5,578)** | 5.87 | 9.39 | 36.59 | 41.31 | 6.32 | 6.59 | 33 | 5.4 | 38.3 | 107.2 | 153.9 | 153.4 | 81.3 | 88.4 |
| | 2.94 | 4.16 | 17.05 | 18.82 | 3.72 | 3.85 | 14 | 3.7 | 17.1 | 47.4 | 65.3 | 103.4 | 49.5 | 45.7 |
| | 1.78 | 1.40 | 5.82 | 5.66 | 2.16 | 2.37 | 4 | 2.5 | 6.3 | 17.6 | 24.3 | 74.3 | 24.6 | 17.6 |
| **5311 Department Stores (845)** | 5.40 | 4.69 | 18.11 | 21.24 | 5.97 | 6.50 | 52 | 6.2 | 47.2 | 87.4 | 146.9 | 141.1 | 81.6 | 78.5 |
| | 2.99 | 2.14 | 9.46 | 10.75 | 3.70 | 4.03 | 24 | 4.5 | 19.0 | 43.8 | 64.0 | 93.7 | 53.9 | 41.1 |
| | 1.97 | .79 | 3.49 | 3.98 | 2.37 | 2.73 | 5 | 3.2 | 7.0 | 18.9 | 25.5 | 62.8 | 31.2 | 13.9 |
| **5651 Family Clothing Stores (2,132)** | 8.04 | 11.01 | 31.26 | 38.03 | 5.26 | 5.26 | 31 | 5.2 | 37.4 | 79.0 | 132.6 | 131.5 | 70.2 | 93.8 |
| | 3.82 | 5.27 | 16.05 | 18.29 | 2.93 | 3.16 | 12 | 3.3 | 15.7 | 31.2 | 51.9 | 95.2 | 38.4 | 51.5 |
| | 2.06 | 1.92 | 6.43 | 7.05 | 1.58 | 1.90 | 3 | 2.2 | 6.2 | 11.1 | 17.1 | 67.4 | 18.4 | 21.0 |
| **5712 Furniture Stores (7,051)** | 6.30 | 9.39 | 33.88 | 39.50 | 6.78 | 7.25 | 72 | 7.1 | 39.1 | 115.3 | 169.6 | 132.4 | 102.8 | 87.1 |
| | 2.96 | 4.48 | 15.51 | 17.20 | 3.38 | 3.75 | 31 | 4.5 | 15.0 | 45.5 | 70.2 | 83.9 | 61.8 | 43.0 |
| | 1.71 | 1.81 | 6.43 | 6.51 | 1.78 | 1.99 | 13 | 3.1 | 5.6 | 15.7 | 25.5 | 47.0 | 30.4 | 14.8 |
| **5541 Gasoline Service Stations (2,976)** | 7.26 | 7.50 | 64.84 | 107.37 | 18.92 | 26.23 | 16 | 40.0 | 81.9 | 86.3 | 137.1 | 96.6 | 153.5 | 207.5 |
| | 2.96 | 3.60 | 29.07 | 49.70 | 8.95 | 12.50 | 7 | 22.6 | 41.1 | 30.6 | 53.0 | 66.6 | 68.8 | 71.7 |
| | 1.49 | 1.46 | 11.85 | 16.33 | 3.82 | 5.54 | 2 | 12.0 | 19.3 | 9.7 | 16.4 | 37.7 | 26.4 | 20.6 |
| **5411 Grocery Stores (4,293)** | 6.78 | 5.00 | 40.26 | 76.08 | 18.08 | 23.07 | 7 | 21.8 | 98.7 | 93.1 | 171.4 | 128.5 | 103.8 | 205.3 |
| | 2.81 | 2.05 | 19.49 | 35.71 | 9.90 | 12.88 | 2 | 15.0 | 48.6 | 37.9 | 67.4 | 90.7 | 53.9 | 91.6 |
| | 1.50 | .87 | 8.85 | 11.09 | 4.74 | 6.32 | | 10.0 | 22.7 | 12.1 | 21.2 | 63.5 | 20.8 | 31.0 |
| **5251 Hardware Stores (3,159)** | 8.95 | 9.65 | 30.49 | 34.36 | 5.66 | 5.16 | 28 | 4.8 | 43.2 | 90.2 | 162.7 | 127.8 | 69.2 | 109.4 |
| | 3.88 | 4.63 | 16.11 | 17.90 | 3.20 | 3.24 | 15 | 3.3 | 17.4 | 37.0 | 63.4 | 95.0 | 35.7 | 57.9 |
| | 2.06 | 1.97 | 7.23 | 7.49 | 1.84 | 2.13 | 7 | 2.4 | 7.4 | 12.4 | 18.6 | 74.0 | 15.4 | 23.0 |
| **5722 Household Appliance Stores (2,238)** | 4.58 | 9.32 | 45.15 | 60.40 | 9.67 | 10.92 | 34 | 8.6 | 49.0 | 181.2 | 231.4 | 184.3 | 117.1 | 110.0 |
| | 2.11 | 3.78 | 19.93 | 25.28 | 4.89 | 5.70 | 18 | 5.2 | 23.0 | 69.8 | 84.6 | 98.2 | 79.0 | 49.1 |
| | 1.36 | 1.29 | 6.98 | 7.36 | 2.45 | 2.95 | 8 | 3.5 | 9.6 | 19.6 | 30.5 | 58.0 | 40.0 | 19.0 |
| **5944 Jewelry Stores (2,298)** | 8.10 | 14.12 | 36.36 | 36.83 | 4.32 | 3.84 | 53 | 3.5 | 32.5 | 106.7 | 151.6 | 131.5 | 70.3 | 71.6 |
| | 3.64 | 7.47 | 18.84 | 19.67 | 2.50 | 2.31 | 26 | 2.4 | 14.1 | 46.4 | 62.7 | 97.5 | 39.8 | 37.6 |
| | 2.08 | 3.45 | 9.61 | 9.32 | 1.45 | 1.45 | 10 | 1.6 | 5.4 | 16.0 | 23.2 | 74.4 | 16.7 | 15.3 |
| **5211 Lumber & Other Bldg. Mtls. Dealers (3,739)** | 4.45 | 6.24 | 32.49 | 38.46 | 8.02 | 8.69 | 51 | 10.3 | 57.4 | 116.8 | 178.3 | 117.6 | 130.8 | 99.6 |
| | 2.50 | 3.49 | 17.08 | 19.35 | 4.60 | 5.10 | 35 | 6.2 | 26.8 | 54.1 | 79.8 | 81.1 | 75.9 | 47.2 |
| | 1.62 | 1.62 | 7.89 | 8.33 | 2.68 | 2.98 | 20 | 4.1 | 11.6 | 22.5 | 32.3 | 52.9 | 40.7 | 17.0 |
| **5399 Miscellaneous General Mdse. Stores (2,295)** | 12.16 | 9.88 | 29.39 | 40.54 | 5.83 | 6.70 | 25 | 7.2 | 37.7 | 67.0 | 109.0 | 123.2 | 64.7 | 100.9 |
| | 4.51 | 4.88 | 15.07 | 19.86 | 3.00 | 3.69 | 10 | 4.1 | 15.1 | 25.4 | 41.5 | 89.5 | 31.8 | 53.4 |
| | 2.24 | 1.89 | 6.44 | 8.51 | 1.54 | 2.11 | 3 | 2.6 | 6.0 | 7.9 | 12.2 | 62.7 | 12.5 | 21.3 |
| **5511 Motor Vehicle Dealers (6,191)** | 1.69 | 2.12 | 26.68 | 33.57 | 21.14 | 25.15 | 9 | 8.0 | 51.6 | 354.2 | 406.9 | 413.7 | 103.3 | 87.9 |
| | 1.37 | 1.03 | 13.60 | 16.12 | 13.75 | 15.82 | 5 | 6.0 | 25.0 | 210.5 | 237.6 | 255.1 | 90.6 | 41.7 |
| | 1.20 | .32 | 4.86 | 4.23 | 8.85 | 9.49 | 3 | 4.5 | 11.7 | 116.9 | 132.4 | 150.6 | 77.3 | 14.7 |
| **5231 Paint, Glass Wallpaper Stores (901)** | 5.79 | 11.35 | 55.31 | 67.45 | 7.49 | 8.94 | 39 | 11.1 | 47.6 | 97.2 | 140.1 | 114.2 | 122.2 | 122.0 |
| | 2.85 | 5.43 | 28.48 | 33.57 | 4.39 | 5.10 | 24 | 6.6 | 23.1 | 42.3 | 60.5 | 78.5 | 65.9 | 51.4 |
| | 1.71 | 1.91 | 10.95 | 11.47 | 2.59 | 3.08 | 12 | 4.2 | 9.7 | 16.5 | 23.0 | 50.0 | 30.0 | 17.2 |
| **5732 Radio & Television Stores (2,391)** | 4.23 | 10.02 | 50.20 | 70.97 | 9.76 | 11.83 | 20 | 8.3 | 56.9 | 172.0 | 219.7 | 198.5 | 106.1 | 129.9 |
| | 2.04 | 4.42 | 23.79 | 28.51 | 5.07 | 5.89 | 10 | 5.0 | 27.0 | 64.6 | 90.9 | 106.5 | 74.2 | 55.5 |
| | 1.35 | 1.44 | 8.81 | 7.64 | 2.54 | 3.07 | 4 | 3.4 | 11.9 | 20.9 | 31.0 | 64.7 | 37.3 | 17.9 |
| **5261 Retail Nurseries, Lawn & Garden Supp. Stores (1,155)** | 5.09 | 10.28 | 47.21 | 64.25 | 8.32 | 9.80 | 24 | 10.0 | 89.4 | 151.8 | 240.9 | 153.8 | 120.2 | 169.3 |
| | 2.21 | 4.79 | 20.75 | 29.17 | 4.06 | 5.12 | 10 | 5.0 | 36.8 | 53.1 | 78.8 | 92.8 | 68.9 | 73.9 |
| | 1.28 | 1.49 | 8.53 | 7.87 | 1.85 | 2.31 | 4 | 3.0 | 12.9 | 13.8 | 25.2 | 52.4 | 29.9 | 21.5 |
| **5661 Shoe Stores (2,987)** | 6.16 | 10.71 | 41.17 | 44.63 | 6.44 | 6.11 | 15 | 4.8 | 37.4 | 110.8 | 169.0 | 159.1 | 72.4 | 96.1 |
| | 3.04 | 5.54 | 21.02 | 22.98 | 3.73 | 3.73 | 6 | 3.3 | 15.3 | 45.2 | 61.8 | 108.6 | 43.5 | 49.9 |
| | 1.78 | 2.24 | 9.68 | 9.08 | 2.21 | 2.28 | 2 | 2.3 | 5.7 | 15.9 | 21.2 | 81.5 | 21.4 | 20.1 |
| **5331 Variety Stores (719)** | 7.53 | 9.25 | 29.75 | 36.75 | 6.83 | 6.30 | 10 | 4.7 | 47.4 | 100.6 | 169.3 | 155.9 | 67.2 | 107.7 |
| | 3.72 | 4.54 | 15.65 | 17.99 | 3.83 | 3.93 | 3 | 3.4 | 20.5 | 37.9 | 62.5 | 104.9 | 34.1 | 61.9 |
| | 1.84 | 1.47 | 6.37 | 7.38 | 2.05 | 2.48 | 1 | 2.4 | 8.2 | 12.5 | 19.7 | 84.1 | 16.5 | 24.1 |
| **5621 Women's Ready-to-Wear Stores (9,831)** | 6.85 | 10.51 | 38.63 | 46.22 | 6.03 | 6.55 | 35 | 6.8 | 43.7 | 87.2 | 130.5 | 128.5 | 91.4 | 111.9 |
| | 3.23 | 4.93 | 17.99 | 21.56 | 3.44 | 3.83 | 16 | 4.4 | 19.3 | 36.4 | 52.5 | 90.4 | 50.3 | 54.8 |
| | 1.83 | 1.61 | 6.45 | 6.69 | 1.92 | 2.25 | 5 | 3.0 | 7.6 | 12.6 | 18.5 | 58.3 | 23.3 | 20.6 |

# WHOLESALING

| Line of Business (and number of concerns reporting) | Current assets to current debt | Net profits on net sales | Net profits on tangible net worth | Net profits on net working capital | Net sales to tangible net worth | Net sales to net working capital | Collection period | Net sales to inventory | Fixed assets to tangible net worth | Current debt to tangible net worth | Total debt to tangible net worth | Inventory to net working capital | Current debt to inventory | Funded debts to net working capital |
|---|---|---|---|---|---|---|---|---|---|---|---|---|---|---|
| | Times | Per cent | Per cent | Per cent | Times | Times | Days | Times | Per cent | Per cent | Per cent | Per cent | Per cent | Per cent |
| 5075 Air Heating & Air Condtg. (355) | 3.54 | 5.72 | 47.09 | 53.89 | 10.99 | 14.04 | 62 | 18.8 | 38.7 | 181.2 | 212.7 | 133.3 | 206.9 | 71.2 |
| | 1.91 | 2.84 | 20.11 | 22.64 | 6.07 | 6.95 | 40 | 7.7 | 20.2 | 84.2 | 93.4 | 74.1 | 112.6 | 24.0 |
| | 1.43 | 1.16 | 8.40 | 7.63 | 3.32 | 3.89 | 22 | 4.6 | 7.3 | 29.4 | 34.5 | 38.5 | 66.0 | 10.0 |
| 5013 Automotive Parts & Supplies (3,340) | 4.88 | 6.75 | 33.65 | 37.18 | 7.99 | 7.96 | 40 | 7.7 | 42.4 | 120.7 | 175.1 | 126.2 | 102.8 | 78.2 |
| | 2.73 | 3.55 | 18.06 | 19.35 | 4.81 | 4.83 | 28 | 5.1 | 19.2 | 54.3 | 76.0 | 91.1 | 61.6 | 39.6 |
| | 1.73 | 1.71 | 9.10 | 9.11 | 2.96 | 3.15 | 18 | 3.6 | 8.4 | 24.9 | 31.3 | 67.0 | 33.5 | 13.6 |
| 5181 Beer & Ale (490) | 4.23 | 4.72 | 40.96 | 70.49 | 12.18 | 19.82 | 18 | 19.4 | 77.4 | 104.3 | 154.1 | 147.9 | 124.5 | 148.0 |
| | 2.10 | 2.91 | 23.25 | 36.16 | 7.87 | 11.47 | 8 | 13.6 | 43.2 | 48.4 | 69.2 | 90.0 | 83.7 | 63.7 |
| | 1.48 | 1.40 | 10.67 | 17.16 | 4.67 | 7.01 | 1 | 9.7 | 20.2 | 17.2 | 25.8 | 52.7 | 45.8 | 16.3 |
| 5161 Chemicals and Allied Products (622) | 3.41 | 7.62 | 49.33 | 64.27 | 13.45 | 15.62 | 61 | 27.7 | 59.6 | 200.0 | 241.9 | 100.0 | 297.2 | 93.2 |
| | 1.91 | 3.63 | 26.29 | 33.82 | 7.24 | 8.31 | 41 | 13.0 | 27.1 | 97.6 | 126.6 | 60.9 | 156.8 | 38.8 |
| | 1.34 | 1.41 | 12.61 | 13.22 | 3.63 | 3.92 | 26 | 7.8 | 10.9 | 38.2 | 48.1 | 31.1 | 82.7 | 12.9 |
| 5137 Clothing & Accessories, Women's and Children's (621) | 4.39 | 6.39 | 40.03 | 51.14 | 11.48 | 12.64 | 59 | 14.5 | 25.4 | 169.7 | 193.5 | 135.3 | 182.0 | 61.8 |
| | 2.15 | 2.97 | 20.12 | 24.58 | 5.71 | 6.30 | 34 | 7.9 | 10.9 | 74.5 | 89.8 | 80.3 | 93.3 | 32.9 |
| | 1.51 | 1.34 | 9.08 | 9.56 | 3.00 | 3.38 | 12 | 4.4 | 4.7 | 26.3 | 33.2 | 46.0 | 44.0 | 8.5 |
| 5136 Clothing and Furnishings, Men's & Boys' (560) | 3.84 | 6.83 | 39.40 | 46.48 | 12.91 | 12.63 | 60 | 11.0 | 29.7 | 227.1 | 266.6 | 163.5 | 161.3 | 63.1 |
| | 1.94 | 2.94 | 19.91 | 21.89 | 6.75 | 6.49 | 34 | 6.2 | 11.7 | 102.9 | 121.5 | 93.4 | 97.0 | 35.5 |
| | 1.40 | 1.16 | 9.18 | 9.95 | 3.43 | 3.36 | 17 | 3.7 | 4.2 | 38.2 | 41.4 | 52.4 | 55.2 | 10.2 |
| 5081 Commercial Machines & Equipment (1,854) | 4.29 | 8.73 | 54.62 | 64.87 | 10.19 | 11.49 | 51 | 13.6 | 50.0 | 163.1 | 223.2 | 123.0 | 164.4 | 89.4 |
| | 2.22 | 4.18 | 26.98 | 28.03 | 5.70 | 6.10 | 33 | 7.7 | 21.8 | 66.7 | 89.7 | 78.4 | 96.1 | 39.0 |
| | 1.42 | 1.69 | 11.47 | 10.77 | 3.38 | 3.57 | 21 | 4.9 | 8.7 | 25.5 | 36.2 | 45.9 | 50.0 | 12.1 |
| 5145 Confectionery (348) | 4.85 | 4.34 | 32.24 | 47.39 | 14.51 | 18.91 | 22 | 20.8 | 58.8 | 99.0 | 135.5 | 122.2 | 116.3 | 95.4 |
| | 2.60 | 1.98 | 17.13 | 21.37 | 8.16 | 10.04 | 13 | 12.3 | 25.1 | 45.9 | 66.0 | 85.4 | 68.5 | 42.7 |
| | 1.65 | .86 | 10.00 | 11.11 | 4.34 | 5.83 | 6 | 7.7 | 9.1 | 18.9 | 23.6 | 52.6 | 34.0 | 12.9 |
| 5143 Dairy Products (199) | 2.57 | 3.32 | 26.55 | 67.34 | 24.88 | 39.30 | 31 | 92.7 | 98.0 | 233.1 | 372.4 | 120.6 | 627.8 | 209.1 |
| | 1.49 | 1.71 | 14.26 | 31.34 | 10.65 | 16.68 | 21 | 42.7 | 49.0 | 85.5 | 98.6 | 48.0 | 300.9 | 58.9 |
| | 1.07 | .45 | 7.95 | 8.86 | 5.65 | 6.54 | 12 | 16.2 | 23.1 | 34.6 | 39.9 | 10.7 | 139.3 | 10.9 |
| 5122 Drugs, Proprietaries and Sundries (412) | 3.31 | 5.27 | 28.90 | 36.80 | 12.24 | 12.62 | 49 | 11.2 | 47.3 | 208.3 | 266.0 | 151.3 | 148.8 | 78.4 |
| | 1.96 | 2.21 | 14.05 | 18.10 | 6.75 | 7.08 | 31 | 7.1 | 22.7 | 96.1 | 120.3 | 98.7 | 94.5 | 39.5 |
| | 1.43 | .73 | 5.91 | 7.64 | 3.59 | 3.86 | 18 | 5.0 | 7.8 | 40.2 | 50.2 | 56.1 | 56.8 | 17.5 |
| 5063 Electrical Apparatus and Equipment (1,597) | 3.70 | 6.55 | 40.88 | 48.21 | 10.41 | 11.53 | 55 | 12.7 | 38.3 | 168.2 | 213.4 | 124.2 | 165.3 | 69.3 |
| | 2.11 | 3.35 | 20.73 | 21.94 | 6.22 | 6.30 | 40 | 7.3 | 18.7 | 84.8 | 99.6 | 83.3 | 101.2 | 30.9 |
| | 1.50 | 1.59 | 11.85 | 11.60 | 3.51 | 3.56 | 27 | 4.6 | 8.3 | 34.5 | 43.0 | 52.5 | 58.0 | 11.3 |
| 5064 Electrical Appliances, TV and Radio Sets (588) | 3.08 | 4.98 | 40.83 | 47.28 | 12.44 | 13.50 | 47 | 11.2 | 37.6 | 239.0 | 278.4 | 183.2 | 151.7 | 66.0 |
| | 1.87 | 2.39 | 16.67 | 19.78 | 7.10 | 7.13 | 34 | 6.5 | 15.3 | 98.7 | 128.0 | 98.8 | 104.7 | 26.0 |
| | 1.31 | .90 | 7.41 | 6.54 | 3.98 | 3.87 | 19 | 4.3 | 6.0 | 42.5 | 50.7 | 54.5 | 61.2 | 5.1 |
| 5065 Electronic Parts and Equipment (936) | 4.33 | 7.11 | 44.15 | 54.34 | 11.02 | 11.72 | 56 | 15.5 | 40.5 | 160.6 | 226.0 | 121.4 | 189.5 | 73.3 |
| | 2.30 | 3.73 | 22.46 | 25.22 | 5.91 | 6.09 | 38 | 7.1 | 16.1 | 69.3 | 95.8 | 78.9 | 99.2 | 30.1 |
| | 1.47 | 1.55 | 11.12 | 10.50 | 3.28 | 3.26 | 23 | 4.7 | 6.6 | 25.0 | 31.5 | 41.9 | 48.7 | 9.7 |
| 5083 Farm Machinery & Equipment (3,310) | 2.28 | 5.43 | 33.81 | 38.05 | 10.19 | 10.68 | 30 | 5.5 | 51.4 | 305.1 | 355.2 | 324.1 | 102.4 | 84.0 |
| | 1.55 | 2.94 | 18.52 | 20.54 | 6.08 | 6.43 | 17 | 3.3 | 25.0 | 151.6 | 176.9 | 181.0 | 84.6 | 41.2 |
| | 1.26 | 1.42 | 9.27 | 9.75 | 3.60 | 3.80 | 9 | 2.3 | 12.4 | 63.5 | 74.6 | 91.9 | 63.7 | 13.7 |
| 5139 Footwear (177) | 3.15 | 4.15 | 41.98 | 46.07 | 11.94 | 12.03 | 85 | 9.9 | 24.0 | 274.4 | 316.9 | 163.2 | 175.6 | 51.0 |
| | 1.94 | 2.70 | 22.29 | 20.49 | 5.96 | 5.61 | 54 | 6.0 | 7.0 | 98.2 | 110.2 | 90.2 | 102.9 | 19.4 |
| | 1.30 | 1.41 | 7.80 | 6.67 | 3.43 | 3.61 | 32 | 3.7 | 1.9 | 37.0 | 39.9 | 61.2 | 57.2 | 4.7 |
| 5148 Fresh Fruits & Vegetables (609) | 2.89 | 3.45 | 43.13 | 58.20 | 19.79 | 31.32 | 37 | 123.8 | 82.6 | 167.5 | 231.9 | 68.9 | 736.9 | 125.8 |
| | 1.74 | 1.74 | 20.40 | 28.29 | 10.65 | 14.36 | 22 | 57.6 | 40.0 | 73.4 | 92.5 | 25.9 | 330.5 | 50.5 |
| | 1.21 | .72 | 9.47 | 9.14 | 4.79 | 6.13 | 12 | 27.5 | 14.1 | 27.2 | 33.3 | 8.7 | 144.0 | 8.4 |

| Line of Business (and number of concerns reporting) | Current assets to current debt | Net profits on net sales | Net profits on tangible net worth | Net profits on net working capital | Net sales to tangible net worth | Net sales to net working capital | Collection period | Net sales to inventory | Fixed assets to tangible net worth | Current debt to tangible net worth | Total debt to tangible net worth | Inventory to net working capital | Current debt to inventory | Funded debts to net working capital |
|---|---|---|---|---|---|---|---|---|---|---|---|---|---|---|
| | Times | Per cent | Per cent | Per cent | Times | Times | Days | Times | Per cent | Per cent | Per cent | Per cent | Per cent | Per cent |
| **5021 Furniture** (687) | 3.59 **1.98** 1.40 | 6.19 **3.10** 1.46 | 41.27 **24.08** 10.53 | 58.89 **27.47** 10.92 | 13.32 **7.06** 3.93 | 15.18 **7.40** 3.96 | 54 **35** 19 | 18.7 **8.5** 5.1 | 43.3 **16.7** 7.2 | 198.0 **87.9** 32.8 | 235.5 **107.0** 42.1 | 136.9 **77.8** 40.0 | 208.2 **116.0** 67.0 | 90.3 **42.6** 12.0 |
| **5141 Groceries, General Line** (874) | 3.50 **2.04** 1.40 | 2.75 **1.10** .41 | 26.01 **12.92** 5.73 | 35.65 **14.76** 5.43 | 21.68 **11.34** 6.16 | 27.70 **12.57** 6.76 | 27 **15** 8 | 18.5 **12.1** 8.1 | 71.3 **28.7** 10.5 | 183.5 **76.8** 33.0 | 245.1 **105.7** 41.9 | 165.7 **108.6** 72.0 | 135.7 **85.9** 47.3 | 109.0 **49.0** 16.1 |
| **5072 Hardware** (824) | 4.42 **2.52** 1.66 | 5.99 **3.21** 1.64 | 37.47 **18.70** 8.80 | 42.43 **18.44** 8.67 | 8.70 **5.15** 3.08 | 8.66 **5.31** 3.24 | 52 **38** 26 | 10.3 **6.2** 3.9 | 31.8 **16.0** 6.4 | 138.0 **60.0** 28.4 | 166.9 **75.1** 33.9 | 117.0 **80.8** 53.7 | 132.9 **81.3** 42.5 | 66.9 **27.9** 10.5 |
| **5084 Industrial Machinery and Equipment** (2,879) | 3.33 **1.95** 1.38 | 6.26 **3.27** 1.73 | 44.71 **23.34** 12.45 | 53.58 **26.92** 12.85 | 11.65 **6.63** 3.79 | 13.53 **7.21** 3.95 | 56 **40** 23 | 18.3 **8.6** 5.2 | 52.1 **22.8** 9.6 | 190.5 **89.0** 37.2 | 246.9 **108.1** 44.7 | 129.0 **75.6** 38.2 | 210.6 **120.2** 71.6 | 80.0 **33.9** 9.7 |
| **5031 Lumber Plywood and Mill Work** (1,359) | 3.33 **1.99** 1.39 | 4.76 **2.29** .99 | 34.75 **18.60** 9.69 | 45.63 **22.11** 9.59 | 14.16 **7.46** 4.20 | 17.15 **8.11** 4.57 | 50 **35** 23 | 20.7 **9.5** 5.8 | 47.6 **22.0** 9.0 | 193.3 **83.0** 35.7 | 242.6 **107.7** 46.8 | 130.9 **80.0** 43.9 | 215.6 **120.9** 68.9 | 72.9 **33.9** 12.5 |
| **5147 Meats and Meat Products** (456) | 3.30 **1.86** 1.21 | 3.33 **1.47** .50 | 38.13 **18.73** 10.03 | 53.99 **26.35** 9.17 | 29.08 **14.73** 7.55 | 35.28 **16.40** 7.08 | 28 **18** 10 | 61.6 **35.0** 20.9 | 94.1 **39.4** 17.8 | 205.5 **81.8** 33.4 | 257.6 **108.4** 45.1 | 96.1 **43.7** 18.4 | 331.8 **179.9** 92.9 | 109.1 **38.7** 10.3 |
| **5051 Metals Service Centers and Offices** (747) | 3.10 **1.80** 1.27 | 6.23 **2.91** 1.25 | 41.30 **19.08** 10.22 | 55.08 **23.04** 11.11 | 13.78 **6.30** 3.78 | 16.38 **7.35** 4.15 | 62 **45** 29 | 16.6 **7.7** 5.0 | 53.9 **25.4** 10.3 | 225.4 **98.8** 39.4 | 283.3 **121.2** 49.4 | 157.0 **88.2** 41.8 | 224.3 **128.1** 80.2 | 73.0 **32.8** 11.7 |
| **5198 Paints, Varnishes and Supplies** (274) | 4.56 **2.68** 1.58 | 7.02 **3.37** 1.51 | 46.55 **17.85** 6.27 | 35.97 **18.37** 5.24 | 10.39 **5.34** 3.36 | 9.87 **5.02** 3.24 | 48 **35** 25 | 10.5 **6.8** 4.8 | 49.6 **16.9** 7.2 | 152.0 **63.6** 25.5 | 189.9 **80.3** 37.2 | 106.0 **75.3** 46.9 | 138.5 **86.1** 46.3 | 75.8 **29.8** 12.1 |
| **5111 Printing and Writing Paper** (133) | 3.66 **2.32** 1.61 | 5.23 **2.53** 1.22 | 35.17 **20.41** 6.24 | 64.13 **23.50** 5.68 | 12.13 **5.76** 3.46 | 13.04 **6.94** 4.30 | 51 **40** 26 | 14.6 **9.8** 7.1 | 50.7 **24.5** 9.5 | 160.5 **59.2** 30.4 | 204.0 **80.8** 31.9 | 109.8 **77.2** 52.1 | 175.9 **114.1** 68.9 | 73.6 **37.8** 8.9 |
| **5171 Petroleum Bulk Stations & Terminals** (1,469) | 2.88 **1.76** 1.25 | 4.00 **1.91** .97 | 36.82 **18.85** 9.84 | 55.12 **29.11** 11.73 | 17.48 **8.84** 4.41 | 25.62 **12.14** 5.69 | 36 **23** 14 | 42.2 **23.3** 13.8 | 99.5 **58.1** 29.0 | 145.0 **67.4** 29.7 | 210.0 **99.3** 44.7 | 103.7 **55.4** 27.8 | 306.7 **171.8** 100.9 | 148.4 **64.1** 20.6 |
| **5133 Piece Goods** (776) | 3.22 **1.90** 1.36 | 3.64 **1.98** .93 | 29.59 **15.30** 8.37 | 31.56 **16.59** 8.06 | 12.47 **6.84** 3.46 | 13.81 **6.58** 3.52 | 68 **40** 16 | 13.4 **7.3** 4.3 | 16.7 **6.4** 2.0 | 240.1 **102.5** 42.9 | 254.4 **115.2** 47.8 | 149.8 **90.1** 50.9 | 212.0 **117.0** 69.0 | 50.1 **21.5** 6.0 |
| **5074 Plumbing & Hydronic Heating Supplies** (1,170) | 3.76 **2.35** 1.60 | 5.68 **3.06** 1.43 | 31.43 **17.18** 9.55 | 35.95 **18.10** 9.15 | 9.06 **5.28** 3.30 | 9.63 **5.63** 3.43 | 52 **39** 26 | 10.4 **6.4** 4.2 | 37.0 **16.9** 7.7 | 150.3 **66.7** 31.8 | 190.0 **87.9** 37.7 | 125.4 **85.4** 55.8 | 141.5 **87.7** 52.7 | 65.7 **30.6** 11.5 |
| **5144 Poultry & Poultry Products** (186) | 3.01 **1.63** 1.18 | 2.86 **1.07** .42 | 39.60 **17.64** 9.38 | 69.47 **25.26** 7.46 | 24.51 **12.80** 6.03 | 36.63 **16.47** 6.48 | 27 **19** 12 | 87.5 **45.0** 16.4 | 93.4 **46.0** 19.4 | 176.5 **82.8** 29.2 | 225.5 **99.1** 40.8 | 94.5 **44.6** 12.7 | 472.6 **239.0** 117.7 | 137.2 **55.4** 6.0 |
| **5093 Scrap & Waste Materials** (475) | 4.06 **1.99** 1.34 | 9.22 **4.17** 1.76 | 47.64 **23.06** 11.82 | 86.58 **31.65** 6.36 | 9.68 **4.95** 2.58 | 14.42 **6.73** 2.57 | 45 **26** 12 | 33.1 **13.8** 7.0 | 90.1 **45.8** 18.0 | 111.8 **49.9** 20.0 | 149.5 **68.0** 27.3 | 102.7 **56.1** 16.0 | 277.1 **145.5** 60.7 | 129.5 **45.1** 8.2 |
| **5014 Tires & Tubes** (501) | 2.65 **1.63** 1.29 | 5.20 **2.60** 1.13 | 34.61 **17.34** 8.02 | 46.34 **22.98** 9.40 | 11.93 **6.74** 4.00 | 13.32 **7.31** 4.34 | 49 **33** 21 | 9.3 **6.0** 4.3 | 56.8 **29.7** 12.5 | 244.3 **119.1** 56.4 | 291.0 **149.7** 69.2 | 201.6 **114.2** 75.1 | 156.4 **110.1** 67.1 | 88.7 **40.9** 11.5 |
| **5194 Tobacco & Tobacco Products** (313) | 3.97 **2.47** 1.67 | 1.91 **.95** .36 | 20.11 **11.70** 5.70 | 26.05 **13.20** 6.55 | 21.22 **12.46** 7.93 | 21.78 **12.58** 8.81 | 18 **13** °9 | 20.2 **13.8** 9.4 | 34.0 **15.0** 7.6 | 139.7 **65.7** 34.5 | 176.0 **86.3** 37.5 | 136.5 **94.0** 66.9 | 110.2 **70.7** 41.2 | 57.8 **26.0** 7.0 |

# MANUFACTURING

| Line of Business (and number of concerns reporting) | Current assets to current debt | Net profits on net sales | Net profits on tangible net worth | Net profits on net working capital | Net sales to tangible net worth | Net sales to net working capital | Collection period | Net sales to inventory | Fixed assets to tangible net worth | Current debt to tangible net worth | Total debt to tangible net worth | Inventory to net working capital | Current debt to inventory | Funded debts to net working capital |
|---|---|---|---|---|---|---|---|---|---|---|---|---|---|---|
| | Times | Per cent | Per cent | Per cent | Times | Times | Days | Times | Per cent | Per cent | Per cent | Per cent | Per cent | Per cent |
| **2873** **Agricultural Chemicals,** **Nitrogenous (56)** | 2.33<br>1.63<br>1.27 | 4.88<br>2.56<br>1.03 | 16.31<br>9.03<br>4.33 | 38.55<br>21.39<br>6.48 | 6.97<br>4.08<br>2.27 | 12.60<br>7.00<br>3.83 | 77<br>49<br>24 | 14.4<br>7.2<br>5.3 | 126.0<br>84.3<br>42.8 | 168.9<br>76.3<br>49.3 | 208.9<br>107.9<br>61.1 | 146.8<br>90.2<br>49.1 | 275.4<br>150.7<br>88.9 | 204.9<br>80.5<br>22.7 |
| **3563** **Air and Gas** **Compressors (35)** | 3.20<br>2.04<br>1.49 | 9.89<br>6.25<br>2.27 | 64.25<br>29.68<br>8.14 | 59.97<br>24.76<br>8.87 | 8.23<br>4.27<br>3.08 | 6.53<br>4.69<br>2.88 | 54<br>41<br>28 | 12.0<br>4.0<br>3.8 | 63.9<br>18.9<br>10.3 | 134.7<br>88.6<br>34.3 | 158.4<br>99.5<br>37.4 | 171.3<br>80.3<br>35.1 | 126.0<br>99.6<br>66.4 | 58.4<br>23.2<br>1.8 |
| **3724** **Airplane Parts** **& Accessories (35)** | 4.40<br>2.30<br>1.50 | 9.28<br>6.75<br>5.23 | 23.37<br>20.30<br>14.11 | 42.79<br>26.40<br>19.53 | 4.89<br>3.11<br>2.07 | 8.28<br>5.38<br>3.25 | 68<br>54<br>29 | 20.0<br>6.3<br>4.5 | 95.3<br>55.1<br>22.4 | 114.3<br>53.3<br>23.8 | 163.6<br>85.1<br>36.1 | 90.2<br>60.4<br>13.4 | 306.8<br>107.5<br>54.5 | 163.8<br>74.5<br>32.6 |
| **2051** **Bakery Products,** **Bread, Cake (134)** | 3.79<br>1.75<br>1.05 | 6.94<br>3.20<br>1.30 | 27.80<br>17.23<br>6.65 | 114.96<br>34.39<br>-5.43 | 9.43<br>6.42<br>3.77 | 23.17<br>12.12<br>5.71 | 28<br>20<br>11 | 59.9<br>35.2<br>21.2 | 150.5<br>90.1<br>49.1 | 113.5<br>43.2<br>13.6 | 208.5<br>71.5<br>25.4 | 66.6<br>36.0<br>6.8 | 484.3<br>250.9<br>126.8 | 185.1<br>83.9<br>1.5 |
| **3312** **Blast Furnaces and** **Steel Mills (99)** | 2.54<br>1.74<br>1.43 | 6.92<br>3.96<br>2.23 | 34.22<br>15.87<br>7.67 | 35.48<br>23.87<br>13.59 | 7.62<br>4.36<br>2.89 | 11.63<br>7.20<br>4.55 | 50<br>43<br>35 | 15.5<br>8.6<br>5.5 | 122.4<br>80.2<br>39.7 | 125.5<br>59.3<br>39.7 | 125.5<br>59.3<br>36.6 | 193.3<br>104.4<br>66.3 | 120.3<br>84.4<br>40.0 | 191.8<br>136.9<br>86.3 |
| **2331** **Blouses & Waists:** **Women's & Misses' (285)** | 2.78<br>1.75<br>1.30 | 4.63<br>2.37<br>.86 | 41.63<br>21.04<br>7.01 | 47.64<br>22.00<br>4.37 | 14.54<br>8.13<br>4.97 | 17.11<br>9.41<br>5.02 | 56<br>34<br>15 | 19.0<br>11.3<br>6.9 | 42.5<br>17.3<br>5.7 | 237.7<br>122.8<br>50.9 | 261.5<br>137.1<br>60.3 | 143.4<br>83.0<br>41.4 | 262.4<br>162.4<br>97.9 | 70.5<br>24.3<br>10.7 |
| **2731** **Book Publishing (270)** | 5.93<br>2.58<br>1.58 | 14.42<br>6.60<br>3.18 | 36.97<br>17.70<br>6.99 | 55.56<br>24.20<br>7.03 | 5.16<br>2.62<br>1.19 | 6.58<br>2.94<br>1.54 | 90<br>49<br>28 | 10.0<br>4.6<br>2.8 | 60.7<br>20.9<br>6.5 | 108.2<br>40.0<br>12.8 | 163.0<br>64.6<br>22.7 | 90.8<br>61.3<br>29.9 | 181.5<br>95.9<br>40.0 | 100.4<br>43.8<br>9.8 |
| **2211** **Broad Woven Fabrics,** **Cotton (111)** | 4.54<br>2.70<br>1.71 | 7.20<br>3.89<br>1.56 | 35.08<br>15.61<br>8.57 | 56.99<br>23.95<br>7.92 | 6.81<br>3.82<br>2.57 | 8.89<br>5.08<br>3.57 | 64<br>41<br>23 | 16.4<br>8.1<br>5.4 | 76.0<br>45.2<br>20.5 | 113.4<br>42.8<br>18.5 | 131.5<br>79.9<br>28.9 | 104.1<br>68.9<br>36.4 | 157.6<br>85.6<br>48.8 | 92.3<br>31.0<br>11.9 |
| **2033** **Canned Fruits &** **Vegetables (108)** | 2.90<br>1.64<br>1.20 | 5.21<br>3.13<br>.89 | 26.08<br>12.38<br>2.75 | 61.13<br>16.89<br>3.58 | 7.98<br>4.73<br>2.88 | 14.85<br>6.80<br>3.53 | 33<br>22<br>16 | 7.9<br>4.6<br>3.1 | 106.0<br>61.8<br>32.4 | 187.0<br>82.7<br>30.8 | 261.5<br>117.0<br>48.5 | 321.5<br>125.6<br>67.2 | 134.9<br>93.0<br>63.3 | 132.5<br>58.3<br>12.9 |
| **2812** **Chemicals: Alkalies** **and Chlorine (5)** | 2.17<br>1.62<br>1.31 | 5.04<br>1.80<br>.73 | 21.96<br>11.25<br>2.65 | 60.81<br>9.54<br>3.33 | 6.71<br>3.46<br>2.62 | 18.04<br>10.22<br>8.38 | 59<br>53<br>43 | 44.88<br>14.1<br>7.7 | 127.6<br>82.1<br>68.2 | 127.6<br>72.5<br>38.2 | 376.2<br>145.4<br>75.8 | 135.9<br>36.9<br>18.1 | 5593.9<br>237.2<br>152.8 | 697.3<br>273.7<br>113.9 |
| **2751** **Commercial Printing** **except Lithographic (1,277)** | 4.37<br>2.28<br>1.36 | 11.18<br>5.97<br>2.50 | 49.43<br>23.80<br>11.86 | 94.46<br>36.17<br>10.40 | 7.08<br>4.21<br>2.55 | 11.41<br>6.36<br>3.39 | 51<br>36<br>25 | 41.1<br>20.4<br>11.5 | 118.0<br>68.0<br>34.4 | 95.0<br>41.3<br>16.5 | 157.6<br>70.1<br>27.9 | 64.5<br>33.1<br>10.0 | 444.4<br>187.6<br>91.0 | 185.9<br>74.2<br>17.8 |
| **3271** **Concrete Block and** **Brick (149)** | 3.35<br>2.15<br>1.48 | 8.10<br>4.88<br>2.32 | 27.52<br>15.55<br>5.75 | 50.78<br>30.03<br>15.23 | 5.04<br>3.35<br>2.31 | 9.37<br>6.40<br>3.82 | 54<br>40<br>28 | 16.1<br>9.0<br>6.0 | 99.8<br>65.8<br>36.8 | 85.6<br>48.5<br>22.4 | 147.6<br>67.3<br>29.7 | 102.3<br>63.5<br>34.4 | 242.8<br>122.7<br>73.0 | 161.4<br>72.8<br>15.1 |
| **2065** **Confectionery** **Products (89)** | 7.27<br>2.79<br>1.53 | 8.33<br>5.75<br>2.87 | 41.65<br>17.84<br>12.00 | 63.91<br>36.12<br>10.57 | 7.71<br>4.16<br>2.70 | 11.75<br>7.01<br>4.36 | 28<br>18<br>8 | 15.4<br>9.9<br>6.6 | 78.4<br>56.9<br>27.1 | 86.2<br>31.9<br>12.2 | 135.9<br>38.4<br>18.3 | 112.1<br>68.4<br>36.4 | 137.5<br>70.8<br>34.8 | 110.8<br>47.5<br>12.5 |
| **3531** **Const., Min., & Handling** **Machy. & Equipt. (144)** | 3.15<br>1.95<br>1.33 | 8.33<br>4.71<br>2.31 | 37.14<br>20.37<br>11.14 | 50.38<br>22.20<br>11.57 | 8.04<br>4.07<br>2.68 | 8.67<br>4.23<br>2.47 | 59<br>43<br>29 | 10.0<br>5.7<br>3.1 | 68.1<br>39.6<br>18.2 | 172.8<br>71.1<br>34.1 | 233.2<br>104.1<br>48.3 | 141.1<br>86.4<br>41.3 | 158.1<br>100.8<br>62.7 | 78.6<br>42.1<br>11.3 |
| **2649** **Convtd. Paper & Paperboard** **Products (89)** | 3.78<br>2.38<br>1.56 | 6.30<br>3.64<br>1.61 | 41.83<br>20.09<br>11.47 | 61.32<br>25.25<br>13.86 | 7.00<br>5.12<br>2.70 | 10.55<br>5.62<br>3.25 | 48<br>36<br>29 | 17.0<br>11.0<br>4.4 | 84.5<br>47.0<br>19.9 | 99.2<br>41.5<br>21.3 | 152.7<br>76.6<br>25.2 | 86.5<br>51.7<br>22.7 | 246.8<br>114.3<br>62.2 | 113.3<br>57.6<br>8.8 |
| **3421** **Cutlery (18)** | 7.09<br>3.81<br>2.39 | 17.28<br>10.53<br>6.38 | 29.21<br>17.79<br>-5.60 | 22.82<br>15.22<br>1.31 | 3.55<br>2.45<br>1.82 | 4.14<br>2.64<br>2.06 | 78<br>50<br>15 | 5.6<br>4.1<br>2.4 | 62.5<br>12.0<br>6.1 | 58.8<br>34.9<br>16.4 | 70.2<br>43.3<br>20.2 | 104.4<br>85.9<br>34.2 | 101.3<br>68.6<br>28.1 | 86.6<br>57.6<br>36.2 |
| **2026** **Dairy Products: Milk,** **Fluid (109)** | 1.78<br>1.37<br>1.06 | 1.85<br>1.09<br>.34 | 17.95<br>12.12<br>5.95 | 62.16<br>25.46<br>2.90 | 14.20<br>9.35<br>6.67 | 54.17<br>20.57<br>9.57 | 31<br>26<br>21 | 51.9<br>31.9<br>21.3 | 104.6<br>73.0<br>45.7 | 153.4<br>82.1<br>54.0 | 187.8<br>107.0<br>68.8 | 127.0<br>60.0<br>14.8 | 560.3<br>298.1<br>202.1 | 185.5<br>63.8<br>8.1 |
| **2335** **Dresses: Women's,** **Misses' & Juniors' (497)** | 2.78<br>1.71<br>1.31 | 4.75<br>2.27<br>.72 | 40.40<br>21.79<br>7.20 | 48.45<br>21.89<br>7.53 | 14.68<br>8.34<br>4.54 | 17.05<br>9.67<br>4.92 | 62<br>41<br>14 | 20.4<br>11.5<br>6.7 | 38.1<br>16.3<br>5.2 | 211.7<br>100.2<br>38.6 | 235.6<br>119.8<br>46.4 | 131.1<br>76.9<br>37.3 | 261.0<br>161.1<br>89.4 | 61.6<br>29.9<br>5.9 |
| **3641** **Electric Lamps (33)** | 6.80<br>3.58<br>2.06 | 6.04<br>3.63<br>1.74 | 25.64<br>16.13<br>6.79 | 26.62<br>15.46<br>3.19 | 8.67<br>5.11<br>2.57 | 6.15<br>4.22<br>3.23 | 53<br>42<br>27 | 11.7<br>6.4<br>4.4 | 73.5<br>30.3<br>14.4 | 102.7<br>40.0<br>17.2 | 205.8<br>61.3<br>17.3 | 97.2<br>64.6<br>36.0 | 141.6<br>60.3<br>27.5 | 89.8<br>54.6<br>14.4 |
| **3612** **Electric Transformers (77)** | 4.28<br>2.59<br>1.64 | 6.61<br>4.80<br>1.95 | 41.49<br>17.69<br>11.42 | 38.92<br>21.76<br>11.42 | 7.61<br>4.23<br>2.73 | 7.08<br>4.65<br>3.23 | 71<br>57<br>37 | 11.5<br>6.6<br>4.2 | 81.7<br>32.2<br>16.9 | 116.6<br>54.9<br>27.5 | 183.3<br>76.6<br>36.5 | 101.0<br>65.0<br>48.4 | 146.4<br>88.5<br>45.9 | 84.4<br>34.9<br>8.4 |
| **1731** **Electrical Work (4,585)** | 4.62<br>2.30<br>1.50 | 11.47<br>5.67<br>2.46 | 60.01<br>30.66<br>13.32 | 84.00<br>37.29<br>13.41 | 8.85<br>5.37<br>3.15 | 11.52<br>6.46<br>3.55 | 68<br>45<br>27 | 52.1<br>22.3<br>10.1 | 60.6<br>32.1<br>16.2 | 125.8<br>56.0<br>21.0 | 162.1<br>74.0<br>28.6 | 61.3<br>29.0<br>10.8 | 548.5<br>216.6<br>86.8 | 90.3<br>37.3<br>11.0 |
| **3811** **Engineering & Scientific** **Instruments (152)** | 4.98<br>2.74<br>1.80 | 8.70<br>5.70<br>3.04 | 30.99<br>20.92<br>10.85 | 49.79<br>23.54<br>9.64 | 5.31<br>3.50<br>2.12 | 5.75<br>3.61<br>2.44 | 84<br>55<br>39 | 8.7<br>5.3<br>3.4 | 56.1<br>32.1<br>13.5 | 109.1<br>49.8<br>20.4 | 159.4<br>76.3<br>23.6 | 90.9<br>65.4<br>38.4 | 135.1<br>87.2<br>43.2 | 69.6<br>43.3<br>17.5 |

# MANUFACTURING

| Line of Business (and number of concerns reporting) | Current assets to current debt | Net profits on net sales | Net profits on tangible net worth | Net profits on net working capital | Net sales to tangible net worth | Net sales to net working capital | Collection period | Net sales to inventory | Fixed assets to tangible net worth | Current debt to tangible net worth | Total debt to tangible net worth | Inventory to net working capital | Current debt to inventory | Funded debts to net working capital |
|---|---|---|---|---|---|---|---|---|---|---|---|---|---|---|
| | Times | Per cent | Per cent | Per cent | Times | Times | Days | Times | Per cent | Per cent | Per cent | Per cent | Per cent | Per cent |
| **3441** **Fabricated Structural** **Met. (533)** | 2.92 / 1.85 / 1.38 | 7.06 / 3.87 / 1.78 | 37.13 / 19.51 / 8.40 | 60.36 / 28.76 / 11.59 | 8.30 / 5.19 / 3.30 | 12.41 / 6.89 / 4.06 | 67 / 48 / 33 | 25.1 / 12.9 / 6.7 | 82.1 / 44.4 / 22.1 | 146.9 / 80.1 / 38.2 | 195.5 / 106.5 / 52.0 | 105.1 / 58.8 / 26.5 | 345.3 / 177.2 / 96.9 | 94.8 / 38.4 / 12.2 |
| **3523** **Farm Machinery &** **Equipment (401)** | 3.66 / 2.05 / 1.34 | 7.96 / 4.57 / 2.47 | 36.58 / 20.98 / 9.67 | 45.69 / 24.73 / 9.13 | 7.48 / 4.37 / 2.86 | 8.53 / 4.86 / 2.85 | 52 / 34 / 18 | 8.2 / 4.9 / 3.1 | 93.2 / 48.8 / 22.6 | 180.0 / 76.9 / 30.7 | 261.6 / 114.8 / 44.4 | 154.3 / 97.8 / 58.4 | 133.3 / 85.4 / 46.0 | 107.6 / 60.4 / 20.8 |
| **3143** **Footwear: Men's Except** **Athletic (58)** | 3.09 / 2.39 / 1.86 | 5.48 / 3.27 / 1.76 | 22.45 / 13.26 / 5.92 | 22.76 / 13.88 / 5.06 | 7.91 / 4.47 / 3.29 | 7.37 / 4.40 / 3.41 | 65 / 44 / 24 | 6.1 / 4.8 / 3.4 | 48.1 / 27.7 / 18.5 | 147.3 / 62.3 / 35.8 | 228.7 / 84.7 / 47.9 | 134.8 / 99.9 / 75.6 | 100.3 / 70.7 / 53.9 | 71.3 / 35.6 / 15.2 |
| **3144** **Footwear: Women's Except** **Athletic (36)** | 3.24 / 2.23 / 1.62 | 6.23 / 3.71 / 2.33 | 40.36 / 17.53 / 11.19 | 45.29 / 21.92 / 13.59 | 6.55 / 4.21 / 2.80 | 7.09 / 4.88 / 3.02 | 59 / 52 / 33 | 12.4 / 6.6 / 4.6 | 30.0 / 14.9 / 7.9 | 141.1 / 62.5 / 35.7 | 168.1 / 68.7 / 35.7 | 112.2 / 72.1 / 40.6 | 165.8 / 111.5 / 73.5 | 24.4 / 12.8 / 1.2 |
| **3361** **Foundries: Aluminum** **(133)** | 4.18 / 2.15 / 1.39 | 7.86 / 5.01 / 3.05 | 34.62 / 21.89 / 13.68 | 58.93 / 31.92 / 19.59 | 6.95 / 4.55 / 3.26 | 12.09 / 7.15 / 4.45 | 56 / 43 / 30 | 28.1 / 18.2 / 9.2 | 95.7 / 55.6 / 24.6 | 113.5 / 51.8 / 21.6 | 156.7 / 77.7 / 26.8 | 84.6 / 49.0 / 20.3 | 373.3 / 178.7 / 84.8 | 148.6 / 60.6 / 12.7 |
| **3362** **Foundries: Brass, Bronze** **and Copper (77)** | 4.36 / 2.34 / 1.52 | 9.21 / 5.39 / 2.36 | 34.34 / 15.96 / 10.79 | 49.09 / 29.10 / 9.99 | 5.68 / 3.50 / 2.40 | 11.11 / 6.22 / 3.36 | 59 / 44 / 35 | 28.4 / 13.9 / 7.4 | 74.4 / 45.5 / 24.6 | 74.4 / 38.6 / 13.3 | 134.7 / 49.8 / 16.2 | 89.2 / 41.5 / 19.7 | 305.4 / 144.6 / 89.6 | 122.3 / 48.3 / 15.2 |
| **3321** **Foundries: Gray Iron** **(136)** | 3.76 / 2.46 / 1.63 | 8.20 / 5.49 / 3.11 | 25.63 / 16.26 / 10.87 | 65.92 / 35.80 / 17.23 | 4.86 / 3.45 / 2.28 | 10.79 / 6.67 / 4.04 | 52 / 43 / 33 | 35.9 / 19.6 / 11.1 | 90.5 / 59.4 / 35.7 | 55.7 / 31.5 / 17.1 | 100.7 / 47.1 / 20.7 | 69.7 / 33.9 / 15.1 | 353.6 / 187.9 / 100.2 | 123.0 / 41.0 / 8.7 |
| **2041** **Grain Mill Products:** **Flour (65)** | 3.34 / 1.88 / 1.35 | 3.30 / 2.29 / .93 | 18.51 / 10.46 / 4.59 | 23.52 / 16.56 / 2.21 | 7.17 / 5.60 / 3.55 | 13.21 / 7.95 / 4.35 | 44 / 28 / 15 | 18.5 / 10.8 / 6.4 | 103.9 / 70.4 / 40.7 | 109.6 / 67.2 / 28.7 | 158.6 / 95.7 / 37.9 | 166.0 / 92.6 / 47.5 | 163.5 / 110.1 / 57.7 | 141.0 / 82.0 / 32.8 |
| **2251** **Hosiery: Women's (33)** | 4.16 / 2.16 / 1.42 | 8.26 / 3.01 / .86 | 33.58 / 7.52 / 2.99 | 54.21 / 8.59 / 3.00 | 10.26 / 5.55 / 2.71 | 12.07 / 7.38 / 3.04 | 51 / 37 / 26 | 18.8 / 9.4 / 6.4 | 69.6 / 28.0 / 11.7 | 101.9 / 48.9 / 19.8 | 101.9 / 57.7 / 23.6 | 150.7 / 81.9 / 33.0 | 265.9 / 96.0 / 63.2 | 96.2 / 70.7 / 6.3 |
| **3632** **Household Appliances (5)** | 3.71 / 1.57 / 1.30 | 2.94 / 1.39 / -3.09 | 33.36 / 13.84 / -16.56 | 26.29 / 14.07 / -91.52 | 20.08 / 10.60 / 5.42 | 22.96 / 17.01 / 7.34 | 42 / 24 / 17 | 35.9 / 12.5 / 4.8 | 237.6 / 131.5 / 95.8 | 336.4 / 74.2 / 41.7 | 466.7 / 360.7 / 122.9 | 270.5 / 135.7 / 61.3 | 142.2 / 128.1 / 92.3 | 259.2 / 137.1 / 78.9 |
| **3634** **Housewares and Fans:** **Electric (46)** | 4.16 / 2.58 / 1.72 | 8.65 / 4.18 / 1.89 | 35.92 / 16.80 / 8.45 | 35.29 / 19.75 / 5.61 | 8.54 / 3.92 / 2.70 | 8.36 / 4.03 / 2.80 | 67 / 41 / 29 | 8.1 / 5.9 / 4.0 | 82.1 / 35.0 / 12.1 | 160.5 / 55.8 / 40.4 | 274.8 / 98.8 / 45.4 | 118.5 / 83.0 / 41.6 | 134.7 / 89.8 / 62.7 | 77.5 / 40.8 / 17.7 |
| **1623** **Heavy Const: Water,** **Sewer, Utility (1,195)** | 2.66 / 1.62 / 1.17 | 12.58 / 6.32 / 2.94 | 52.89 / 30.29 / 14.48 | 100.54 / 49.50 / 13.49 | 7.54 / 4.73 / 2.77 | 15.09 / 7.05 / 3.11 | 82 / 52 / 30 | 185.5 / 60.6 / 25.1 | 112.6 / 73.1 / 41.2 | 131.3 / 69.0 / 29.3 | 188.4 / 98.6 / 41.6 | 38.4 / 10.5 / 2.9 | 2461.5 / 858.4 / 319.4 | 120.4 / 46.2 / 9.5 |
| **1541** **Industrial Buildings and** **Warehouses (1,563)** | 2.41 / 1.55 / 1.24 | 6.67 / 3.11 / 1.46 | 50.00 / 24.72 / 12.42 | 66.27 / 32.75 / 13.06 | 13.90 / 8.12 / 4.37 | 18.87 / 10.42 / 4.92 | 70 / 44 / 23 | 290.1 / 98.8 / 26.9 | 61.5 / 29.0 / 13.6 | 220.4 / 109.5 / 43.3 | 254.3 / 132.7 / 56.0 | 35.7 / 9.2 / 2.1 | 4733.6 / 1196.8 / 292.7 | 78.9 / 30.0 / 8.1 |
| **2813** **Industrial Gas (23)** | 3.48 / 2.11 / 1.34 | 12.04 / 7.93 / 5.58 | 24.55 / 15.72 / 12.19 | 87.70 / 44.97 / 17.45 | 2.20 / 1.90 / 1.59 | 8.87 / 6.37 / 3.25 | 67 / 45 / 25 | 46.5 / 16.2 / 8.8 | 135.1 / 66.4 / 36.3 | 44.2 / 23.7 / 10.5 | 83.9 / 35.3 / 13.6 | 66.6 / 36.3 / 2.6 | 795.5 / 261.6 / 107.2 | 145.9 / 44.7 / 1.3 |
| **2253** **Knit Outerwear** **Mills (180)** | 2.92 / 1.82 / 1.35 | 4.34 / 1.82 / .57 | 31.28 / 13.55 / 5.42 | 41.29 / 11.62 / -1.70 | 11.84 / 6.31 / 3.67 | 12.78 / 7.32 / 3.88 | 53 / 30 / 16 | 22.1 / 10.8 / 5.3 | 88.5 / 30.4 / 6.2 | 199.2 / 82.0 / 29.5 | 233.2 / 105.4 / 38.3 | 130.2 / 77.4 / 38.3 | 231.0 / 124.7 / 79.9 | 86.3 / 30.9 / 9.4 |
| **3561** **Machinery, Except Electrical:** **Pumps and Equipment (80)** | 4.28 / 2.98 / 1.87 | 9.46 / 5.98 / 3.00 | 30.56 / 18.91 / 9.12 | 35.93 / 25.49 / 12.80 | 5.63 / 2.77 / 2.15 | 8.18 / 4.00 / 2.79 | 59 / 47 / 29 | 9.1 / 6.6 / 3.8 | 63.4 / 39.2 / 15.2 | 96.7 / 42.4 / 24.2 | 131.7 / 65.7 / 30.4 | 111.2 / 69.0 / 36.7 | 121.7 / 81.2 / 42.2 | 66.6 / 29.4 / 14.1 |
| **2082** **Malt Liquors (12)** | 2.32 / 1.63 / 1.14 | 5.47 / 1.34 / .22 | 21.56 / 9.40 / 1.50 | 52.82 / 10.57 / -19.21 | 7.21 / 5.62 / 2.99 | 25.13 / 9.93 / 3.19 | 24 / 14 / 11 | 16.8 / 13.6 / 10.3 | 114.3 / 95.4 / 79.2 | 96.5 / 51.2 / 33.7 | 141.7 / 89.4 / 60.4 | 180.1 / 76.6 / 35.9 | 196.1 / 136.1 / 111.0 | 237.3 / 74.9 / 2.8 |
| **2515** **Mattresses &** **Bedsprings (135)** | 4.11 / 2.44 / 1.64 | 6.91 / 3.54 / 1.08 | 36.86 / 12.66 / 4.81 | 60.56 / 17.97 / 6.23 | 9.13 / 5.43 / 2.73 | 10.89 / 6.66 / 3.98 | 42 / 28 / 15 | 14.4 / 9.3 / 6.5 | 79.3 / 34.4 / 17.4 | 110.9 / 53.5 / 18.4 | 162.8 / 71.2 / 24.0 | 112.4 / 70.3 / 39.6 | 140.4 / 90.7 / 45.9 | 120.3 / 50.9 / 11.7 |
| **2011** **Meat Packing** **Plants (234)** | 3.91 / 1.79 / 1.25 | 2.61 / 1.04 / .43 | 26.95 / 13.75 / 4.39 | 59.46 / 24.08 / 6.02 | 21.07 / 11.06 / 5.96 | 34.79 / 18.73 / 10.52 | 19 / 14 / 9 | 55.1 / 32.9 / 18.1 | 125.0 / 67.0 / 41.4 | 127.9 / 58.6 / 20.6 | 211.8 / 92.2 / 32.2 | 98.5 / 58.5 / 22.2 | 291.3 / 155.5 / 74.7 | 195.2 / 83.2 / 16.7 |
| **3465** **Metal Stampings (91)** | 3.07 / 1.91 / 1.15 | 4.72 / 3.43 / 1.65 | 30.94 / 16.08 / 6.79 | 42.00 / 24.39 / 11.40 | 7.84 / 4.51 / 3.23 | 9.77 / 6.92 / 3.41 | 47 / 37 / 25 | 15.4 / 8.7 / 6.7 | 92.3 / 59.9 / 26.4 | 142.6 / 56.0 / 21.6 | 156.1 / 79.1 / 23.4 | 122.8 / 79.4 / 32.8 | 229.5 / 133.8 / 83.4 | 80.8 / 47.4 / 4.4 |
| **2431** **Millwork (429)** | 3.93 / 2.25 / 1.48 | 8.45 / 4.35 / 2.32 | 42.59 / 23.40 / 12.59 | 64.44 / 30.63 / 13.13 | 8.38 / 4.90 / 2.93 | 10.73 / 6.11 / 3.94 | 52 / 36 / 25 | 16.4 / 9.0 / 6.0 | 72.0 / 42.2 / 20.3 | 121.4 / 54.7 / 21.6 | 178.1 / 77.2 / 29.2 | 109.3 / 70.9 / 35.2 | 193.1 / 114.9 / 56.9 | 113.9 / 47.4 / 10.3 |
| **3714** **Motor Vehicle Parts** **& Accessories (335)** | 3.61 / 2.21 / 1.47 | 8.71 / 4.94 / 2.48 | 43.69 / 24.03 / 12.78 | 56.58 / 30.45 / 12.60 | 6.25 / 4.09 / 2.88 | 8.97 / 5.30 / 3.12 | 53 / 39 / 25 | 13.4 / 7.4 / 4.8 | 77.8 / 45.7 / 23.9 | 98.7 / 52.7 / 28.6 | 143.2 / 76.8 / 33.3 | 119.4 / 79.8 / 43.9 | 186.6 / 103.0 / 61.8 | 79.6 / 45.8 / 13.7 |

147

# MANUFACTURING

| Line of Business (and number of concerns reporting) | Current assets to current debt (Times) | Net profits on net sales (Per cent) | Net profits on tangible net worth (Per cent) | Net profits on net working capital (Per cent) | Net sales to tangible net worth (Times) | Net sales to net working capital (Times) | Collection period (Days) | Net sales to inventory (Times) | Fixed assets to tangible net worth (Per cent) | Current debt to tangible net worth (Per cent) | Total debt to tangible net worth (Per cent) | Inventory to net working capital (Per cent) | Current debt to inventory (Per cent) | Funded debts to net working capital (Per cent) |
|---|---|---|---|---|---|---|---|---|---|---|---|---|---|---|
| **3573 Office, Computing & Accounting Machines** (276) | 3.13 / 1.98 / 1.51 | 10.50 / 6.24 / 2.62 | 40.67 / 21.38 / 11.73 | 58.10 / 26.52 / 10.41 | 6.73 / 3.50 / 2.16 | 7.73 / 4.23 / 2.58 | 89 / 64 / 38 | 10.1 / 5.0 / 3.3 | 64.0 / 31.7 / 16.0 | 146.6 / 68.5 / 31.4 | 206.4 / 106.4 / 44.1 | 119.1 / 75.1 / 43.2 | 180.1 / 118.9 / 72.2 | 94.2 / 50.3 / 18.9 |
| **2363 Outerwear: Children's & Infants'** (23) | 2.74 / 1.74 / 1.43 | 10.37 / 2.84 / 2.00 | 36.48 / 20.06 / 12.28 | 69.24 / 21.68 / 10.97 | 8.78 / 6.65 / 4.22 | 10.73 / 7.71 / 3.92 | 58 / 43 / 18 | 18.9 / 8.0 / 5.4 | 25.4 / 11.8 / 5.5 | 196.1 / 70.0 / 46.7 | 238.5 / 87.0 / 47.5 | 122.9 / 75.8 / 35.4 | 277.6 / 148.2 / 62.0 | 67.5 / 26.5 / 16.9 |
| **2851 Paints and Allied Products** (236) | 3.74 / 2.42 / 1.65 | 5.83 / 3.57 / 2.13 | 26.38 / 15.13 / 9.61 | 45.93 / 21.36 / 12.50 | 7.07 / 4.53 / 3.04 | 8.67 / 5.64 / 3.69 | 54 / 43 / 33 | 10.9 / 7.5 / 5.3 | 62.0 / 35.3 / 20.0 | 101.1 / 53.4 / 29.6 | 147.3 / 79.2 / 34.9 | 106.9 / 75.4 / 48.6 | 143.3 / 93.5 / 60.5 | 74.2 / 36.8 / 15.0 |
| **2621 Paper Mills, except. Building Paper** (49) | 2.93 / 1.97 / 1.52 | 9.57 / 6.34 / 3.10 | 24.64 / 17.10 / 12.40 | 78.50 / 37.96 / 19.74 | 6.43 / 3.62 / 2.15 | 10.57 / 6.62 / 4.47 | 50 / 34 / 26 | 11.9 / 9.7 / 6.2 | 139.7 / 91.0 / 53.7 | 72.9 / 38.9 / 27.0 | 155.5 / 100.2 / 61.0 | 99.3 / 73.5 / 49.7 | 158.3 / 113.9 / 63.6 | 181.6 / 94.6 / 51.5 |
| **2651 Paperboard Boxes: Folding** (82) | 3.01 / 2.11 / 1.36 | 5.16 / 3.03 / 2.03 | 30.78 / 17.06 / 9.77 | 43.97 / 22.40 / 11.82 | 7.57 / 5.03 / 3.17 | 9.28 / 5.92 / 4.22 | 46 / 39 / 29 | 14.15 / 8.5 / 6.0 | 112.0 / 68.5 / 43.2 | 106.0 / 59.4 / 34.2 | 190.8 / 107.3 / 36.1 | 118.3 / 91.2 / 36.0 | 207.6 / 115.3 / 73.2 | 144.4 / 70.6 / 30.1 |
| **3713 Parts and Accessories: Truck and Bus Bodies** (120) | 3.60 / 2.32 / 1.46 | 7.28 / 4.83 / 2.91 | 46.15 / 24.79 / 13.04 | 57.28 / 32.31 / 16.94 | 8.05 / 5.04 / 3.13 | 10.90 / 5.64 / 3.63 | 46 / 30 / 20 | 9.7 / 5.9 / 4.2 | 64.1 / 31.5 / 17.9 | 140.8 / 56.5 / 26.7 | 198.3 / 93.6 / 36.5 | 146.1 / 87.8 / 58.1 | 144.5 / 84.6 / 51.1 | 119.5 / 60.7 / 17.7 |
| **2911 Petroleum Refining** (74) | 1.85 / 1.36 / 1.14 | 6.73 / 4.32 / 2.12 | 49.49 / 26.34 / 18.87 | 104.19 / 50.59 / 17.91 | 11.74 / 5.95 / 4.26 | 23.46 / 11.18 / 5.40 | 59 / 39 / 27 | 21.7 / 15.2 / 8.0 | 153.9 / 98.4 / 56.3 | 188.2 / 94.5 / 61.1 | 288.0 / 156.8 / 82.5 | 149.7 / 46.9 / 18.5 | 440.0 / 266.4 / 160.5 | 206.0 / 61.2 / 17.8 |
| **2821 Plastics Materials & Resins** (99) | 2.84 / 1.98 / 1.37 | 6.46 / 4.31 / 2.46 | 37.26 / 19.68 / 14.51 | 63.35 / 29.22 / 18.61 | 8.14 / 4.76 / 3.10 | 11.94 / 6.76 / 3.71 | 62 / 50 / 33 | 14.9 / 10.0 / 6.9 | 83.6 / 48.1 / 23.3 | 129.4 / 68.0 / 28.0 | 189.8 / 84.7 / 36.6 | 102.4 / 67.5 / 26.6 | 249.5 / 138.7 / 99.1 | 118.1 / 42.6 / 15.6 |
| **1711 Plumbing, Heating & Air Conditioning** (6,581) | 3.90 / 2.07 / 1.38 | 10.18 / 4.62 / 2.05 | 54.23 / 27.09 / 11.78 | 83.62 / 36.33 / 12.55 | 10.01 / 5.81 / 3.26 | 13.25 / 7.34 / 3.97 | 62 / 41 / 24 | 51.5 / 22.5 / 10.6 | 68.4 / 35.2 / 17.1 | 143.8 / 61.1 / 21.4 | 184.8 / 80.9 / 30.3 | 68.0 / 32.4 / 11.1 | 552.0 / 218.7 / 99.6 | 96.7 / 36.0 / 10.0 |
| **2421 Sawmills & Planing Mills** (458) | 3.99 / 1.91 / 1.14 | 10.92 / 6.49 / 3.17 | 36.86 / 20.81 / 11.23 | 61.56 / 29.83 / 4.92 | 5.99 / 3.60 / 2.01 | 10.96 / 5.00 / 2.34 | 34 / 20 / 12 | 17.0 / 9.8 / 5.6 | 116.1 / 74.0 / 35.5 | 92.3 / 46.3 / 18.9 | 172.3 / 76.3 / 30.6 | 107.6 / 59.5 / 20.6 | 245.9 / 114.3 / 54.5 | 181.3 / 60.2 / 8.9 |
| **3451 Screw Machine Products** (275) | 4.56 / 2.34 / 1.50 | 9.38 / 6.79 / 3.41 | 36.12 / 24.92 / 15.24 | 86.66 / 42.58 / 22.12 | 6.30 / 3.72 / 2.32 | 10.42 / 5.72 / 3.75 | 54 / 41 / 31 | 30.6 / 14.0 / 7.5 | 106.2 / 66.6 / 37.8 | 91.8 / 42.4 / 17.4 | 163.1 / 59.5 / 23.5 | 79.4 / 48.3 / 17.1 | 299.2 / 153.8 / 83.7 | 152.1 / 59.6 / 14.3 |
| **2321 Shirts & Nightwear: Men's & Boys'** (156) | 3.27 / 1.88 / 1.43 | 4.94 / 2.40 / 1.07 | 34.80 / 15.95 / 6.02 | 39.01 / 17.63 / 6.02 | 12.05 / 6.72 / 3.50 | 12.31 / 6.35 / 3.74 | 57 / 34 / 15 | 14.3 / 7.1 / 4.6 | 49.4 / 19.6 / 7.6 | 229.0 / 96.5 / 36.5 | 308.3 / 138.0 / 62.2 | 142.6 / 90.4 / 44.6 | 174.4 / 109.6 / 70.0 | 88.1 / 37.4 / 6.8 |
| **2311 Suits and Coats: Men's and Boys** (135) | 3.45 / 2.03 / 1.39 | 5.05 / 2.43 / 1.36 | 28.87 / 12.67 / 4.11 | 43.60 / 14.99 / 4.27 | 8.49 / 4.87 / 2.94 | 9.06 / 5.26 / 3.18 | 71 / 40 / 18 | 10.4 / 5.6 / 3.8 | 39.6 / 16.5 / 5.0 | 203.8 / 73.1 / 33.1 | 223.7 / 90.3 / 42.9 | 131.8 / 89.8 / 56.0 | 165.6 / 95.0 / 57.9 | 61.2 / 23.7 / 4.8 |
| **2841 Soap and Other Detergents** (55) | 3.89 / 2.40 / 1.75 | 8.16 / 5.78 / 2.44 | 41.10 / 28.16 / 14.88 | 49.15 / 28.16 / 14.67 | 6.80 / 4.03 / 3.08 | 8.92 / 5.81 / 4.52 | 49 / 39 / 30 | 14.5 / 8.9 / 7.1 | 58.5 / 28.8 / 16.5 | 88.3 / 43.6 / 28.8 | 129.8 / 59.4 / 31.1 | 88.5 / 73.3 / 35.8 | 177.5 / 101.7 / 70.7 | 56.7 / 30.1 / 9.9 |
| **2086 Soft Drinks: Bottled & Canned** (162) | 4.04 / 2.33 / 1.36 | 7.54 / 4.30 / 1.81 | 29.34 / 17.31 / 10.25 | 98.06 / 38.50 / 12.26 | 7.39 / 4.55 / 2.84 | 15.64 / 8.39 / 5.62 | 27 / 21 / 13 | 23.0 / 15.3 / 11.8 | 117.5 / 72.8 / 45.4 | 71.3 / 33.3 / 12.5 | 134.8 / 53.5 / 18.1 | 101.6 / 60.9 / 35.2 | 214.1 / 126.3 / 65.9 | 206.8 / 69.5 / 8.9 |
| **3552 Textile Machinery** (85) | 3.18 / 2.06 / 1.52 | 6.59 / 4.84 / .98 | 28.03 / 15.06 / 3.54 | 43.83 / 26.15 / 9.93 | 6.54 / 3.37 / 2.42 | 10.94 / 5.53 / 3.25 | 59 / 40 / 29 | 19.8 / 10.3 / 5.4 | 74.4 / 40.8 / 24.0 | 110.5 / 54.0 / 27.5 | 132.3 / 70.3 / 33.5 | 112.8 / 69.7 / 29.9 | 242.4 / 135.0 / 79.6 | 114.4 / 43.5 / 14.2 |
| **2341 Women's & Children's Underwear** (130) | 2.72 / 1.71 / 1.38 | 4.29 / 1.75 / .76 | 23.74 / 13.43 / 3.21 | 26.80 / 15.52 / 5.76 | 11.64 / 6.97 / 4.12 | 13.48 / 7.54 / 4.52 | 60 / 45 / 26 | 14.6 / 7.4 / 5.1 | 37.3 / 18.0 / 5.6 | 202.6 / 112.6 / 47.0 | 224.9 / 120.5 / 53.8 | 168.6 / 96.4 / 49.3 | 183.6 / 130.2 / 88.0 | 64.5 / 23.3 / 7.7 |
| **2337 Women's & Misses' Suits & Coats** (232) | 2.79 / 1.72 / 1.34 | 4.64 / 2.22 / .87 | 37.56 / 16.97 / 9.01 | 42.25 / 18.69 / 7.80 | 13.95 / 8.68 / 4.80 | 16.33 / 8.52 / 5.01 | 62 / 40 / 19 | 14.9 / 7.9 / 5.5 | 36.4 / 14.2 / 4.8 | 234.5 / 122.0 / 49.3 | 256.1 / 137.3 / 60.4 | 143.1 / 93.3 / 50.7 | 223.5 / 127.1 / 80.5 | 68.4 / 33.7 / 11.3 |
| **3949 Sporting and Athletic Goods** (288) | 4.77 / 2.36 / 1.46 | 10.26 / 4.59 / 1.83 | 41.52 / 20.02 / 7.28 | 64.81 / 19.70 / 2.45 | 7.17 / 4.04 / 2.42 | 7.39 / 4.39 / 2.36 | 62 / 40 / 20 | 10.7 / 5.7 / 3.5 | 72.8 / 36.2 / 14.1 | 136.8 / 50.9 / 16.2 | 190.0 / 82.1 / 23.1 | 111.2 / 72.8 / 38.0 | 166.8 / 90.0 / 36.0 | 96.5 / 44.8 / 13.5 |
| **2327 Trousers: Men's & Boys'** (92) | 3.12 / 2.00 / 1.47 | 5.50 / 1.69 / .97 | 29.59 / 13.03 / 5.64 | 29.35 / 8.22 / 2.87 | 10.94 / 5.45 / 3.30 | 11.70 / 5.56 / 3.64 | 59 / 41 / 17 | 18.9 / 5.9 / 4.4 | 45.8 / 19.0 / 7.1 | 141.7 / 81.0 / 28.3 | 200.2 / 89.6 / 37.9 | 126.5 / 80.5 / 47.3 | 162.5 / 96.6 / 59.6 | 59.5 / 31.9 / 7.0 |
| **2511 Wood Household Furniture** (364) | 5.12 / 2.52 / 1.48 | 11.42 / 5.45 / 2.64 | 58.25 / 22.60 / 9.70 | 86.59 / 30.89 / 10.69 | 8.39 / 4.68 / 2.47 | 11.82 / 6.29 / 3.49 | 51 / 31 / 14 | 16.1 / 8.5 / 4.7 | 72.7 / 41.2 / 18.8 | 91.5 / 34.6 / 16.0 | 139.8 / 64.5 / 23.8 | 109.4 / 71.0 / 35.6 | 134.0 / 78.7 / 40.0 | 118.0 / 36.8 / 10.2 |
| **2328 Work Clothing: Men's & Boys'** (60) | 3.16 / 1.96 / 1.35 | 4.44 / 2.59 / .74 | 22.17 / 11.93 / 5.14 | 42.51 / 12.84 / 6.67 | 7.57 / 4.38 / 2.93 | 11.50 / 5.21 / 3.20 | 61 / 40 / 24 | 9.2 / 5.1 / 3.8 | 60.1 / 23.7 / 12.4 | 226.6 / 77.5 / 35.2 | 270.9 / 109.3 / 48.4 | 189.9 / 94.5 / 53.1 | 138.1 / 100.0 / 60.2 | 62.4 / 35.4 / 6.4 |

# APPENDIX C.   HOW TO USE THE LIBRARY FOR CASE ANALYSIS

In case analysis students may be required to look up data on economics and industries. This appendix contains most of the common sources of such data. In order to find information in the library one should start with a strategy for researching library information. Figure 1 presents such a strategy.

Figure 1.   STRATEGY FOR LIBRARY INFORMATION

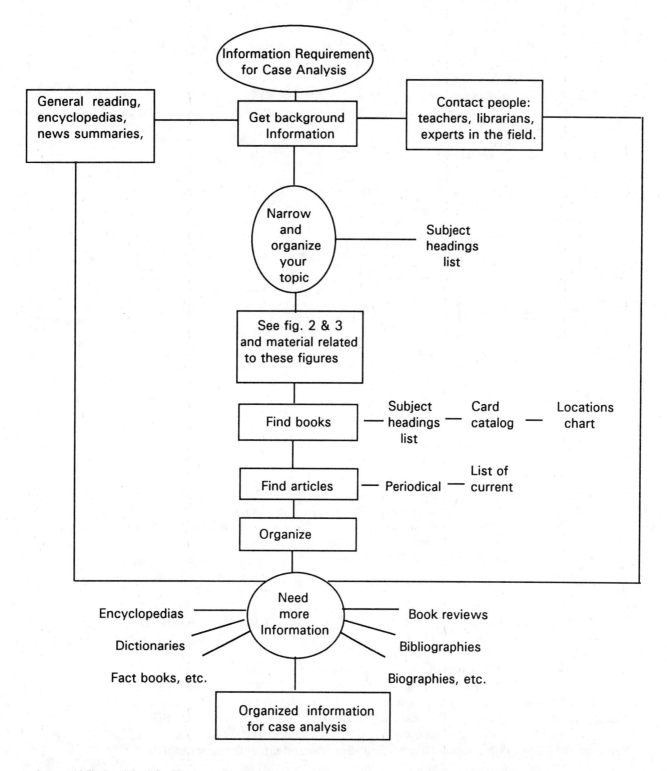

Source:  Milutinovich, J.S.  "Business Facts for Decision Makers: Where to Find Them, Business Horizons, March-April 1985.

In some case classes students are required to limit their analysis to the information provided in the case, however, instructors will often require/allow outside research. Timely and reliable information about past and present conditions, constraints, and opportunites in the analysis of a case may be appropriate. Because of time constraints, students need a selected list of available sources of information.

Data sources can be divided into four major categories[1]:

1. Government publications;
2. General reference sources of business information and ideas;
3. Specialized sources of specific data;
4. Statistical sources.

Figure 2 presents the organization of government publications and Figure 3 presents the organization of general business references.

Figure 2. GOVERNMENT PUBLICATIONS

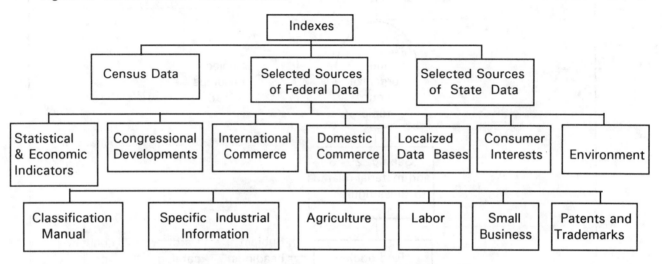

Source: Milutinovich j. S., "Business Facts For DecisionMakers: Where to Find Them", Business Horizons, March-April 1985.

No one collects more business information than the United States government. Tremendous quantities of primary data for governments use become secondary data for the business community. Due of its scope, citations are divided into four categories: Indexes; Census Data; Selected Sources from Federal Government and Selected Sources from State Government. Because of the limitations of this guide we only provide the key indexes associated with Government Publications

INDEXES

Adler, James B. C/S/Index to Publications of U.S. Congress (U.S. Government, Wash. D.C.)
Andriot, John L., ed., Guide to U.S. Government Publications (U.S. Gov., McLean,Va.: Documents Index).
Business Service Checklist (Wash. D.C.: Department of Commerce).
Business Service & Information: The Guide to Federal Gov. (N.Y.: Mgt. Inf. Exchange, Wiley, 1987).
The Federal Register ( Wash., D.C.: Division of Fed. Register, National Archives).
Monthly Catalog of U.S. Gov. Publications (Wash.,DC: U.S. Gov. Printing Office)
Monthly Checklist of State Publications (Wash. DC: Superintendent of Documents, GPO).
Selected U.S. Gov. Publications (Wash., DC: Superintendent of Documents, GPO).

## SOURCES OF BUSINESS INFORMATION

The source to consult as a time-saving first step in collecting information for case analysis is the business reference librarian. Generally this specialist has the best sources at his or her fingertips and can give expert guidance. They have compiled booklists concerning specific areas, identify special library collections, and are aware of books scheduled for publication.

A likely second step in many libraries today is the use of an on-line data base. Computer technology has revolutionized the search for business facts. By using a data base, which is an organized collection of information in a particular subject area, the analyst benefits from accessibility and adaptability of massive resources now available. Figure 3 diagrams these business sources.

Figure 3   GENERAL BUSINESS REFERENCE SOURCES

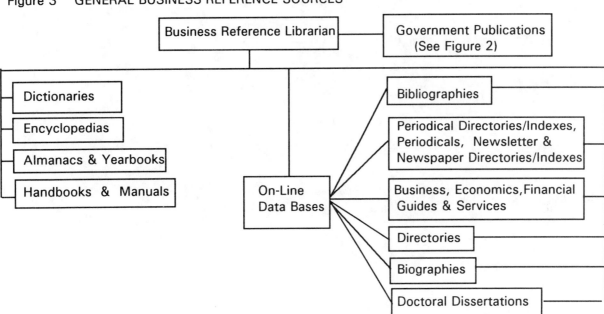

Source:   Milutinovich, J. S., "Business Facts for Decision Makers: Where To Find Them", Business Horizons, March-April 1985.

151

**NOTES:**

**NOTES:**